THE

FUTURE

OF

ACADEMIC

FREEDOM

THE
FUTURE
OF
ACADEMIC
FREEDOM

Edited by
Louis Menand

THE UNIVERSITY OF CHICAGO PRESS   CHICAGO & LONDON

LOUIS MENAND is Professor of English at the Graduate Center of the City
University of New York. He is Contributing Editor of the *New York Review of Books*
and the author of *Discovering Modernism: T. S. Eliot and His Context* (1987).

The University of Chicago Press, Chicago 60637
The University of Chicago Press Ltd., London
© 1996 by The American Association of University Professors
Chapter 1 © 1996 by Louis Menand
Chapter 3 © 1996 by Thomas L. Haskell
Chapter 5 © 1996 by Henry Louis Gates Jr.
Chapter 7 © 1996 by Ronald Dworkin
Chapter 9 © 1996 by Edward W. Said
All rights reserved. Published 1996
Printed in the United States of America
05 04 03 02 01 00 99 98 97 96   1 2 3 4 5
ISBN 0-226-52004-8 (cloth)

Library of Congress Cataloging-in-Publication Data

The future of academic freedom / edited by Louis Menand.
       p.   cm.
    Includes bibliographical references and index.
    ISBN 0-226-52004-8 (cloth : alk. paper)
    1. Academic freedom—United States.   2. College teaching—United
States—Philosophy.   3. Education, Higher—Aims and objectives—
United States.   I. Menand, Louis.
LC72.2.F88   1996
878.1'21—dc20   96-8510
                                                                      CIP

⊗ The paper used in this publication meets the minimum requirements
    of the American National Standard for Information Science—
Permanence of Paper for Printed Library Materials, ANSI Z39.48-1984

This collection of essays grew out of confusion and need. By 1990, the growing controversies within the academic disciplines had spilled into the popular press and the political arena. Academic practices and values, always subject to misunderstanding by those outside the academy, were increasingly suspected of having a political agenda designed to undermine traditional American values. Many faculty, recalling the public anger with the academy that had been expressed at times during the most intense years of the Cold War, and during the war in Vietnam especially, waited for the issue to play itself out and go away. Few wanted to face the attacks head on. But with institutions as different as Dartmouth and the University of Texas in the headlines, the criticism only intensified. Speech codes, multicultural curricula, affirmative action, sexual harassment, women's studies, deconstruction, and every meeting of the Modern Language Association excited new rounds of attacks. The changes in the universities that the public didn't like were collectively categorized as "political correctness," a label that resonated with the history of repressive thought that the Right associated with communism and the Left with McCarthyism.

The polemics that ensued did little credit to any tradition of scholarly debate or dialogue. If the attacks of many nonacademic critics seemed unfair and misinformed, the defense from those within universities was often ragged and hasty. Almost invisible in the midst of the public controversy was the extent to which arguments were as divisive and contentious within the academy as they were on the outside. The academy could not get control of the "PC" problem because it was deeply embedded in philosophical questions that had been developing for many years rather than in the politics of a particular season. This "paradigm shift," as one writer called it, had led to significant intellectual and methodological transformations in the ways scholars thought about knowledge, language, and truth—changes that altered assumptions about teaching, writing, and education itself.

Professors and their critics addressed the nature of the changes in higher education in different contexts, but a common concern was academic freedom. However difficult it has been to preserve, the academic community, both administrators and faculty, continues to believe that the free exchange of ideas, in research and teaching, is essential to the university in any society that aspires to being a democracy. This cornerstone value has seemed at risk in the current controversy, and the deeply rooted sense of its importance to intellectual life has fueled the intensity of the anger and anxiety. Even in the hottest and meanest moments of the debates, almost everyone, on all sides, has affirmed the necessity of protecting academic freedom. But with such intense agreement on the principle, how was it that academic freedom suddenly seemed so vulnerable?

The American Association of University Professors (AAUP), the faculty association founded in 1915 by such prominent academics as Arthur Lovejoy and John Dewey for the purpose of defending academic freedom, initially underestimated the depth of the issues involved in the PC controversy. Following the general perspectives of Dewey's Pragmatist philosophy, the AAUP had from its founding defined the university as "an intellectual experiment station" in which ideas "distasteful" to the larger community might germinate. The vehemence of the argument about the relativity of "truth" and the attack on academic freedom as conceptually invalid if not based on a truth standard forced many within the academy, including the AAUP, to rethink familiar issues. In 1915 many of the leading scholars and intellectuals of the day had met to draft the first "General Declaration of Principles" of the fledgling association of university professors. Now, with almost eighty years of history behind it, it seemed appropriate for the AAUP again to bring some of the best minds to bear on these issues. Was the practice of academic freedom consistent with the principles? Could the principles be defended in the context of poststructuralist philosophy? Was the traditional practice possible in a charged political climate? The essays collected in this volume represent the AAUP's effort to sponsor a reexamination of such questions by some of the people whose work has set the terms of the recent debate.

For two years the authors of these essays presented lectures to the national meetings of the AAUP, debating with the members and with the other contributors the questions posed by the series. Perhaps the most encouraging thing to emerge from the discussion is the confidence that good academic practice offers a means whereby academic freedom can be protected in circumstances in which philosophical viewpoints cannot be reconciled. These essays also challenged the AAUP to reexamine the early Pragmatism implicit in the association's founding documents and the neo-Pragmatism of some of the figures at the center of the current controversy.

I wish to acknowledge three people who were essential in the effort to arrange the lecture series and edit the book. Jordan Kurland, the AAUP's senior staff member in the national office, provided encouragement and guidance that secured funding from the AAUP's Academic Freedom Foundation. Robert Post, professor of law from Berkeley who was then serving as the AAUP's general counsel, helped to conceptualize the project, select speakers, and articulate our purpose to the AAUP's diverse and interdisciplinary membership. Louis Menand, professor of English at the Graduate Center of the City University of New York, had come to our attention through his many essays as one of the best of the new public intellectuals from within the academy. Convincing Menand to act as editor for the series and the book was our greatest good fortune. His familiarity with contemporary controversies and his balanced critique of the academy enabled him to frame the issues intellectually and dispassionately. If academic freedom was to be important to the emerging generation of scholars, it had to be addressed within the philosophical context of their values. We sought a cross section of intellectuals and disciplines to represent the views that were shaping the contemporary discourse. The scholars we approached seemed to share our sense that important issues were at stake, and they were remarkably generous in giving us their time and thoughts. They brought to the work high seriousness and passionate commitment. To all of them I wish to express the appreciation and pleasure that members of the AAUP took in hearing and debating their ideas. This book will, I hope, extend that conversation to all those who are concerned about the integrity of academic freedom in our changing colleges and universities.

Linda Ray Pratt
President of the American Association of University Professors, 1992–94

PART 1

WHAT

DOES

ACADEMIC

FREEDOM

PROTECT?

ONE

The Limits of Academic Freedom

Louis Menand

I

Coercion is natural; freedom is artificial. Freedoms are socially engineered spaces in which parties engaged in specified pursuits enjoy protection from parties who would otherwise naturally seek to interfere in those pursuits. One person's freedom is therefore always another person's restriction: we would not have even the concept of freedom if the reality of coercion were not already present. Since freedoms are socially constructed and socially maintained, their borders are constantly patrolled, and on both sides. Those on the inside are vigilant about external threats of interference; those whose interests naturally impel them toward intervention are keen to find some means of influencing behavior inside the protected space.

Some of this patrolling is practical, and involves negotiations over the regulations that define the protected space and that sanction attempts to compromise the freedom enjoyed within it. But much of the patrolling is philosophical. Those inside the space are continually articulating rationales for maintaining, or even expanding, their sphere of activity; those whose activities or interests place them on the outside are continually questioning those rationales, or proposing rationales of their own for restricting or re-defining the freedom in question. When the rationales articulated on the inside appear weak, the advantage swings to those on the outside.

This seems to many people today to be the case with the American university. Even people friendly to the university have begun to feel that it has brought its troubles on itself by failing to agree on an account of its activities that merits continued social commitment. They worry that forces eager to reduce public support for universities or (what amounts to the same thing) to restrict access to higher education have been handed the rhetorical weapons they need by the very people who stand to suffer from those reductions—by academics themselves.

At the heart of the political and economic battles over the future of the university is the concept of academic freedom. Academic freedom is not simply a kind of bonus enjoyed by workers within the system, a philosophical luxury universities could function just as effectively, and much more efficiently, without. It is the key legitimating concept of the entire enterprise. Virtually every practice of academic life that we take for granted—from the practice of allowing departments to hire and fire their own members to the practice of not allowing the football coach to influence the quarterback's grade in math class—derives from it. Any internal account of what goes on in the academic world must at the same time be a convincing rationale for maintaining the space defined by academic freedom. The alternative is a political free-for-all, in which decisions about curricula, funding, employment, classroom practice, and scholarly merit are arrived at through a process of negotiation among competing interests. The power in such negotiations will not be wielded by the professors.

The debate over the contemporary university has become absorbed by two issues. The first is the so-called politicization of the humanities—the notion that since all knowledge is political and furthers the interests of some person or some group, teaching and scholarship ought to be undertaken with their political intentions firmly in mind, and specifically with a view to redressing the disparagement or neglect of subordinate groups. The second is epistemological relativism—the notion that judgments and values cannot be objective or universal, and that ideals like "disinterestedness," "reason," and "truth" are insupportable abstractions which we would be better off abandoning in favor of more frankly relational and historicist terms like "perspective," "understanding," and "interpretation." The journalistic shorthand for the first issue is "multiculturalism," with the implication of an anti-Western animus; the shorthand for the second is "postmodernism" (sometimes, even less accurately, "deconstruction"), with the suggestion that it underwrites an "anything goes" nihilism.

The university's critics have succeeded in reducing the debate over higher education to a debate over these catch-terms, and in nearly all the full-scale attacks on the contemporary academy the persistence of postmodernism and multiculturalism is adduced as a reason for trustees, alumni, administrators, and public officials to intervene in the internal academic affairs of universities. This recommendation is quite explicit, for example, in Dinesh D'Souza's best-selling *Illiberal Education* (1991) and in Lynne Cheney's *Telling the Truth* (1992).[1] The consequence is that people outside the university who are alarmed by the specter of encroachments on academic freedom—people who are distressed by the, so to speak, politicization of "the politicization of the humanities"—tend to assume that a defense of the freedom of academics to determine the content of their own work must entail a defense of postmodernism and multiculturalism. Since those notions seem antithetical to the traditional values of academic activity, the values on which the rationale for academic freedom has conventionally seemed to rest, any defense appears hopelessly compromised from the start.

The university does have internal problems that threaten the future of academic freedom, but postmodernism and multiculturalism, however those terms are defined,[2] are not among them, and it is a mistake to assume that the practices and ideas they stand for, even in the minds of critics like D'Souza and Cheney, somehow transgress the limits of the kind of activity academic freedom is designed to protect. They may—they do—pose a public relations problem for universities that is not insignificant.[3] But it should be obvious that the fact that multiculturalism and postmodernism will probably never enjoy majority popular acclaim is irrelevant to their status as ideas deserving of the usual protections of academic freedom. If it was only popularly acclaimed ideas that merited protection, we would not need the protection in the first place.

A more deeply misleading assumption informing the debate over the future of the university is the notion that there exists some unproblematic conception of academic freedom that is philosophically coherent and that will conduce to outcomes in particular cases which all parties will feel to be just and equitable. No such conception exists, and the reason has to do with the social origins of all freedoms. It has been customary since Isaiah Berlin's famous essay "Two Concepts of Liberty" to distinguish between "negative" liberty, which Berlin defines as freedom *from* interference in one's pursuits, and "positive" liberty, which is freedom *for* a predefined end.[4] Berlin was describing two traditions of political thought, but he made it clear that negative liberty was the stronger liberal conception, since it acknowledges the incommensurability of ultimate ends in modern life. Under a regime of negative freedoms, individuals are treated as autonomous moral agents who are capable of choosing their own ends and whose destinies are therefore (to that extent) in their own keeping, *for good or for ill.*

In actual practice, though, every freedom has both positive and negative dimensions, because every freedom is created and is created for a purpose. Freedoms (or rights, in the legal vocabulary) do not preexist civil society like so much virgin forest which civil libertarians, like environmentalists, strive to preserve from the encroachments of social interests. Freedoms are, in effect, manufactured by civil societies in order to further some conception of the good life, even if that conception of the good life is (as Michael Walzer has suggested it is for American society)[5] simply the belief that individuals should be free, in the negative sense, to pursue their own ends without being required to answer to those who favor different ends.

Academic freedom is obviously such a two-faced concept. It establishes a zone of protection and self-regulation in the interests of furthering the ends of academic activity—that is, of teaching and inquiry. The argument over the propriety of campus hate speech codes—regulations sanctioning expressions presumed to give offense—is an argument that points up the positive aspect (in Berlin's sense) of the concept. For the question of whether academic freedom countenances such regulations is separate from the question of whether the First Amendment countenances them. Freedom of expression and academic freedom are not the same freedoms; each is designed in furtherance of somewhat differently defined goods. On the other hand, making this distinction does not dispose of the question of whether hate speech codes are compatible with academic freedom, since although it can be argued that hate speech falls outside the protection of academic freedom on the grounds that such speech serves no plausible educational purpose, it can also be argued that hate speech is protected by academic freedom, on the grounds that no educational purpose is served by censoring expressions which, since they enjoy constitutional protection, students will have to live with in the nonacademic world.[6] There is clearly no single definition of academic freedom that will satisfy both sides of this disagreement: the concept will tip the scales on either side depending on how it is defined and on which of the many things that go on in universities it is thought to protect. This does not, just as clearly, mean that definitions of academic freedom are useless.

The concept of academic freedom, in short, has always been problematic. It is *inherently* problematic. Like any ideal concept, it requires a willing suspension of disbelief in order properly and efficiently to do its work. In times of stress, it becomes easier to see the ways in which ideal concepts don't have all four feet on the ground at the same time, and this is what we are seeing now in the case of the concept of academic freedom. Insuring that the concept continues to work properly, and to provide the protections it has traditionally provided to members of academic communities, is not something that can be accomplished by tinkering with its inner philosophical workings—by coming up with an abstract construction that *will* run with all four feet on the ground. When the ideal of academic freedom enters the reality of institutional practice, inequities in the distribution of that freedom inevitably result. When John Dewey helped launch the American Association of University Professors in 1915, he dismissed the notion that the organization's primary function would be to arbitrate disputes over, and to protest against abridgments of, academic freedom. But in his presidential report at the end of the association's first year, he acknowledged that a surprising number of cases had arisen which required protest and arbitration. He hoped, he said, that the first year was an aberration.[7] But it seems likely that these cases will always arise, for the reason that freedom is always at the expense of something.

II

Most people share pretty much the same idea of the sorts of coercions academic freedom is a freedom from. But the concept has different implications and yields different consequences in different contexts, and it is useful to examine a few of these contexts in order to see just how academic freedom operates simultaneously as a liberty and a restriction. The concept has, for example, implications for the vocational status of professors. What makes universities different from other places in which people work with their brains? The answer is that so far as the content of the work that goes on in them is concerned, universities are essentially self-regulating. The university professor is a professional. He or she works in a business whose standards and practices are, to every extent possible, established and enforced by its own practitioners. Professions aspire to self-regulation for the same reason that the Hollywood film industry has its own rating system: because if a profession doesn't undertake to regulate itself, it exposes itself to the possibility of regulation by the state or some other external agency.

The modern research university, the university created by Charles William Eliot, Andrew White, Daniel Gilman, and their contemporaries, emerged in the second half of the nineteenth century, the period in which many of the modern professions were first organizing themselves. One of the intentions of those founders was, in fact, to help train new members of the professional class. Charles Eliot, who became president of Harvard in 1869, is famous for implementing the first undergraduate free elective system in the country. He did this in order to allow students to acquire not a general but a specialized education, to enable them to track themselves in the direction of their future careers. He later created the Harvard Graduate School of Arts and Sciences (modeled on Johns Hopkins, the first pure research institution in the United States, which opened its doors in 1876) in order to produce the specialists needed to train future specialists.

No professional, no lawyer or doctor or architect, wants to have the terms of his or her practice dictated by someone other than his or her peers, people who have the interests of the profession, rather than the interests of some group outside the profession, at heart. In the case of the academic professional, interference by outside political or economic interests is considered repugnant to a unique degree, and elaborate measures are taken to insulate the university teacher and researcher from them. Universities have, essentially, a compact with the rest of society on this matter: society agrees that research which doesn't have to answer to some standard of political correctness, economic utility, or religious orthodoxy is a desirable good, and agrees to allow professors to decide among themselves the work it is important for them to undertake.

The protections that have been erected with the intention of guaranteeing this freedom are embodied in all the special peculiarities of academic life: doctoral programs, peer review, tenure. Academics decide who is to be permitted to enter the profession by requiring candidates to complete doctoral degree granting programs. They certify the legitimacy of scholarly work by requiring that it be submitted to peer review before it is published. And they create permanent members of the profession by requiring junior professors to submit their work to the approval of senior professors before awarding them tenure—which is regarded, of course, as the ultimate protection of their freedom to pursue their research interests as they see fit. The research university is thus a virtual paradigm of professionalism: specialists within each specialized field have wide authority to determine who the new specialists will be, and in what the work of the specialization properly consists. This authority insures a commensurately wide freedom of inquiry; but (and this is the important point) *only for the specialist.* For people who do not become members of the profession, this system constitutes not a freedom but an almost completely disabling restriction.

In this respect, the academic profession is like every other profession. On the one hand, professions are democratic. They open careers to talents. Even the sons and daughters of the wealthy must pass the bar exam; even the relatives of university presidents have to defend their dissertations. But professionalism also gives the individual practitioner, once certification has been acquired, the official protection of the professional group; and this means that the weakest professional enjoys, automatically, a huge advantage in the market for his or services over the strongest amateur operating alone. The professional scholar has access to resources—to fresh scholarship presented at professional conferences, to the minds of students, to the attention of other professionals in the pages of refereed journals and through professional contacts, to sanctuary in the case of occupational difficulties, and, most importantly, to a virtually guaranteed income—which the uncredentialed scholar must somehow survive without. When we talk about the freedom of the academic to dictate the terms of his or her work, we are also and unavoidably talking about the freedom to exclude, or to limit the exposure of, work that is not deemed to meet academic standards. Academic freedom is, at a basic level, an expression of self-interest: it is a freedom for academics. Nonacademic intellectuals and scholars are required to operate without it.

The concept of academic freedom operates in a similarly double-edged way in the case of graduate students, junior professors, and other untenured members of the profession. The doctoral student and the assistant professor are free to write what they choose, but what they write had better accord with their senior colleagues' idea of what counts as acceptable scholarship in the field. It is expected that those senior colleagues will make their judgments in a disinterested spirit—in the spirit, indeed, of academic freedom. But they perform a judgment, not a measurement—the dissertation is read, not weighed—and no one who is an assistant professor coming up for tenure is likely to feel a strong association between that experience and the concept of intellectual freedom. Again, in being free to regulate itself, the profession is free to reject what does not intellectually suit it and essentially to compel, by withholding professional rewards (including monetary ones like promotions and merit increases), the production of work that does.

Academics are sometimes oblivious to the effect this exclusivity has, especially in fields such as literary criticism that naturally attract many nonacademic practitioners. It is notable that a number of the most widely publicized attacks on the contemporary university—for example, D'Souza's *Illiberal Education,* Roger Kimball's *Tenured Radicals,* David Lehman's *Signs of the Times,* and Richard Bernstein's *Dictatorship of Virtue*—were written by people who had once been enrolled in graduate programs but did not go on to have academic careers. It would be an exaggeration to say that resentment made them do it, but there is a lot of resentment in their pages.

The situation of the untenured academic belongs to a second context in which the concept of academic freedom has practical implications, and that is the intradisciplinary context. There are many complaints today about disciplinary and departmental factionalism, about groups of professors exerting pressure on colleagues to conform to certain expectations about what they ought properly to be working on or teaching. Course proposals are rejected as insufficiently "diverse" by departmental curriculum committees, article submissions and grant proposals are turned down by peers for weak politics or for insufficient theoretical couture, tenure candidates are sandbagged because of their politics—or their lack of politics—and sometimes because of their race or their gender, and so forth.

Whether the problem of factionalism is or isn't worse than it was at any other time in the history of the academic profession, it is clear that the concept of academic freedom, when it is applied to the activities of a particular department or to the activities of scholars within a particular discipline, requires a balancing act. Not everyone is protected equally. Ideally, the discipline or the department governs itself, choosing the direction or directions it thinks most worthwhile, while at the same time continuing to respect the right of the individual scholar to differ. But practice is often another matter. The scholar who chooses to differ may not, after all, choose to differ silently. He or she may undertake to interfere with the designs of his or her colleagues—with their plans to hire the like-minded, or to redesign the curriculum, or to devise a particular prerequisite for their majors. It is, given the uneven distribution of political energy in most departments, often not terribly difficult to do this, which is why many professors complain that their departments or their disciplines have been "taken over" by minority parties. But this is a phenomenon that has nothing necessarily to do with politicization. Quantitative versus qualitative, positivist versus metahistorical, Robertsonian versus Lévi-Straussian, realist versus Leo Straussian: the academic life has always been an endless series of turf battles. Giving departments and disciplines the freedom to determine their own course of action means giving professors the freedom to interfere with one another's professional designs. Disciplines are "communicative spaces" and "interpretive communities," but there is rarely anything particularly "ideal" about them.

The history of debates over the "correct" direction for the field to be heading illuminates the essentially contestatory nature of life within a discipline. The New Criticism, for example, was once attacked for subverting the integrity of the discipline of literary studies in very much the same spirit that poststructuralist criticism is attacked today by people who regard the academic legitimacy of the New Criticism as beyond even the shadow of a suspicion.[8] It is, of course, poststructuralism (or, more popularly, postmodernism) that is blamed for the epistemological relativism that is supposed to be undermining the claim of scholarship in the humanities to deserve the protection of academic freedom. Their academic origins in departments of literature is a clue to the appeal those theories hold. For the writers whose names are most often associated with poststructuralism, Jacques Derrida and Michel Foucault, were not literary critics or literary theorists at all; and yet it was largely through literature departments that their ideas penetrated the American academy. One of the reasons for this may be that the criticism of literature has, of all the major fields of study, the weakest case for inclusion in the professional structure of the research university. The notion that literary criticism is a disinterested, "scientistic" activity would have seemed absurd to almost any critic before the twentieth century. So that to the extent that postmodernist theory subverts the sort of activities academics are traditionally thought to pursue—that is, investigating phenomena with the goal of arriving at true and impartial understandings of them—the study of literature was the field most vulnerable.

For the professionalist attributes of academic life—the doctoral dissertation and defense, refereed journals, procedures for tenure and promotion, and so on—were not established only to insure self-governance and to protect professors from the interference of outside authorities in the content of their work. They also exist because it was once assumed that it is through such procedures that genuine knowledge is produced.[9] Scholars work in fields, they study with established experts in those fields, they produce their own contributions to knowledge about their fields, and their contributions are judged by their peers in the field. If their contributions are judged genuine, those scholars are rewarded with the power to judge the efforts of the next generation of epigones. The model is one of the models of science: knowledge develops by the accumulation of research findings, brick piled onto brick, monograph onto monograph, until the arch of knowledge about a field stands clearly defined against the background of mere undisciplined information. All these professional requirements were established in part to encourage the production of more bricks, to provide a tube, as it were, from which more toothpaste could endlessly be squeezed.

There was in the beginning no place in this model for literary criticism, since the appreciation and interpretation of works of literature are not obviously scientific. At the time the modern university was developed, literary criticism did not even pretend to be, or want to be, a scientistic enterprise. The first members of the Modern Language Association (founded in 1883) were philologists, scholars whose work on language did conform to a scientific model and could therefore be evaluated "objectively." The philological conception of the field was so dominant that specialists in English at Johns Hopkins were in the beginning members of the German department.

It is therefore not entirely surprising that literary criticism, even after it had defined itself in a manner compatible with the institutional requirements of the research university, remained a breeding ground for skepticism about the positivistic implications of those requirements. Postmodernism, in this light, is simply the apotheosis of that skepticism. It has led to the conventional wisdom, among many professors in the humanities, that, contrary to the understanding of knowledge and inquiry associated with work in the sciences, knowledge in the humanistic fields is necessarily partial and perspectival, historically contingent, politically and psychologically determined—in no sense bricklike except in its potential to do harm.

This view has gained adherents in departments of literature and in other disciplines as well. Yet the institutional structure remains unchanged. Vast quantities of bricks are still produced. They are ponderously weighed and inspected by committees and referees and other professional weighers and inspectors. Their manufacturers are duly rewarded or punished. And then the bricks get thrown onto the heap. No one expects an arch to sprout up, since it is understood and accepted by everyone that the brickmakers' work will change with the interests and fashions of the times. People have already made careers by theorizing about the inevitability of the obsolescence of their own theorizing.

It is this state of intellectual affairs that has made it seem so difficult to argue that professors need the protections associated with the concept of academic freedom, since so many professors in the humanities are now willing to assert that their work is not about reaching the truth about a field, but about intervening in a conversation—a "discourse"—that is already partial and political. The dilemma cuts in both directions. A professor who believes that "truth" is simply a name for what a particular group finds it advantageous to regard as given or universal, and who regards universities as sites for social indoctrination, can hardly have much use for a concept grounded on the premise that intellectual inquiry is a neutral and disinterested activity. On the other hand, a professor who believes in the value and the possibility of unconstrained intellectual inquiry, and in the importance of protecting that inquiry with the concept of academic freedom, is in no position to condemn the activities of colleagues who see knowledge as principally political, since that would mean interfering with those colleagues' own freedom of inquiry.

It is not hard to see why these disputes are more fraught than disputes between Robertsonian Chaucerians and structuralist Chaucerians, or between quantitative sociologists and ethnomethodologists. For the disputants in those quarrels at least imagined themselves to be standing on the same ground: they had a philosophical faith in things like appeals to evidence and scholarly demonstrations. They agreed that they were both trying to get to a true, or at least superior, knowledge of their subjects; they just disagreed about which horse knew the way. In the contemporary quarrel, though, one of the disputants actually appears to be burrowing away under the ground on which the other is trying to stand.[10]

But how radical is the poststructuralist challenge? Contemporary skepticism about conventional notions of truth and knowledge is often discussed as though it were a recent eruption, an unexpected and hideous intrusion into a world that had never before thought to question the idea that there is a truth we can arrive at beyond our local, subjective, and political interests, or the idea that the pursuit of knowledge can be a purely disinterested activity, or the idea that facts and values can always be made distinct. This is generational myopia. John Dewey, who helped compose the first articulation of the principle of academic freedom, did not regard truth as an absolute, determinate entity. He did not believe that the pursuit of knowledge could be an activity unconnected with the desire to fulfill practical needs. Nor did he believe that facts could be usefully separated from the values and the moral significance we attach to them. His whole philosophy was designed to explain not only why the traditional metaphysics of truth are unsustainable, but why we are better off without them. He didn't think that this makes academic freedom impossible. He thought that this is exactly what makes academic freedom necessary. We don't need universities in order to preserve a static knowledge from the forces of change. We need them to insure that knowledge will not remain static in the service of some vested interest.

Although postmodernism is popularly associated with the spirit of "anything goes," it has had no such consequence in the academy. "Anything goes" is the last sentiment a reasonable observer would be likely to associate with a contemporary literature department. Like every new idea intended to shatter old vessels, postmodernism (like multiculturalism) has undergone disciplinization. It isn't a threat to academic freedom. It is what many academics today do, in the same way that they once did structuralist analysis or literary biography or close reading: they argue with each other about it, they publish articles to support or refute it, and they wonder where the next wave is coming from. Postmodernism has, as every academic in the humanities is perfectly aware, its own stock of unquestioned assumptions and methodological orthodoxies and its own canonical texts. If those assumptions and orthodoxies cease to generate interesting or useful work, the whole movement should, if the machinery of academic freedom is working properly, collapse of its own weight. Many people feel, of course, that the machinery is not working properly because professors no longer play fairly with one another, and work that doesn't fit the reigning paradigms doesn't get rewarded. But work that doesn't fit the reigning paradigms has never been rewarded until it succeeds in persuading enough practitioners of its superiority to the work that does. No one understands this better than a postmodernist.

III

Discussions of academic freedom tend to concentrate on the work of professors, but there is another kind of academic freedom in the university which is not always compatible with the academic freedom of professors, and that is the academic freedom of students. It is been pointed out by some critics of the contemporary academy that there seems to be a contradiction between the freedom of speech professors allow themselves and the restrictions which a few of them appear to be willing to place on the speech of their students.[11] But like every other issue associated with the concept of academic freedom, this is a complicated matter.

In his fine history of academic freedom in the era of the American university, Walter Metzger notes that there were two assumptions about knowledge which were prevalent in the era of the American college but which were largely abandoned after the emergence of the research university in the period following the Civil War. The first of these, he says, was "that character was a function of belief." The second was the conviction "that an idea was warranted and verified by proof of its moral advantages."[12] These principles, Metzger observes, were discredited, or made to seem irrelevant, by the advent of modern scientific thought, spurred to a great extent by the rapid acceptance and wide influence of Darwinism. With the eclipse of these assumptions about the moral bearing of knowledge went the parental function of institutions of higher education and the assumption that one of the principal purposes of college is to produce morally sound young men.

The notion that an idea is "warranted and verified by proof of its moral advantages" certainly sounds unscientific. We do not expect the scientist to bring his or her inquiries to a halt at the frontiers of moral heterodoxy, or even to speculate about the possible moral bearing of his or her research. At the same time, is there any teacher who does not believe that, to some degree, character *is* a function of belief, or that the ideas he or she shares with students ought not to conduce to their moral advantage? Professors do not just hand knowledge over disembodied, leaving students to make moral sense of it as they will. This is not to say that they are in the habit of dictating to students what to believe; but they do think that there is a positive moral component to their teaching. Why else would they teach?

The pedagogical attitude caricatured as "politically correct" thinking constitutes a rather dramatic reversion to this premodern conception of the moral mission of higher education, but it is just one way of doing what all professors try to do, which is to imbue students with the knowledge and habits of mind they regard as useful for the conduct of life. There are many professors today who would agree quite readily with the proposition that "an idea [is] warranted and verified by proof of its moral advantages." The moral advantages they have in mind may not be the moral advantages that, say, James McCosh had in mind. But they are willing to apply the same test. So that to the objection that speech codes are coercive, it can be replied that there are many ways in which professors coerce their students into accepting their own point of view, or into "thinking like" a critic or a scientist or a lawyer, and it is not always easy, as a theoretical matter, to explain why one type of coercion is permissible while another is not.

Lionel Trilling once wrote a short story called "Of This Time, Of That Place," in which a student submits a hopelessly off-base interpretation of a poem to a young, presumably Trillingesque English professor. The professor gives the paper a C−. The student returns and, in the most ingratiating manner, pleads his case on the grounds that interpretation is subjective and not a science. The professor wilts a little under this assault, and agrees to reread the paper and to reconsider the grade. He reads the paper again, and changes the grade to an F. We would say, from the point of view of the academic freedom of the parties involved, that the student was free to say what he liked, and the professor was free to judge its merit. Should the boundaries of those two freedoms be unlimited?

There would seem to be a point at which a limit is reached, and the term "advocacy" has been adopted by a number of people as the name for this point. The term is implicitly counterposed to a notion of standard pedagogical practice as neutral, balanced, expository, and nondoctrinaire; and it is suggested that advocacy—that is, instruction undertaken with the intention of persuading students to adopt a particular political view—is undeserving of the protection of academic freedom because it is not disinterested. If the professor proposes to transgress the limits of the free space of the academy in order to intervene in the political realm outside the university, the assumption goes, the political realm is thereby entitled to transgress back.

But the concept of advocacy is extremely puzzling. There are some hypothetical classroom situations in which what is called "advocacy" clearly arises as a problem: the situation in which the professor deliberately misreads a text, or suppresses what he or she knows to be valid evidence, in order to compel a "correct" political reading, or the situation in which the professor lectures about the demerits of affirmative action policies in what is supposed to be a class on the differential calculus. Both of these pedagogical practices are obviously wrong, but not for reasons having anything to do with advocacy. The first case is essentially unheard of, since it requires a professor to express a point of view he or she knows is not supported by the evidence: the problem, in other words, isn't politics but dishonesty. In the second case, the behavior is unprofessional, and it does not matter what the professor is filling the class hour with. It might be his recipe for egg salad. The matter is clearly regulable, and it is unrelated to issues about politics, ethics, or academic freedom.

Apart from these virtually nonexistent cases, there remains only the basic pedagogical question, Should professors attempt to put across their own point of view about the material they teach in the classroom? But what else could they do? It is because professors have views about their subjects that they have been hired to teach them. Their ethical constraint is only that they teach what they honestly believe the significance of the material to be. Every professor teaches in order to enable his or her students to have some degree of control over their lives. Some believe that a posture of skepticism serves as a useful model in this respect; some believe a posture of engagement does. But very few professors conduct their classes in anything resembling a spirit of indoctrination, for the simple reason that indoctrination isn't just bad pedagogy; it's bad advocacy.

Concern about advocacy seriously underestimates the instincts of college students. Students know perfectly well when they're being expected to toe an intellectual line. They've spent their entire lives reading these kinds of signals from grown-ups. They know what their professor's take on the subject is, and if they find that take disagreeable or uninteresting, or feel that nothing of interest remains after discounting for it, they advise their friends to register for someone else's course. One would imagine that, on the whole, students feel rather well-equipped intellectually to have learned the "enlightened" view that art and ideas have political motives and consequences, and that truths are relative constructions, useful in some contexts and deconstructible in others. If this is not good equipment to have, it is the business of the professor down the hall to persuade them otherwise. It is hard to see why it should be the business of a trustee.

IV

The threat that multiculturalism and postmodernism pose to academic freedom is not epistemological or political. It is, much more banally, administrative. Universities differ. They service different student populations, they have different academic strengths and weaknesses, they have been shaped by different histories. But professors are, professionally speaking, all the same. Professors within each discipline, regardless of where they teach, have had essentially the same graduate training, they participate in the same scholarly conversations, they put pretty much the same books on their reading lists, they structure the requirements for the major and for advanced degrees in roughly the same way, and they (often) look to move on to more prestigious schools in the expectation that their new colleagues will not differ in any of these respects from their old ones. Students are local; research is global. Although colleges are demographically diverse, the disciplines are national, and they are national because they are professionalized. A professor's loyalty is ordinarily much greater to his or her discipline than it is to the particular campus he or she happens to have ended up working at—just as a lawyer's loyalty to "the law" is meant to supersede his or her loyalty to the particular firm he or she happens to practice in. That is what professional identity consists in, and one of the ways disinterestedness is supposed to be created.

Academic freedom, as it is now structured, depends crucially on the autonomy and integrity of the disciplines.[13] For it is the departments, and the disciplines to which they belong, that constitute the spaces in which rival scholarly and pedagogical positions are negotiated. Academic freedom not only protects sociology professors from the interference of trustees and public officials in the exercise of their jobs as teachers and scholars; it protects them from physics professors as well. It mandates that decisions about what counts as good work in sociology shall be made by sociologists. And, practically speaking, "sociologists" means the department of sociology. That is the self-governing professional community.

In theory, it is perfectly possible to do multiculturalist sociology or postmodernist sociology. But multiculturalism and postmodernism are epiphenomena of a development that arises from a number of causes, and that presents a much more serious risk to academic freedom than advocacy or relativism. This is the meltdown of disciplinary boundaries. The key point about the various "studies" fields which have emerged as intellectual focal points for scholarly activity in the humanities over the last ten or fifteen years—Women's Studies, African-American Studies, Science and Technology Studies, Cultural Studies, and so on—is that those fields are interdisciplinary *by definition*. It is even possible to say that they are antidisciplinary, since in bringing together specialists from various disciplines, they have managed to produce a kind of scholarship that flourishes in the cracks between disciplines, and that is directed, in certain respects, by a critique of the traditional disciplines.

The collapse of the disciplines is not a philosophical crisis; after all, the academic disciplines originally arose, in the late nineteenth century, out of much more holistic organizations of knowledge. The modern disciplines are splinters of more comprehensive wholes, so that what was once social science has become sociology, history, political science, economics, and anthropology, each an academic specialty with its own internal system of self-governance, each immune to the interference of the others. There is nothing inevitable about these arrangements, just as there is nothing inevitable about the segregation of the criticism of literature from social theory, politics, theology, moral philosophy, or any other nonliterary form of knowledge. Disciplinarity depended on a kind of formalism, and formalism is no longer in high philosophical repute. The discipline of English, for example, is neither natural nor inevitable, and it is very easy to see all the ways in which, by essentializing the object of its study and by marginalizing nonliterary approaches, it limits and even distorts the understanding of literature.

But when disciplines and departments dissolve, the machinery of self-governance becomes more difficult to maintain. For even if there is no "field" for contributions to knowledge to be measured against, and no department to determine which of its subspecialties needs staffing and who is qualified to undertake the job, decisions about hiring, promotion, and curricula have to be made somewhere, and that somewhere is likely to be the office of the dean or the provost. Administrators faced with allocating dwindling resources in the period of retrenchment that now seems upon the American university will be delighted to see the disciplines lose their authority, for it means spreading fewer faculty farther, and it gives them far greater control over the creation and elimination of staff positions.

Postmodernism and multiculturalism obviously abet this skepticism about the legitimacy of traditional disciplinary distinctions, and even some professors who do not regard themselves as postmodernists or multiculturalists see the usefulness of stepping outside the paradigms the disciplines have generated and of approaching their work in a less specialized, even a less professional, spirit. But specialization and professionalism are today still at the core of the institutional arrangements that make academic freedom possible: they help determine who counts as a member of the self-regulating community of practitioners and, negatively, who counts as an external meddler in the community's affairs. It would be a great benefit to universities, in every aspect of their mission, if the principle of academic freedom operated less invidiously—if universities could become intellectually more cosmopolitan places, but without sacrificing the side of the principle intended to protect ideas from majoritarian prejudice and political or financial expediency.

The structure of disciplinarity that has arisen with the modern research university is expensive; it is philosophically weak; and it encourages intellectual predictability, professional insularity, and social irrelevance. It deserves to be replaced. But if it is replaced, it is in the interests of everyone who values the continued integrity of teaching and inquiry to devise a new institutional structure that will perform the same function. Otherwise academic freedom will be killed by the thing that, in America, kills most swiftly and surely: not bad ideas, but lack of money.

NOTES

1. "Liberal education is too important to entrust to these self-styled revolutionaries. Reform, if it comes, requires the involvement of intelligent voices from both inside and outside the university—students who are willing to take on reigning orthodoxies, professors and administrators with the courage to resist the activist high tide, and parents, alumni, and civic leaders who are committed to applying genuine principles of liberal learning to the challenges of the emerging multicultural society." Dinesh D'Souza, *Illiberal Education: The Politics of Race and Sex on Campus* (New York: Free Press, 1991), p. 257. "Just as members of corporate boards have begun to educate themselves and exert influence over the companies they oversee, so, too, can those who sit on the governing boards of colleges and universities. And surely there is important reason for them to do so. . . . Trustees are often people who have made their mark in law or business, journalism or philanthropy. They are not usually professional intellectuals, but that should not be seen as a disadvantage. Indeed, it can be an asset." Lynne Cheney, *Telling the Truth: A Report on the State of the Humanities in Higher Education* (Washington, D.C.: National Endowment for the Humanities, 1992), p. 50. Cheney cites Martin Anderson and Gertrude Himmelfarb as writers who also recommend this strategy.

2. For the purposes of this argument, these terms may be defined in their widest journalistic sense. I will continue to use them in that sense, despite the obvious oversimplification (and even distortion) this entails, since my point is that even if the caricatured version of these ideas were correct, it would not matter to the question of whether the people who espoused them were deserving of the protection of academic freedom.

3. I try to sketch this public relations problem, as I see it, in "Marketing Postmodernism," in *The Condition of American Liberal Education: Pragmatism and a Changing Tradition,* ed. Robert Orrill (New York: The College Board, 1995), pp. 140–44.

4. Isaiah Berlin, "Two Concepts of Liberty" (1958), in *Four Essays on Liberty* (New York: Oxford University Press, 1969), pp. 118–72.

5. See Michael Walzer, "Comment," in Charles Taylor, *Multiculturalism: Examining the Politics of Recognition,* expanded edition, ed. Amy Gutmann (Princeton: Princeton University Press, 1994), pp. 99–103.

6. These divergent interpretations are discussed and weighed in the essays by Cass Sunstein and Henry Louis Gates Jr. in this volume.

7. See John Dewey, "Introductory Address to the American Association of University Professors" (1915) and "Annual Address of the President to the American Association of University Professors" (1915), in *John Dewey: The Middle Works, 1899–1924* (Carbondale: Southern Illinois University Press, 1978), 6:88–108.

8. The landmark document in the attack on the New Criticism is Douglas Bush's 1948 presidential address to the Modern Language Association, "The New Criticism: Some Old-Fashioned Queries," *PMLA* 64, suppl., pt. 2 (March 1949): 18–21. On the quarrel between historical scholars and critics, see Gerald Graff, *Professing Literature: An Institutional History* (Chicago: University of Chicago Press, 1987), pp. 183–94.

9. The history of this idea is outlined in Thomas Haskell's essay in this volume.

10. The question of whether the concept of academic freedom requires traditional epistemological foundations is discussed in the essays by Richard Rorty and Thomas Haskell in this volume. A nonepistemological basis for academic freedom is argued for in the final essays of the volume, by Joan Scott, Ronald Dworkin, Evelyn Fox Keller, and Edward Said.

11. See, for example, Cheney, *Telling the Truth,* pp. 9–17.

12. Richard Hofstadter and Walter Metzger, *The Development of Academic Freedom in the United States* (New York: Columbia University Press, 1955), pp. 287–88.

13. Joan Scott's essay in this volume discusses the connection between academic freedom and disciplinarity.

TWO

Does Academic Freedom Have Philosophical Presuppositions?

Richard Rorty

As Americans use the term, "academic freedom" names some complicated local folkways that have developed in the course of the past century, largely as a result of battles fought by the American Association of University Professors. These customs and traditions insulate colleges and universities from politics and from public opinion. In particular, they insulate teachers from pressure from the public bodies or private boards who pay their wages.

One way to justify such customs is to start from the premise that the search for objective truth is something quite distinct from politics, and indeed distinct from almost all other cultural activities. So, the argument goes, if politics or passion intrudes on that search, the purposes of colleges and universities—the accumulation of knowledge—will not be served. In particular, if universities are politicized, they will no longer be worthy of trust, just as doctors who care more for their fees than for their patients, or judges who care more about popularity than about justice, are no longer worthy of trust. A politicized university will be likely to produce merely opinion, rather than knowledge.

A number of contemporary philosophers, including myself, do their best to complicate the traditional distinctions between the objective and the subjective, reason and passion, knowledge and opinion, science and politics. We offer contentious reinterpretations of these distinctions, draw them in nontraditional ways. For example, we deny that the search for objective truth is a search for correspondence to reality, and urge that it be seen instead as a search for the widest possible intersubjective agreement. So we are often accused of endangering the traditions and practices that people have in mind when they speak of "academic freedom" or "scientific integrity" or "scholarly standards."

This charge assumes that the relation between a belief about the nature of truth and certain social practices is presuppositional. A practice presupposes a belief only if dropping the belief constitutes a good reason for altering the practice. For example, the belief that surgeons do not perform operations merely to make money for themselves or their hospitals, but do so only if there is a good chance that the operation will be beneficial to the patient, is presupposed by current practices of financing health care. The belief that many diseases are caused by bacteria and viruses, and that few can be cured by acupuncture, is presupposed by current practices of disbursing public funds for medical research.

The question of whether academic freedom rests on philosophical presuppositions raises the general question of whether *any* social practice has *philosophical,* as well as empirical, presuppositions. Beliefs about surgeons' motives and about the causes and cures of diseases are empirical presuppositions. Although the empirical–philosophical distinction is itself pretty fuzzy, it is generally agreed that a belief is on the empirical end of the spectrum to the extent that we are clear about what would falsify it. In the medical examples I have used, we are clear about this. Various specific revelations about the success rate of acupuncture, or about the secret protocols of the American College of Surgeons, could have an immediate, devastating, effect on current practices. But when it comes to a philosophical belief like "The truth of a sentence consists in its correspondence to reality," or "Ethical judgments are claims to knowledge, rather than mere expressions of feeling," nobody is very clear about what it would take to make us believe or disbelieve it. Nobody is sure what counts for or against such propositions.

The reasons they are unsure are the same as those why it is unclear whether, if we stopped believing these propositions, we should need to change our practices. Philosophical views are not tied very closely either to observation and experiment or to practice. This is why they are sometimes dismissed as *merely* philosophical, where "merely" suggests that views on these subjects are optional—that most people, for most purposes, can get along without any. But precisely to the extent that such views are in fact optional, social practices do *not* have philosophical presuppositions. The philosophical propositions said to be presuppositional turn out to be rhetorical ornaments of practice, rather than foundations of practice. This is because we have much more confidence in the practice in question than in any of its possible philosophical justifications.

In a culture which regards debates among philosophers with appropriate insouciance, purported philosophical foundations would suffer the same fate as has, in the two centuries since the Enlightenment, overtaken theological foundations. As American society has become more and more secular, the conviction has grown that a person's religious beliefs, and perhaps even her lack of any such beliefs, are irrelevant to her participation in most of our social practices. But it was not always that way. Article 6 of the Constitution of the United States, which forbids religious tests for office, was hardly uncontroversial. The conservatives who had doubts about Jefferson's Virginia Statute of Religious Freedom were convinced that participation in many of our institutions and practices presupposed Christian belief. They had a plausible case. But Jefferson, we now say with the benefit of hindsight, had a better case.

One useful example of the change in the relation between religious and other social practices is the gradual shift in attitudes toward oath taking between Jefferson's time and our own. Taking oaths has always been integral to legal practice, but there has been considerable disagreement about what an oath is, what sort of people can take it, and what presuppositions taking it involves. At the beginning of our century the *Encyclopædia Britannica* still defined an oath as "an asseveration or promise made under non-human penalty or sanction." The author of the relevant article offered dozens of instances of the relevance of belief in such sanctions—for example, Siamese Buddhists who made themselves eligible as witnesses in court by praying that, if they lied, they be punished by five hundred reincarnations as a beast and five hundred more as a hermaphrodite.

Nowadays most of us who are called upon to be witnesses in court, atheists and theists alike, solemnly and sincerely swear to tell the whole truth without giving much thought to the existence or nature of nonhuman penalties or sanctions. We atheists no longer even bother to distinguish between swearing and affirming, although that distinction was of great concern to the British House of Commons when the atheist Charles Bradlaugh asked to be seated, and was written into British law in 1888 only after anguished debate. No bailiff asks us about our religious beliefs before administering the oath. The suggestion that she do so would be regarded by the court as an absurd waste of time. Truthfulness under oath is, by now, a matter of our civic religion, our relation to our fellow Americans rather than to a nonhuman power. The relation between belief in the existence of a certain kind of God and the practice of oath taking used to be presuppositional, but now it is not.

As I see it, it is with truth as it is with truth telling: philosophical debates about the nature of truth should become as irrelevant to academic practices as debates about the existence and forms of postmortem punishment are to present-day judicial practices. Just as we have much more confidence in our judicial system than we do in any account of the afterlife, or the workings of divine Providence, so we have, or at least should have, much more confidence in our colleges and universities than we do in any philosophical view about the nature of truth, or objectivity, or rationality.

More specifically, I shall argue in what follows that philosophers who deny that there is any such thing as the correspondence of a belief to reality, and thus seem to many nonphilosophers to have denied the existence of truth, are no more dangerous to the pursuit of truth than theologians who deny the existence of hellfire. Such theologians put neither morality nor Christianity in danger, and such philosophers endanger neither the university nor society. Those theologians did, however, change our sense of what Christianity was—of what it takes to be a good Christian. We now have a conception of Christianity which would have seemed perverse and outrageous to many of our eighteenth-century ancestors, though not to Jefferson. Analogously, these philosophers may gradually change our sense of what a university is and what its role in society is. We may wind up with a conception of the university and its social role that might have seemed outrageous to von Humboldt and to Nicholas Murray Butler, though not to John Dewey.

I view it as a mark of moral and intellectual progress that we are more and more prepared to judge institutions, traditions, and practices by the good they seem to be doing rather than by the philosophical or theological beliefs invoked in their defense. More generally, I view it as a mark of such progress that we are coming to think of such beliefs as abbreviations of practices rather than as foundations for practices, and that we are able to see many different beliefs as equally good abbreviations for the same practice. My view of the nonpresuppositional relation of any given set of philosophical convictions to academic freedom is of a piece with President Eisenhower's famous dictum that America is firmly founded in religious belief, and that it doesn't matter which religion it is. I think that there are a lot of different philosophical beliefs about the nature of truth and rationality that can be invoked to defend the traditions and practices that we call "academic freedom," and that in the short run, at least, it does not greatly matter which ones we pick.[1]

A distinguished fellow-philosopher, John Searle, sharply disagrees with me on this point. Outside of philosophy, Searle and I agree on a great deal. We are equally suspicious of the mannered posturing and the resentful self-righteousness of the academic Left in the United States. We are equally suspicious of attempts to require courses which will shape students' socio-political attitudes, the sort of courses which students at Berkeley now refer to as "compulsory chapel." We are equally nostalgic for the days when leftist professors concerned themselves with issues in real politics (such as the availability of health care to the poor, or the need for strong labor unions) rather than with academic politics. But Searle and I disagree over the relevance of our professional specialty—philosophy—to the phenomena we both dislike.

In an article entitled "Rationality and Realism: What Is at Stake?" Searle describes what he calls "the Western Rationalistic Tradition," and says that it is under attack from such philosophers as Thomas Kuhn, Jacques Derrida, and myself.[2] Searle goes on to say that

> The biggest single consequence of the rejection of the Western Rationalistic Tradition is that it makes possible an abandonment of traditional standards of objectivity, truth, and rationality, and opens the way for an educational agenda one of whose primary purposes is to achieve social and political transformation.[3]

Searle lists a number of philosophical positions that he regards as central to the Western Rationalistic Tradition, but I shall discuss only two: the claim that, in Searle's words, "knowledge is typically of a mind-independent reality," and the claim that knowledge is expressed in "propositions which are true because they accurately represent that reality." I disagree with both claims. I agree with Kuhn that we should

> deny all meaning to claims that successive scientific beliefs become more and more probable or better and better approximations to the truth and simultaneously suggest that the subject of truth claims cannot be a relation between beliefs and a putatively mind-independent or "external" world.[4]

I agree with Hilary Putnam that

> Elements of what we call "language" or "mind" penetrate so deeply into what we call "reality" that the very project of representing ourselves as being "mappers" of something "language-independent" is fatally compromised from the start. Like Relativism, Realism is an impossible attempt to view the world from Nowhere.[5]

Kuhn, Putnam, Derrida, and I could all agree with Donald Davidson that

> It is futile either to reject or accept the idea that the real and the true are "independent of our beliefs." The only evident positive sense we can make of this phrase, the only use that derives from the intentions of those who prize it, derives from the idea of correspondence, and this is an idea without content.[6]

The detailed arguments which go on between philosophers like Davidson, Putnam, Derrida, Kuhn, and myself—philosophers who think that "correspondence to reality" is a term without content—and philosophers like Searle, are as baffling to nonspecialists as those between theologians who debate transubstantiation, or who ask whether it is worse to be reincarnated as a hermaphrodite than as a beast. The technical, nit-picking character of both sets of arguments is itself a reason for suspecting that the issues debated are not very closely tied in with our social practices.

If what Searle calls "traditional standards of objectivity, truth, and rationality" are simply the normal practices of the academy—or, to give Searle the benefit of the doubt, those practices as they were before people like Kuhn, Derrida, and I began to muddy the waters—then I see no more reason to think that abandoning a belief in correspondence will make one a less honest scholar than to think that abandoning a belief in God will make one a less honest witness. The loyalty of philosophers on both sides of the argument about correspondence to these "traditional standards" is much greater than their attachment to the significance, or the insignificance, of the idea of "correspondence."

Searle is right, however, that the bad guys tend to favor my side of the argument. There really are people around who have no qualms about converting academic departments and disciplines into political power bases. These people do not share Searle's and my reverence for the traditions of the university, and they would like to find philosophical support for the claim that such reverence is misplaced. Here is an example of the kind of rhetoric which Searle quotes with relish as an illustration of the evil influence of views like mine: "As the most powerful modern philosophies and theories have been demonstrating, claims of disinterest, objectivity and universality are not to be trusted, and themselves tend to reflect local historical conditions."[7] I have to admit to Searle that the committee which produced that dreadful sentence included people who really do believe that the philosophical views I share with Kuhn and Derrida entail that the universities have no further use for notions like "disinterest" and "objectivity."

But these people are wrong. What we deny is that these notions can be explained or defended by reference to the notion of "correspondence to mind-independent reality." Philosophers on my side of the argument think that we can only explain what we mean when we say that academic research should be disinterested and objective by pointing to the ways in which free universities actually function. We can only defend such universities by pointing to the good which these universities do, to their role in keeping democratic government and liberal institutions alive and functioning.

The distinction I am drawing is analogous to that between saying "we have no further use for Christianity" and saying "we cannot explain the Eucharist by reference to Aristotelian notions of substance and accident." At the time of the Council of Trent, many intelligent people thought that if we gave up on the Aristotelian-Thomistic account of the Eucharist, then the Christian religion, and thus the stability of the European sociopolitical order, would be endangered. But they were mistaken. Christianity survived the abandonment of this account, and survived in what Protestants think of as a desirably purified form.

Philosophers on my side of the argument think that if we stop trying to give epistemological justifications for academic freedom, and instead give sociopolitical justifications, we shall be both more honest and more clear-headed. We think that disinterested, objective inquiry would not only survive the adoption of our philosophical views but might survive in a desirably purified form. One result of the adoption of our views might be, for example, that physics-envy will become less prevalent, and that distinctions between disciplines will no longer be drawn in phallogocentric terms, such as "hard" and "soft." Biologists and historians might stop looking down their noses at colleagues in other departments who cannot produce experimental or archival data in support of their conclusions. We might stop debating the pointless and tiresome question of whether doctoral dissertations in English literature constitute contributions to knowledge, rather than being merely expressions of opinion. Sociologists and psychologists might stop asking themselves whether they are following rigorous scientific procedures and start asking themselves whether they have any suggestions to make to their fellow citizens about how our lives, or our institutions, should be changed.

The crucial move made by people on my side of the argument about the nature of objectivity is that, just as the only difference between unconsecrated and consecrated bread is in the social practices appropriate to each, so the only difference between desirable objectivity and undesirable politicization is the difference between the social practices conducted in the name of each. The point, we say, is not whether Christ is Really Present in the bread, but whether we should treat a consecrated Host as we would a snack. The point is not whether disinterested and objective inquiry will lead to correspondence to mind-independent reality, but how to keep the Old Guard from freezing out the Young Turks while simultaneously preventing the Young Turks from wrecking the university.

A healthy and free university accommodates generational change, radical religious and political disagreement, and new social responsibilities as best it can. It muddles through. There are no rules for this muddling through, any more than there are rules that our appellate judges follow when they accommodate old constitutional provisions to new sociopolitical situations. Debate at English department faculty meetings is no less, and no more, rational than at the conferences where justices of the Supreme Court discuss pending cases. As many philosophers of law advise us, attempts to draw nice clean lines between law and morality, or between jurisprudence and politics, meet with little success. The question of whether the judges of the higher courts explain what the law already is, or instead make new law, is as idle as the philosophical question about whether literary criticism produces knowledge or opinion. But recognizing the idleness of the first question does not make philosophers of law, or the rest of us, value the ideal of a free and independent judiciary any the less. Nor does it make us less able to tell good judges from bad judges, any more than our lack of an epistemology of literary criticism makes us less able to tell good critics from bad critics, boring pedants from original minds.

More generally, the experience that each of us has had with decisions about curriculum and appointments should persuade us that the distinction between academic politics and the disinterested pursuit of truth is pretty fuzzy. But that fuzziness does not, and should not, make us treasure free and independent universities any the less. Neither philosophers nor anyone else can offer us nice sharp distinctions between appropriate social utility and inappropriate politicization. But we have accumulated a lot of experience about how to keep redrawing this line, how to adjust it to meet the needs of each new generation. We have managed to do so in ways that have kept our colleges and universities healthy and free.

One of the things this accumulated experience has taught us is that universities are unlikely to remain healthy and free once people outside the universities take a hand in redrawing this line. The one thing that has proved worse than letting the university order its own affairs—letting its members quarrel constantly and indecisively about what shall count as science or as scholarship—is letting somebody else order those affairs. As long as we keep this lesson in mind and manage to keep the traditions of civility alive within the academy, what Searle calls "traditional standards of objectivity, truth, and rationality" will take care of themselves. These standards are not under the guardianship of the philosophers, and changes in opinion among the philosophy professors will not cause us to abjure or change them. As Nelson Goodman said about logic, all the logician can do is tell you what deductive arguments people usually accept as valid; she cannot correct their notions of deductive validity. Similarly, all we philosophers can do when asked for standards or methods of disinterested and objective inquiry is to describe how the people we most admire conduct their inquiries. We have no independent information about how objective truth is to be obtained.

So much for the overall argument I should like to offer. I want to turn now to the more technical aspects of the disagreement between myself and Searle. The central question that Searle raises is whether, if we do not believe in mind-independent reality, we can still believe in, and insist upon, objectivity.[8] Philosophers on my side of the argument answer that objectivity is not a matter of corresponding to objects but of getting together with other subjects—that there is nothing to objectivity except intersubjectivity. So when Searle says "If there is no such thing as objective truth and validity, then you might as well discuss the person making the statement and his motives for making it," we rejoin that nobody ever said there was no such thing as objective truth and validity. What we say is that you gain nothing for the pursuit of such truth by talking about the mind-dependence or mind-independence of reality. All there is to talk about are the procedures we use for bringing about agreement between inquirers.

One reason that the question of mind-independent reality is so vexed and confusing is an ambiguity in the notion of "independence." Searle sometimes writes as if philosophers who, like myself, do not believe in mind-independent reality must deny that there were mountains before people had the idea of "mountain" in their minds, or the word "mountain" in their language. But nobody denies that. Nobody thinks that there is a chain of causes which makes mountains an effect of thoughts or words. What people like Kuhn, Derrida, and I believe is that it is pointless to ask whether there really are mountains or whether it is merely convenient for us to talk about mountains.

We also think it pointless to ask, for example, whether neutrinos are real entities or merely useful heuristic fictions. This is the sort of thing we mean by saying that it is pointless to ask whether reality is independent of our ways of talking about it. Given that it pays to talk about mountains, as it certainly does, one of the obvious truths about mountains is that they were here before we talked about them. If you do not believe that, you probably do not know how to play the usual language-games that employ the word "mountain." But the utility of those language-games has nothing to do with the question of whether Reality as It Is In Itself, apart from the way it is handy for human beings to describe it, has mountains in it. That question is about the other, *non*causal, sense of "independence." My side thinks nothing could possibly turn on the answers to questions of independence in *that* sense, and that therefore we can get along quite nicely without the notion of Reality as It Is In Itself.

Davidson says that the question of whether the real is "independent of our beliefs" should not be asked because he thinks that the only relevant sense of independence is not "causal antecedence" but "existence in itself." He thinks that the notion of "correspondence to reality" is useless because the relevant reality is reality "as it is in itself." We who agree with Davidson think that the whole project of distinguishing between what exists in itself and what exists in relation to human minds—the project shared by Aristotle, Locke, Kant, and Searle—is no longer worth pursuing.[9] This project, like the project of underwriting the sanctity of the Eucharist, once looked interesting, promising, and potentially useful. But it did not pan out. It has turned out to be a dead end.

Another semitechnical point I need to make concerns an ambiguity lurking in the notion of "accurate representation." Searle says, you recall, that the Western Rationalistic Tradition holds that knowledge is expressed in "propositions which are true because they accurately represent that [mind-independent] reality." We Davidsonians want to distinguish between two senses of the term "accurately represent." In the nonphilosophical sense of this term, to ask a witness if she has accurately represented a situation is to ask about her truthfulness or her carefulness. When we say that good historians accurately represent what they find in the archives, we mean that they look hard for relevant documents, do not discard documents tending to discredit the historical thesis they are propounding, do not misleadingly quote passages out of context, tell the same historical story among themselves that they tell us, and so on. To assume that a historian accurately represents the facts as she knows them is to assume that she behaves in the way in which good, honest historians behave. It is not to assume anything about the reality of past events, or the truth-conditions of statements about such events, or about the necessarily hermeneutical character of the *Geisteswissenschaften,* or about any other philosophical topic.[10]

But when philosophers discuss the question of whether knowledge consists in accuracy of representation, they are not concerned with honesty or carefulness. The question at issue between representationalists like Searle and antirepresentationalists like me is merely this: Can we pair off parts of the world with parts of beliefs or sentences, so as to be able to say that the relations between the latter match the relations between the former? Can true beliefs or sentences be treated on the model of realistic portraiture? There are obviously some cases which can be so treated, such as the immortal "The cat is on the mat." There are lots of other cases, such as the sentence "Neutrinos have no mass" or "The pursuit of scholarly truth requires academic freedom," to which the notion of "parts of the world" has no evident application. We philosophers haggle endlessly about whether the notions of "correspondence" and "representation" can be extended to these harder cases. When we are tired of haggling about that, we start haggling over whether there is any criterion for whether a belief accurately represents reality other than its coherence with the rest of our beliefs and, if not, whether we should distinguish between the *criterion* of true belief and the *nature* of true belief.

Searle's claim that the correspondence theory of truth has moral or social importance runs together the philosophical and nonphilosophical senses of "accurate representation." If we antirepresentationalists and anti-correspondentists ever win our argument with Searle, that will give historians and physicists no reason to behave differently than they presently do. Nor, I suspect, will their morale or their efficiency improve if Searle and his fellow representationalists should win. Honesty, care, truthfulness, and other moral and social virtues are just not that closely connected with what we philosophy professors eventually decide to be the least problematic way of describing the relationship between human inquiry and the rest of the universe.

The claim about a lack of close connection which I have just made is not put forward as a philosophical truth about the necessary, ahistorical relation of philosophy to the rest of culture. It is simply a sociological truth about the lack of interest which most people, intellectuals as well as nonintellectuals, currently have in philosophy. It is like the truth that the adoption of the ethics of love suggested by St. Paul does not depend upon the Orthodox, as opposed to the Arian, position on the relation between the First and

Second Persons of the Trinity. That is a sociological truth about contemporary Christians, not an ahistorical truth about the relation between ethics and theology. Things were otherwise in the days when not only your physical safety but your choice of which charioteers to cheer for in the hippodrome depended upon your theological allegiance.

If Searle has his way—if he succeeds in persuading us (or even in persuading funding agencies) that the relation between the Western Rationalistic Tradition and current academic practices is in fact presuppositional, and that refuting Kuhn, Derrida, and me is an urgent social need—then the academy will divide up into those who cheer for the representationalist philosophical team and those who (selflessly sacrificing grants for the sake of philosophical correctness) cheer for their opponents. Scholars and scientists will go around asking each other, and being asked by grant givers, "Which side are you on?"

I think that would be unfortunate, if only because it would be a waste of people's time and of their emotional energy. It would be better to distinguish the ethics of the academy—the customs and practices that help to determine the attitude of students to books, faculty to students, administrators to faculty and donors, and so on—from the private theological or philosophical convictions of any of the persons involved. To help keep the academy free and depoliticized, we should, for example, make sure that professors do not mock the beliefs of their students, that donors do not designate particular persons to fill the chairs they endow, and that a scholar's conclusions about controversial issues within her field, or about political or philosophical matters, continue to be irrelevant to her membership in the university. But we should not worry about whether true sentences accurately represent mind-independent reality.

So far I have been arguing that philosophy does not make much difference to our practices, and that it should not be allowed to do so. But this may seem a strange position for somebody who calls himself a Pragmatist. We Pragmatists say that every difference must make a difference to practice. Yet we think it important to argue that the Western Rationalistic Tradition, as Searle defines it, is *wrong*. We insist on trying to develop another, better, tradition. So how can we, without dishonesty, say that philosophical controversies do not matter all that much?

We Pragmatists can make our position consistent, I think, by saying that although such controversies don't matter much in the short run, they may well matter a lot in the long run. The Christian who believes that God will punish him with hellfire if he lies under oath and the atheist who believes that he will be unable to live with himself if betrays the social compact by committing perjury will, in the short run, do the same thing. But in the long run it may make a lot of difference whether a society is regulated by its members' fear of nonhuman sanctions or by secular sentiments of pride, loyalty, and solidarity. The physicist who describes himself as uncovering the absolute, intrinsic, in-itself character of reality and his colleague who describes herself as assembling better instruments for prediction and control of the environment will, in their race to solve the same problem, do much the same things. But in the long run physicists whose rhetoric is Pragmatist rather than Western Rationalistic might be better citizens of a better academic community.

Deep emotional needs are fulfilled by the Western Rationalistic Tradition, but not all such needs should be fulfilled. Deep emotional needs were fulfilled by belief in nonhuman judges and nonhuman sanctions. These were the needs that Dostoyevsky evinced when he said that if God did not exist, everything would be permitted. But these needs should be, and to some extent have been, sublimated or replaced, rather than gratified. I have pressed the analogies between theological and philosophical belief because I see the Western Rationalistic Tradition as a secularized version of the Western Monotheist Tradition—as the latest twist on what Heidegger calls "ontotheology." We Pragmatists take the same dim view of Absolute Truth, and of Reality as It Is In Itself, as the Enlightenment took of Divine Wrath and Divine Judgment.

John Dewey once quoted G. K. Chesterton's remark that "Pragmatism is a matter of human needs and one of the first of human needs is to be something more than a pragmatist."[11] Chesterton had a point, and Dewey granted it. Dewey was quite aware of what he called "a supposed necessity of the 'human mind' to believe in certain absolute truths." But he thought that this necessity had existed only in an earlier stage of human history, a stage which we might now move beyond. He thought that we had reached a point at which it might be possible, and helpful, to wrench ourselves free of it. He recognized that his suggestion was counterintuitive and would meet the kind of opposition which Searle mounts. But he thought that the long-run good done by getting rid of outdated needs would outweigh the temporary disturbance caused by attempts to change our philosophical intuitions.

As Dewey saw it, the need to distinguish between the pursuit of truth "for its own sake" and the pursuit of what Bacon called "the improvement of man's estate" arose out of particular social conditions.[12] These conditions prevailed in ancient Greece and made it useful to draw certain distinctions that became, in the course of time, part of our common sense. These included, for example, the distinctions between theory and practice, mind and body, objective and subjective, morality and prudence, and all the others which Derrida groups together as "the binary oppositions of Western metaphysics."

Dewey was happy to admit that these distinctions had, in their time, served us well. In their time, they were neither confusions, nor repressive devices, nor mystifications. On the contrary: they were instruments which Greek thinkers used to change social conditions, often for the better. But over a couple of millennia these instruments outlived their usefulness. Dewey thought that, just as many Christians have outgrown the need to ask whether the sentences of the Creed correspond to objective reality, so civilization as a whole might outgrow the supposed necessity to believe in absolute truths.

Dewey learned from Hegel to historicize everything, including Hegel's own picturesque but outdated story of the union of subject and object at the end of History. Like Marx, Dewey dropped Hegel's notion of Absolute Spirit but kept his insight that ideas and movements which had begun as instruments of emancipation (Greek metaphysics, Christianity, the Rise of the Bourgeoisie, the Hegelian System) had typically, over the course of time, turned into instruments of repression—into parts of what Dewey called "the crust of convention." Dewey thought that the idea of absolute truths was such an idea, and that the pragmatic theory of truth was "true in the pragmatic sense of truth: it works, it clears up difficulties, removes obscurities, puts individuals into more experimental, less dogmatic, and less arbitrarily sceptical relations to life." "The pragmatist," he continued, "is quite content to have the truth of his theory consist in its working in these various ways, and to leave to the intellectualist the proud possession of [truth as] an unanalyzable, unverifiable, unworking property."[13]

Dewey said that Chesterton's remark "has revealed that the chief objection of absolutists to the pragmatic doctrine of the personal (or 'subjective') factor in belief is that the pragmatist has spilled the personal milk in the absolutist's cocoanut."[14] His point was that Chesterton had implicitly admitted that the best, and perhaps the only argument, for the absolutist view of truth was that it satisfied a human need. Dewey saw that need as one we could outgrow. Just as the child outgrows the need for parental care and the need to believe in parental omnipotence and benevolence, so we may in time outgrow the need to believe in divinities that concern themselves with our happiness, and in the possibility of allying ourselves with a nonhuman power called the Intrinsic Nature of Reality. In doing so, we might outgrow both the need to see ourselves as deeply sinful and guilty and the need to escape from the relative to the absolute. Eventually, Dewey thought, the subjective-objective distinction and relative-absolute distinctions might become as obsolete as the distinction between the soul and the body or between natural and supernatural causes.

Dewey was quite aware, however, that the good work still being done by old distinctions would have to be taken over by new distinctions. He was also quite aware of what Berkeley called the need to "speak with the vulgar and think with the learned," to apply different strokes to different folks. So his writings are a sometimes confusing mixture of invocations of familiar distinctions with counterintuitive, philosophical reinterpretations of those distinctions. His reformulations were often, at least to the vulgar, merely bewildering. So we should not be surprised to find Dewey, at the same time that he was energetically defending the pragmatic theory of truth against his absolutist opponents, writing such sentences as "The university function is the truth-function" and "The one thing that is inherent and essential [to the idea of the university] is the idea of truth."[15]

The nonphilosophers who read these sentences, which appeared in 1902 in an article called "Academic Freedom," probably took "the idea of truth" to mean something like "the idea of an accurate representation of the intrinsic nature of reality." Most people still take it to mean something like that. They automatically contrast the attempt to get such representa-tions—to attain objective truth—with the attempt to make people happy, to fulfill human needs. The latter, they say, involves an element of subjectiv-ity which should be excluded from science and scholarship. When such people are told by Searle and others that Kuhn, Derrida, and I deny that true beliefs represent anything, and deny that reality has an intrinsic nature, they may well believe that the university is endangered, and that the need to preserve academic freedom may require the refutation of these dangerous philosophers.[16]

Dewey, I think, would say that if it should ever come down to a choice between the practices and traditions which make up academic freedom and antirepresentationalist theories of truth and knowledge, we should go for academic freedom. We should put first things first. Change in philosophical opinion is, on Dewey's view, in the service of sociopolitical progress. He would have had no interest in sacrificing free universities to his philosophical convictions. But, of course, he did not think that it would ever come down to any such choice. He saw no tension between his philosophical and his political work. I think that he would have accepted my distinction between the short-run and the long-run effects of change in philosophical opinion.

Nothing, including the nature of truth and knowledge, is worth worrying about if this worry will make no difference to practice. But there are all sorts of ways of making a difference. One of them is by slowly, over a long period of time, changing what Wittgenstein called the pictures that hold us captive. We shall always be held captive by some picture or other, for we shall never escape from language or from metaphor—never see either God or the Intrinsic Nature of Reality face to face. But old pictures may have disadvantages that can be avoided by sketching new pictures. Escape from prejudice and superstition, Dewey thought, is not escape from Appearance to Reality, but escape from the satisfaction of old needs into the satisfaction of new needs. It is a process of maturation, not a progress from darkness to light. On his view, escape from the Western Rationalistic Tradition will indeed be an escape from error to truth, but it will not be an escape from the way things appear to the way things really are. It will merely be an escape from immature needs: the needs Chesterton felt and Dewey did not.

By way of conclusion, I shall put Dewey aside and come back to Searle. Searle sees the difference between himself and me as the difference between someone with a decent respect for hard fact (and other associated intellectual virtues) and someone who relishes, and helps encourage, what he calls "the general air of vaguely literary frivolity that pervades the Nietzscheanized Left."[17] He sees as presuppositional the relationships which I see as largely ornamental. He says that the only argument for his own realist, representationalist, view is that

> it forms the presupposition of our linguistic and other sorts of practices: You cannot coherently deny realism and engage in ordinary linguistic practices, because realism is a condition of the normal intelligibility of those practices. You can see this if you consider any sort of ordinary communication. For example, suppose I call my car mechanic to find out if the carburetor is fixed. . . . Now suppose I have reached a deconstructionist car mechanic and he tries to explain to me that a carburetor is just a text anyway, and that there is nothing to talk about except the textuality of the text. . . . Whatever else is clear about such situations, one thing is clear: communication has broken

down. . . . Give me the assumption that these sorts of communication are even possible between human beings and you will see that you require the assumption of an independently existing reality.[18]

I do not think that this frivolously literary car mechanic is a plausible product of the overthrow of the Western Rationalistic Tradition. The deconstructionist Ph.D.s in English who, after finding themselves unemployable in the academy, lucked into jobs as car mechanics have no trouble telling where their jobs stop and their philosophy begins. They would presumably say, as I would, that the difference deconstruction has made to their lives is, like the difference Methodism or atheism made to their ancestors' lives, atmospheric and spiritual. They might even quote Dewey and say, as I myself would, that they have found Derrida's writings useful for getting "into more experimental, less dogmatic, and less arbitrarily sceptical relations to life."

The more serious question, however, is, as I said earlier, the one about presuppositions. I can go some way with Searle on this question. Thus I agree with him when he makes the Wittgensteinian point that

> For those of us brought up in our civilization, especially the scientific portions of our civilization, the principles that I have just presented as those of the Western Rationalistic Tradition do not function as a *theory*. Rather, they function as part of the taken-for-granted background of our practices. The conditions of intelligibility of our practices, linguistic and otherwise, cannot themselves be demonstrated as truths within those practices. To suppose they could was the endemic mistake of foundationalist metaphysics.[19]

I break off from Searle only at the point where he suggests that our practices would somehow become unintelligible if we described what we are doing in different ways—and in particular if we described them in the nonrealist, nonrepresentationalist terms commended by philosophers like Davidson and Derrida.

Searle and I recognize that certain propositions are intuitively obvious, indemonstrable, and taken for granted. But whereas he sees them as incapable of being questioned without questioning the practices themselves (or, at least, their "intelligibility"), I see them as optional glosses on those practices. Where he sees conditions of intelligibility—presuppositions—I see rhetorical flourishes designed to make practitioners feel that they are being true to something big and strong: The Intrinsic Nature of Reality. On my view, the comfort derived from this feeling is, at this stage in the maturation of Western humanity, as unnecessary, and as potentially dangerous, as the comfort derived from the conviction that one is obeying the Will of God.

It is unnecessary and dangerous because our maturation has consisted in the gradual realization that, if we can rely on one another, we need not rely on anything else. In religious terms, this is the Feuerbachian thesis that God was just a projection of the best, and sometimes of the worst, of humanity. In philosophical terms, it is the thesis that anything that talk of objectivity can do to make our practices intelligible can be done equally well by talk of intersubjectivity. In political terms, it is the thesis that if we can just keep democracy and reciprocal tolerance alive, everything else can be settled by muddling through to some reasonable sort of compromise.

To adopt these various theses, it helps to reflect that nothing in your practices requires you to distinguish an intrinsic from an extrinsic feature of reality.[20] If you give up the intrinsic-extrinsic distinction, the distinction between what things are like apart from human needs and interests and what they are like in relation to those needs and interests, you can also give up the idea that there is a great big difference between seeking for human happiness and seeking for scholarly or scientific truth. For now you will not think of the latter search as the attempt to represent the intrinsic features of reality, without regard to human needs, but as finding descriptions of reality which satisfy certain particular human needs—those which your fellow scientists and scholars have agreed need to be satisfied. The difference between bad subjectivity and sound scholarship will now be glossed as that between the satisfaction of private, idiosyncratic, and perhaps secret needs and the satisfaction of needs which are widely shared, well publicized, and freely debated.

This substitution of objectivity-as-intersubjectivity for objectivity-as-accurate-representation is the key Pragmatic move, the one that lets Pragmatists feel that they can have moral seriousness without "realist" seriousness. For moral seriousness is a matter of taking other human beings seriously, and not taking anything else with equal seriousness. It turns out, Pragmatists say, that we can take each other very seriously indeed without taking the intrinsic nature of reality seriously at all. We shall not change our practices—either political or academic—merely because we have ceased to concern ourselves with epistemology, or because we have adopted nonrepresentationalist philosophies of language and mind. But we may change our attitudes toward these practices, our sense of why it is important to carry them out. Our new sense of what we are doing will be itself as indemonstrable, and as intuitive, as was the Western Rationalistic Tradition. But Pragmatists think it will be better, not just because it will free philosophers from perpetual oscillation between skepticism and dogmatism, but because it will take away a few more excuses for fanaticism and intolerance.

NOTES

1. Eisenhower might have added that any religion that is dubious about American democratic institutions must have something wrong with it. I should claim that any philosophy that is dubious about the folkways that we call "academic freedom" must have something wrong with it.

2. John Searle, "Rationality and Realism: What Is at Stake?" *Daedalus* 122 (Fall 1992): 55–84.

3. Ibid., p. 72.

4. T. S. Kuhn, "Afterwords," in *World Changes: Thomas Kuhn and the Nature of Science,* ed. Paul Horwich (Cambridge, Mass.: MIT Press, 1993), p. 330.

5. Hilary Putnam, *Reality with a Human Face* (Cambridge, Mass.: Harvard University Press, 1990), p. 28. For my differences with Putnam, who considers me a "cultural relativist" and has some sympathy with Searle's criticisms of me and Derrida, if not those of Kuhn, see my "Putnam and the Relativist Menace," *Journal of Philosophy* 90 (September 1993): 443–61.

6. Donald Davidson, "The Structure and the Content of Truth," *Journal of Philosophy* 87 (June 1990): 305.

7. The American Council of Learned Societies, *Speaking for the Humanities,* ACLS Occasional Paper, no. 7 (1989), p. 18; quoted in Searle, "Rationality and Realism," p. 69.

8. Compare Thomas Haskell's remark in chap. 3: "[If] there is no respectable sense . . . in which we are entitled to say that there is a 'nature of things' for inquirers to 'get right,' then one cannot help wondering what the community of inquiry is for." Later in his essay Haskell describes me as differing from Peirce, Lovejoy, and Dewey in that I am unable to say, as they did, that some interpretations were better than others, "better in a strong sense that did not necessarily depend on correspondence and yet was not reducible to perspective." But all I am interested in is getting rid of correspondence, and the notion of the "intrinsic nature" of things which is needed to make sense of correspondence. I do not want to reduce anything to perspective and would not know how to do so. See my remarks on relativism in "Solidarity or Objectivity?" in my *Objectivity, Relativism, and Truth* (Cambridge: Cambridge University Press, 1991) and in "Putnam and the Relativist Menace."

9. For Searle's clearest statement of this distinction, see his *The Rediscovery of the Mind* (Cambridge, Mass.: MIT Press, 1992), p. 211: "It is essential to understand the distinction between features of the world that are *intrinsic* and features that are *observer relative.* The expressions 'mass,' 'gravitational attraction,' and 'molecule' name features of the world that are intrinsic. If all observers and users cease to exist, the world still contains mass, gravitational attraction, and molecules. But expressions such as 'nice day for a picnic' . . . name objects by specifying some feature that has been assigned to them, some feature that is relative to observers and users."

For Pragmatists like me, the feature of being a molecule is just as much or as little "relative to observers and users" as the suitability of a day for a picnic. So we are not sure whether, as Searle goes on to say, "if there had never been any users or observers, there would be no such features as being a nice day for a picnic." We see no useful purpose served by this attempt to distinguish intrinsic from observer-relative features of reality. "Essential," we ask Searle, "for what?"

10. Here I find myself in disagreement with Joyce Appleby, Lynn Hunt, and Margaret Jacob, in their *Telling the Truth about History* (New York: Norton, 1994). They say that "The most distinctive of historians' problems is that posed by temporality itself. . . . The past, insofar as it exists at all, exists in the present; the historian too is stuck in time present, trying to make meaningful and accurate statements about time past. Any account of historical objectivity must provide for this crucial temporal dimension" (p. 253). I am not sure who has had the "debilitating doubts that the past is knowable" (p. 270) of which they speak, nor why we should take such doubts more seriously than Descartes' doubt about the existence of matter. I do not think that there is something called "temporality" which poses a big problem, nor that we require either a "theory of objectivity for the twenty-first century" (p. 254) or a "revitalized and transformed practice of objectivity" (p. 237).

One of the morals of what Kuhn says about the difference between textbook accounts of inquiry, written by people with philosophical axes to grind, and the actual processes of initiation into a disciplinary matrix (such as historiography) seems to me to be that we have never had much of a "theory of objectivity," and that we do not need a new one now. What we have had, and will with luck continue to have, is what Thomas Haskell (following Francis Abbot) calls "communities of the competent," communities which can muddle their way through an unending process of self-transformation without philosophical assistance.

Appleby and her colleagues think philosophy does help, and so they offer, as part of a "combination of practical realism and pragmatism," an "epistemological position that claims that people's perceptions of the world have some correspondence with that world." Philosophers like me think that "correspondence to reality" is just an uncashable and obsolete metaphor. So for us "some correspondence" is like "somewhat pregnant"; we do not think the issue is about *how much* correspondence perception or historiography might have. The epistemological position these three historians propose seems to us to fall between two irreconcilable alternatives, rather than providing a happy synthesis or compromise.

11. G. K. Chesterton, quoted in John Dewey, "A Short Catechism Concerning Truth," *The Middle Works of John Dewey* (Carbondale: Southern Illinois University Press, 1978), 6:11.

12. See, on this point, the opening chapters of Dewey's *The Quest for Certainty* (New York: Minton Balch and Co., 1929); reprinted in *John Dewey: The Later Works, 1925–1953* (Carbondale: Southern Illinois University Press, 1984), vol. 4.

13. Ibid., p. 9.

14. Ibid., p. 11. Robert Westbrook (*John Dewey and American Democracy* [Ithaca, N.Y.: Cornell University Press, 1991], pp. 137–38) cites this passage and points out that it applies to Bertrand Russell's criticisms of Pragmatism as well as to Chesterton's. Pragmatism's radicalism and originality are nicely instanced by its ability to question a presupposition common to Chesterton and Russell, writers who had very little else in common.

15. John Dewey, "Academic Freedom," *John Dewey: The Middle Works, 1899–1924* 2:55.

16. Searle is of course only one of a great number of philosophers who take this line. John Silber, president of Boston University and a well-known Kant scholar, reported to his trustees that "Some versions of critical theory, radical feminism and multiculturalism, among other intellectual positions, are ideological in character and inhospitable to free

intellectual inquiry" and that "We [at Boston University] have resisted relativism as an official intellectual dogma, believing that there is such a thing as truth, and if you can't achieve it, at least you can approach it" (see "New Eruptions at Boston U.," *The Chronicle of Higher Education,* December 8, 1993, p. A27). Nineteen philosophers signed a letter to the *Times* of London saying that Derrida should not receive an honorary degree from Cambridge because his work offers "little more than semi-intelligible attacks upon the values of reason, truth and scholarship" (*The Times* [London], May 9, 1992).

It is instructive to compare such assaults to those written, in the 1930s and 1940s, against logical positivism by C. E. M. Joad, Mortimer Adler, Brand Blanshard, and other philosophers. In its brief heyday, logical positivism was as fanatical, intolerant, and brutal as any intellectual movement has ever been, but by now the cries of "civilization in danger!" that were raised against it seem a bit overwrought. Many of the slogans of poststructuralism now current in our universities, the slogans that Searle sees as exemplifying literary frivolity and dangerous politicization, will come to seem as silly and self-righteously snotty as the youthful excesses of the first generation of logical positivists now seem to us. But the brief reign of poststructuralism will probably do a bit of good, just as the brief reign of logical positivism did. Poststructuralism claims far too much for literature and for politics, just as positivism claimed far too much for science and for philosophy. But intellectual progress is often made by just such violent pendulum swings.

17. Searle, "Rationality and Realism," p. 78. Searle's phrase "literary frivolity," like his reference (quoted below) to "the more scientific portions of our civilization" is characteristic of the traditional alliance of analytic philosophy with the sciences against the humanities. In the 1930s, the heyday of logical positivism and the seedtime of analytic philosophy, the contrast between Carnap's respect for scientists and Heidegger's respect for poets was seen as a contrast between responsibility and frivolous irresponsibility.

If you say that "the university function is the truth function," and if you think of truth as something about which you can expect to get consensus, then, as Louis Menand points out in this volume, "the criticism of literature has the weakest case for inclusion in the professional structure of the research university." The books of F. R. Leavis or Harold Bloom are not happily described as "contributions to knowledge." But this apparent weakness is a product of the mistaken idea that consensus among inquirers—consensus of the sort which Leavis and Bloom knew better than to hope for—is the goal of any responsible intellectual activity.

I hope that this latter idea, and the resulting split between C. P. Snow's "two cultures," will sooner or later become obsolete. We might hasten the process of obsolescence by reflecting that we are much more certain of the value of the departments of English literature than we are about the nature of the research university, or of knowledge. English departments can always be made to look silly by asking them what they have contributed to knowledge lately. But humanists can make biology or mathematics departments look bad by asking what they have done lately for human freedom. The best thing about our universities is the live-and-let-live spirit which lets us wave such pointless questions aside. When outside pressure makes us nervous and self-conscious, we start asking bad questions like "What *is* a university, anyway?" That question is almost certain to be answered by invidious comparisons between disciplines, and especially between the sciences and the humanities.

18. Ibid., p. 81. Searle goes on to say that "One interesting thing about the present theorists who claim to have shown that reality is a social construct, or that there is no

independently existing reality, or that everything is really a text, is that they have denied one of the conditions of intelligibility of our ordinary linguistic practices without providing an alternative conception of that intelligibility." Pragmatists do not think there are such things as conditions of intelligibility. There are only tacit agreements to continue with certain social practices.

19. Searle, "Rationality and Realism," p. 80.

20. But you can still happily agree with common sense that there were dinosaurs and mountains long before anybody described them as dinosaurs and mountains, that thinking doesn't make it so, and that bank accounts and gender roles are social constructions in a sense in which giraffes are not. There would have been no bank accounts or gender roles had there been no human societies, whereas there would have been giraffes. But that is not to say that giraffes are part of Reality as It Is In Itself, apart from human needs and interests. In a wider sense of "social construction," everything, including giraffes and molecules, is socially constructed, for no vocabulary (e.g., that of zoology or physics) cuts reality at the joints. Reality has no joints. It just has descriptions—some more socially useful than others.

THREE

Justifying the Rights of Academic Freedom in the Era of "Power/Knowledge"

Thomas L. Haskell

A hundred years ago, when the old-time colleges seemed to have lost their way and the modern university system was still struggling to be born, American academics worried about an entire range of questions that hardly anyone asks today. Broadly speaking, the questions lay at the intersection of epistemology and intellectual authority. How is knowledge best cultivated? What institutional setting is most conducive to intellectual authority? How is the professoriate to justify its existence to those who pay the bills? What is the university *for?*

Questions of this kind, which carry no special charge today, seemed urgent indeed at the turn of the century, when less than 4 percent of the college-age population was attending college and the university had not yet become securely ensconced as gatekeeper to the professions. The Victorian reformers whom we now remember as the architects of the modern American University—Charles William Eliot of Harvard, Andrew Dickson White of Cornell, Daniel Coit Gilman of Johns Hopkins, and many others whose names are less well known—confronted questions of intellectual authority every day and did not have the luxury of suspending judgment. They had to get on with the practical business of building universities, for expanding enrollments and lavish infusions of capital from a burgeoning industrial economy were opening up a world of new possibilities in higher education.[1]

The same developments also brought crude demands for orthodoxy. *43*

State legislators and wealthy private donors alike took it for granted that "he who pays the piper, calls the tune," an assumption strongly seconded by the prevailing legal doctrines of the era. Faced with contradictory possibilities and pressures, Victorian reformers thought long and hard about authority and professional autonomy. They drew inspiration from ancient precedents of faculty self-governance in England and from the full-bodied traditions of academic freedom that many of them had seen at first hand during their own student days in Germany. Their thinking and worrying bore practical fruit during the decades following the Civil War, and we who teach and work in the American university system today are the beneficiaries of what they wrought. Nowhere is the success of their handiwork more evident than in the easy complacency with which we take for granted the intellectual authority of the university and those who work within it.

My aim is to dispel that complacency, at least momentarily, by doing what historians so often do: tell stories about how things came to be the way they are. The story I will tell draws heavily on the work of Walter Metzger, Mary Furner, William Van Alstyne, and other scholars. I will have little to say about either the captains of industry who financed the modern university, or the educational entrepreneurs, such as Eliot, White, and Gilman, who superintended its construction. Nor will I say much about martyrs to academic freedom, with the single exception of Edward A. Ross. His case deserves special attention because it illustrates the late emergence and fragility of the rights we take for granted, and helps us recall the circumstances under which the American Association of University Professors (AAUP) was founded. The focal point of my story is the emergence of the disciplines, such as history, chemistry, sociology, mechanical engineering, and so forth, in which we academics do our work today. These "communities of the competent" were, I believe, the seed crystals around which the modern university formed. Defending their authority is, in my view, what academic freedom is principally about. What concerns me are two things that imperil that authority: the decay of the epistemological assumptions that originally underwrote the founding of disciplinary communities, and a growing assimilation of academic freedom to First Amendment law, a development that has brought immense benefits but at the expense of obscuring both the function of the disciplinary community and its intimate relation to academic freedom. My aim is not to put forth a new justification for academic freedom but to call attention to the limitations of the old one and hold up for critical examination some of the obstacles that stand in our way as we seek a formulation more adequate to our needs.

Appearances to the contrary notwithstanding, the comfortable state of affairs in which we find ourselves today was not foreordained. What brought it about was a process of institutional development that proceeded in two overlapping phases, each vital to the success of the other. The first created communities of competent inquirers, the second used them to establish authority in specialized domains of knowledge. The history of the community of the competent is long and honorable but only sketchily documented. It has roots that go far back into the history of ecclesiastical establishments, on the one hand, and science, on the other, and which intertwine at every stage with controversies over heresy and communal autonomy. The rudiments of an always edgy and competitive communal solidarity among competent inquirers date back to the founding of the first European universities. By the eighteenth century the changing technology and economics of print culture had decisively surpassed personal acquaintance and private correspondence as a means of knitting inquirers together, giving rise to a nascent division of intellectual labor and prompting much speculation about the growing influence of the "republic of letters."[2]

The nineteenth century brought changes of scale so great as to constitute a qualitative transformation of the conditions of intellectual endeavor.[3] Population growth, rising literacy rates, growing per capita income, and the rapid spread of a predominantly urban form of life joined with immense improvements in the ease and speed of communication to make the fruits of specialized intellectual competence relevant and accessible to a larger public than ever before. Architects of the modern American university such as Daniel Coit Gilman at Hopkins capitalized on these changes, not only by constructing ivy-covered classrooms and dormitories to house an expanding clientele of students but also by founding academic journals, reshaping undergraduate libraries to the needs of research, funding graduate fellowships, and encouraging their faculties to seek reputations of national and international scope. The most visible manifestation of the maturing communities around which the university formed were the specialized disciplinary associations that began organizing on a national basis in the 1880s: the Modern Language Association (MLA; 1883), the American Historical Association (AHA; 1884), the American Economic Association (AEA; 1885), and many others in succeeding years.[4] By the time of World War I, a new intellectual division of labor had taken shape as college and university campuses all over the country reorganized themselves around "departments," local outposts of the fields of learning staked out by the national specialist associations. Neither the departments nor the national professional associations they represented were of any great consequence in themselves, but the maturing communities of the competent for which they stood had profound effects on the lives of their members and utterly transformed the character of higher education in this country.

The importance of these newly defined communities lay in the opportunity they provided for professors to divide their loyalties, thereby complicating their identity and enhancing their authority. Professors would, of course, continue to be teachers, dependent as always on a particular college or university for a salary and for provision of the mainly undergraduate classrooms in which they earned their keep. But they would also become something new: research scholars. As such, their employment credentials, even in their traditional role as teachers of undergraduates, would become contingent upon membership and reputation within translocal communities made up of fellow research specialists. By keeping up a constant exchange of communications in the form of journal articles and books, as well as private correspondence and face-to-face conversations at periodic conventions, the members of these far-flung communities, or *Kommunikations-gemeinschaften* as Karl-Otto Apel calls them, would police each other's opinions and thus provide, in theory at least, a collective warrant for one another's authority.[5] Knit together not by affection but by the respectful attention that experts owe to their peers, these densely interactive communities effectively constitute the specialized universes within which scholarly discourse proceeds today.[6] Although they have undeniably generated their share of ponderous mystifications over the years, when all is said and done they have created a space for originality and critical thinking without which modern culture would almost certainly be the poorer.

The second phase of reform harvested what the first planted. Insofar as a distinct community of competent investigators could be said to exist in a given field, the keystone of professional autonomy was already in place, for the individual members of such a community were empowered by its very existence to speak in a quasi-corporate voice. Having acknowledged one another as peers, and thus relieved one another of the heavy burdens of anonymity and idiosyncrasy, they were well situated to deflect criticism originating outside the community's borders and deflate truth claims unable to win communal support. The result of the sharpened identity and growing solidarity of specialists was an effective monopoly on "sound opinion" within their domain. The cardinal principle of professional autonomy is collegial self-governance; its inescapable corollary is that only one's peers are competent to judge one's performance. "Monopoly" is not an inappropriate term to describe the resulting advantage enjoyed by communally sponsored opinion, yet it carries implications that tend to obscure the defining feature of the community. It is vital to remember that this sort of monopoly comes about by *intensifying* competition between producers (in this case, of ideas), not by sheltering them from it, as in the classic case of economic monopoly. *The price of participation in the community of the competent is perpetual exposure to criticism.* If there is anything at all that justifies the special authority and trustworthiness of community-sponsored opinions, as I believe there is, it lies in the fact that these truth-claims have weathered competition more severe than would be thought acceptable in ordinary human communities.[7]

All that remained was to reach an understanding about the practical limits of solidarity. What degrees and kinds of politically sensitive expression would the professoriate be willing actually to defend through collective action? Where was the pale beyond which the outspoken individual would be left to twist in the wind? That understanding gradually took shape in the political turbulence of the Populist and Progressive eras, as young social scientists, in particular, espoused unpopular views that triggered explosive controversies on campus after campus. Out of this crucible of controversy a tacit set of standards and expectations finally crystallized in 1915, with the founding of the American Association of University Professors and the publication of its first report on Academic Freedom and Tenure.

Although the AAUP code would be severely tested in the patriotic fervor of World War I and placed under heavy strain again in the loyalty controversies of the McCarthy period, it served as a kind of capstone, bringing to completion the institutional edifice the Victorians planned and built out of their concern to provide safe havens for sound opinion. Today, although the professoriate is less influential (and less affluent) than it would like to be, it speaks with unchallenged authority in many spheres of life and is substantially free to play whatever tunes it likes, without begging permission from those who pay the piper. Some recent Supreme Court decisions might even be taken to indicate that professional autonomy, suitably garbed in the lofty language of rights and academic freedom, is today not only secure, but as close to sacred as a secular society can make it. Our Victorian predecessors never dared hope that academic freedom had been high on the agenda of the nation's Founding Fathers. Yet in 1967, speaking for the majority of the Supreme Court in *Keyishian v. Board of Regents,* Justice Brennan did not hesitate to say that "academic freedom . . . is of transcendent value to all of us and not merely to the teachers concerned. That freedom is therefore a special concern of the First Amendment, which does not tolerate laws that cast a pall of orthodoxy over the classroom."[8]

Ironically, even as Justice Brennan crowned the Victorian project with a victory more complete than its architects had envisioned, the tide was running out on the intellectual premises that had sustained it in the first place. None of us today are likely to feel entirely comfortable with the assumptions on which our ancestors built the modern academic order. The problem is most severe for those among us who unreservedly identify themselves as "postmodern," from whose vantage point the assumptions that propelled the Victorians are likely to seem at least naive and possibly sinister. Consider, for example, the familiar Foucauldian notion that power and knowledge, far from constituting a natural opposition, are locked in a mutually supportive embrace so tight that they should be written "power/knowledge," as if two sides of a single coin.[9] Nothing could be more alien to the thinking of our Victorian predecessors, for whom the whole point of academic freedom was to expand the sphere of disinterested knowledge and fence it off from power.[10] Obvious questions present themselves. If a day should come when the premises of academic freedom no longer seem plausible even within the academy, how long can they be expected to prevail in the world at large? And if, as I have contended, academic freedom is but the exposed cutting edge of the drive toward autonomy that every community of the competent must undertake if it is to do its work of authorizing sound opinion, what does the decay of those premises portend for the university?

Turning up the level of magnification a bit will help us gauge the chasm that is opening between the Victorians and ourselves. In 1896, at the height of Populist agitation against the gold standard, Edward A. Ross, a young economist who had just arrived at Stanford, made several speeches in support of William Jennings Bryan and published a campaign pamphlet titled "Honest Dollars." At a time when respectability and Republican Party loyalty were expected to go hand in hand, Ross became the first academic economist to openly endorse the idea of free silver. He was no lightweight. Trained at the University of Berlin and Johns Hopkins University, Ross was married to the niece of social theorist Lester Frank Ward and had recently become secretary of the American Economic Association. Although only thirty years old, he had already achieved high visibility in his field, both as a scholar and as an outspoken reformer at Indiana University and Cornell. When David Starr Jordan left the presidency of Indiana to take over the new university Leland Stanford was building in California, he invited Ross to come along. With Indiana, Stanford, Northwestern, and Cornell all courting him, Ross put Jordan off twice before accepting his third offer.

Jordan's admiration for Ross was soon put to the test by Mrs. Jane Lothrop Stanford, who had been left in sole command of the university by her husband's death. Offended by Ross's activism, she demanded that Jordan dismiss him. Stalling for time, Jordan persuaded Mrs. Stanford to give Ross a sabbatical leave in 1898–99 with the understanding that he would look for another position and resign a year later if still considered unsuitable. Simultaneously Jordan transferred Ross out of economics and made him professor of sociology.

Although he was professionally well connected and had a friend in power, Ross had good reason to wonder how much support he could count on. San Francisco newspapers reported that six out of every seven Stanford faculty members supported McKinley and the gold standard. Leading economists viewed Ross's activism with mixed feelings at best. Frank Taussig of Harvard cautioned Ross that flamboyant popular pronouncements on economic issues were "undignified and objectionable." Taussig was a man of conservative temperament, but even fellow radical Simon Nelson Patten asked: "Have you not been giving a little too much time to politics lately? . . . That miserable money problem gets much more attention than it deserves and I never see an article of yours on it but what I feel that intellectual force has been wasted which might have produced far greater results in other directions." [11]

There was no such thing as tenure at Stanford in 1896, and no one could say just how far an outspoken scholar could go. A colleague of Ross, H. H. Powers, clearly went too far when he had the misfortune not to notice Mrs. Stanford, an orthodox Catholic, sitting in a predominantly student audience as he spoke on religion. The "pessimism and heterodoxy" of his remarks offended her.[12] When Powers added insult to injury by challenging the gold standard as well, she demanded his resignation. Comparatively unpublished and not nearly as well connected as Ross, Powers understandably regarded publicity as a profound threat to his career. He had little choice but to accept his fate in silence. Ross showed him no great sympathy and in fact helped the administration smooth his departure by taking over some of his assignments. By the end of 1897 Ross felt confident that his own safety was assured, as long as he confined himself to questions "about which it was my business to know." [13] Sure enough, at the end of his cooling-off sabbatical Jordan notified him that in spite of Mrs. Stanford's threats, his annual appointment would be resumed in 1899–1900.

By this time Mrs. Stanford had issued a total ban on faculty political activity. Her aim, she said, was to preserve the neutrality of the institution.

Ross flouted the ban so brazenly on his return that one cannot rule out the possibility that he had, perhaps, already made up his mind to leave. Speaking before a group of San Francisco labor leaders in 1900, he condemned coolie immigration and issued a plea for Anglo-Saxon racial purity, going so far as to assert, according to some reports, that vessels bringing Asian laborers to these shores should be fired on to prevent their landing. Ross's ugly racial chauvinism was unexceptional in the context of the times. What made his comments inflammatory was the fact that the Stanford fortune had been built on coolie labor. In another address at about the same time, Ross predicted that in the twentieth century all natural monopolies, including railroads, would pass into public ownership. Outraged once again, concerned about the "socialistic" elements that Ross seemed to be courting, and feeling pressure from her late husband's business associates, Mrs. Stanford ordered Jordan to fire Ross, giving him six months to wrap up his affairs.[14]

Not one to play the passive victim, except when doing so in public might work to his advantage, Ross carefully timed the announcement of his firing to coincide with publication of his major book, *Social Control*. At a well-managed press conference in November 1900, Ross turned on his friend in power, depicting himself as the victim not only of Mrs. Stanford and big money but also of a university president who lacked the courage to defend free speech.[15] His self-conceived role was that of the scientific expert, duty-bound to announce truths arduously wrested from nature and corporately sanctioned by a community of peers. "I cannot with self-respect decline to speak on topics to which I have given years of investigation," he said. "It is my duty as an economist to impart, on occasion, to sober people, and in a scientific spirit, my conclusions on subjects with which I am expert. . . . The scientist's business is to know some things clear to the bottom, and if he hides what he knows he loses his virtue."[16]

George Howard, head of the Stanford history department, went before his French Revolution class two days later and likened the university's termination of Ross to the tyrannies of the *ancien régime*. When subsequently Howard refused to apologize for this outburst, he too was ousted. In the ensuing turmoil, thirty-seven of forty-eight senior faculty members pledged their loyalty to Jordan, but all those in the social sciences who could afford the gesture resigned, virtually wiping out the fields of economics, history, and sociology. Frank Fetter, a prominent economist who had just come from Cornell to take over economics, asked for assurances of free inquiry and expression for all faculty in the future; when it was not forthcoming, he resigned. So did Arthur Lovejoy, Stanford's first and, at the time, only philosopher. Ross may well have shaped the encounter in self-serving ways, but there is no denying that his flair for the dramatic gesture achieved what no other academic freedom case of the era did: it overrode political differences, galvanized opinion, and produced united action by the professoriate to defend one of its own.[17]

At the annual convention of the American Economic Association in December 1900, Edwin R. A. Seligman, one of the most widely respected American economists of his generation, stage-managed a quasi-formal vindication of Ross. The president of the AEA at the time was Richard T. Ely, whose own radicalism had triggered an academic freedom case at Wisconsin in 1894, in which he received only lukewarm support from the profession. Still thought by some to be too much the Chautauqua speaker and Christian socialist and too little the scholar, Ely's name would have had to head the list of signatures if the association had officially declared its support for Ross. Apparently in hopes of avoiding that outcome and bringing together both ends of the political spectrum in defense of Ross, Seligman preferred to act informally, even though that meant not having the official imprimatur of the AEA. Accordingly, Ross made a dramatic appearance before a meeting of about forty economists and then sat silently as Seligman read excerpts from Jordan's letters to show that Ross was being unjustly persecuted. The AEA members present then created a committee to investigate the case. "With this declaration," says Walter Metzger, "the first professorial inquiry into an academic freedom case was conceived and brought into being—the predecessor if not directly the parent of Committee A of the AAUP."[18]

Given the cold shoulder by President Jordan and many members of the Stanford faculty, the inquiry rapidly bogged down in futile efforts to unravel Mrs. Stanford's motives. Lacking the imprimatur of the AEA, its report was fair game for critics. Magazines and newspapers that were unfavorably disposed dismissed it as a partisan document. Thus, in spite of receiving strong support even from conservative economists, the inquiry fell flat. Seligman and others tried to organize a boycott of Stanford. They succeeded in persuading several job candidates to withdraw from consideration, but when it came to a choice between professional solidarity and placing one's graduate students advantageously, solidarity evaporated. Much to the chagrin of Harvard social scientists, new Ph.D.s from Harvard promptly filled the empty slots in Stanford's history department. Although efforts were made to find a desirable post for Ross, he left Palo Alto for the academic wilderness of Nebraska, where another martyr to academic freedom, E. Benjamin

Andrews, was president. Five years later, as memories faded, Ross moved to Wisconsin, where his career flourished for the next thirty years. The warm-hearted historian of the *ancien régime,* George Howard, went to Nebraska for good.[19]

The Ross case was a happy fluke that enabled Ross and his supporters to publicize the issues of academic freedom in uncharacteristically stark, black-and-white terms. The imperious "Dowager of Palo Alto," as sociologist Albion Small called her, could not have played her role better if Ross had been writing the script.[20] Yet even in convenient caricature, the issues of academic freedom are sufficiently murky that the case also illustrates the fragility of intellectual authority and the difficulty of mobilizing effective support on behalf of a scholar confronted with demands for political conformity. Rescuing Ross was no piece of cake. Had events fallen out a little differently, things could have turned out a lot worse than they did. Needless to say, in the absence of a well-organized and highly self-conscious community of the competent, forearmed with values appropriate to the task, there would have been no one to come to Ross's rescue.

Some may imagine that with the resources of the First Amendment at his disposal, Ross and the cause of academic freedom were bound ultimately to prevail. Those resources were not yet available, however. Justice Oliver Wendell Holmes did as much as anyone to make them available, but not until after World War I. Holmes' famous dissent in *Abrams v. United States* came in 1919: "The best test of truth is the power of thought to get itself accepted in the competition of the market. . . . We should be eternally vigilant against attempts to check the expression of opinions that we loathe and believe to be fraught with death, unless they so imminently threaten immediate interference with the lawful and pressing purposes of the law that an immediate check is required to save the country." In contrast, back in 1892, while still a justice of the Massachusetts Supreme Court, Holmes had no compunctions about making freedom of expression contingent upon contractual obligations. In keeping with legal doctrines that prevailed at the time, he then construed the First Amendment only as a prohibition on prior restraint, not a guarantee of immunity against the consequences of expression. In the case of a policeman who had been fired after criticizing his department, Holmes held that

> The petitioner may have a constitutional right to talk politics, but he has no constitutional right to be a policeman. There are few employments for hire in which the servant does not agree to suspend his constitutional right of free

speech, as well as of idleness, by the implied terms of his contract. The servant cannot complain, as he takes the employment on the terms which are offered him.[21]

The Ross case not only was a trial run for the investigative modus operandi that the AAUP would later make its stock in trade, it also brought together the two men who, more than anyone else, brought the AAUP into existence. Arthur Lovejoy, the Stanford philosopher who resigned in protest over Ross's ouster, would become secretary of the organization at its founding in 1915. Edwin R. A. Seligman, the Columbia economist who arranged for Ross's quasi-official vindication, wrote the first draft of the 1915 Report on Academic Freedom and Tenure. Lovejoy then rewrote the text so extensively that Walter Metzger, our premier historian of academic freedom, credits him with being virtually coauthor. Both men later served as president of the organization. It was Lovejoy and a group of seventeen colleagues at Johns Hopkins University who hosted the first intercollegiate meeting aimed at the construction of a national association of university professors. Since Hopkins men had also founded the MLA, the AHA, the AEA, and most of the other specialist organizations that defined the new intellectual division of labor, it was only fitting that they would take the lead in adding this capstone to their professionalizing labors.

The word "capstone" needs stressing. This is how I, as a historian, would *define* academic freedom: as the capstone of the institutional edifice that Victorian reformers constructed in hopes of establishing authority and cultivating reliable knowledge. The metaphor implies a stronger linkage between academic freedom and professionalization than is commonly recognized today. The connection often goes unacknowledged, partly because in our generation professors have been extremely loath to admit their kinship to lawyers, physicians, and other fee-for-service professionals. Here etymological common sense should be our guide: "Professor" could hardly help but be a variety of "professional."[22] The founders of the AAUP were not so skittish about their professional aspirations. They explicitly identified their organization as a complement to the specialist societies and deliberately modeled it on the American Bar Association and the American Medical Association:

> The scientific and specialized interests of members of American university faculties are well cared for by various learned societies. No organization exists, however, which at once represents the common interests of the teaching staffs and deals with the general problems of university policy. Believing that

a society comparable to the American Bar Association and the American Medical Association in kindred professions, could be of substantial service to the ends for which universities exist, members of the faculties of a number of institutions have undertaken to bring about the formation of a national Association of University Professors.[23]

Still more important, the linkage between professionalization and academic freedom has been obscured by the stupendous growth of First Amendment law over the past half century. The rising tide of First Amendment protections has undeniably lifted academic freedom to new heights, and today it does indeed make good sense, legally speaking, to think of academic freedom as a subset of First Amendment liberties. But academic freedom and free speech overlap and reinforce one another only at certain points. Any effort to completely assimilate the former to the latter would be disastrous. Historically speaking, the heart and soul of academic freedom lie not in free speech but in professional autonomy and collegial self-governance. Academic freedom came into being as a defense of the disciplinary community (or, more exactly, the university conceived as an ensemble of such communities), and if it is to do the work we expect of it, it must continue to be at bottom a denial that anyone outside the community is fully competent to pass judgment on matters falling within the community's domain. From my standpoint, no justification for academic freedom can succeed unless it provides ample resources for justifying the autonomy and self-governance of the community. For this task, the First Amendment is ill-suited.[24]

One way to highlight the difference is simply to observe that the founders of the modern university were not so much libertarians as communitarians. They wanted to liberate individual practitioners such as Ross from the dictates of their employers, not as an end in itself, but as a way of enhancing the authority of the entire community of practitioners.[25] This was a generation whose members, like Matthew Arnold, were not much impressed by the freedom merely to do (or say) whatever one pleases. They looked askance at individualistic values and felt no embarrassment about imposing a wholesome discipline on the crude, market-driven society that was growing by leaps and bounds around them. They set out to professionalize higher education because they wanted to establish the good, the true, and the beautiful on a firmer base. Of all the institutions they founded, none are more characteristic or more aptly named than the "disciplines," which even today define the division of intellectual labor within the university.

To sharpen the contrast still more, consider the continuing controversy over the teaching of Darwin's evolutionary theory. If our point of departure were free speech alone, it would not be at all easy to justify the exclusion of "creation science" from the curriculum. After all, when biblical literalists say that evolution is "only a theory," they are not wrong. Like all scientific theories, Darwin's is contestable and will one day be superseded. Why give it a privileged place in the curriculum? The only persuasive answer lies in the authority that inheres in a well-established disciplinary community. Darwin's theory deserves a privileged place because it, unlike "creation science," enjoys the support of a strong consensus of competent biological investigators, who have organized themselves in such a way as to foster mutual criticism and drive out of circulation truth claims that cannot take the heat.

We academics are prone to hide from ourselves the degree to which we rely on authority and count on others to do the same. I once heard a prominent sociologist blithely announce that "authority has no place in the classroom." He meant that teachers should encourage discussion, tolerate dissent, and bend over backwards to avoid silencing or penalizing students whose politics offend them. These are admirable values, too often honored in the breach, but it would be the height of naiveté to think that authority plays no role in the classroom, or that professors and students meet on a level playing field. We professors walk into a classroom and the students cease their chatter, get out pen and paper, and wait dutifully for us to begin. Surely no one dreams that this effect is produced merely by personal charisma or sheer mental power. Teachers occupy one role and students another in an institution cunningly designed to make it in the student's interest to pay attention, to listen up, to defer to our authority. We appear before them not as mere citizens but as delegates of a community of inquiry, made up of members who earn their keep by engaging in mutual criticism. When we defend academic freedom, we are defending that authority.

The very mention of authority makes late-twentieth-century academics nervous, yet we all routinely defer to the authority of experts. Deference undergirds even our most fundamental assumptions about ourselves and the world we inhabit. For example, I believe in evolution with nearly the same degree of confidence I feel about the existence of the table I am writing on, or the accuracy of an account I might give of some episode in my own life, based on personal experience and recollection. Yet my belief in evolution rests on no firmer basis than deference to expert authority. I have not inspected the fossil record for myself, or worked my way through the intricate details of Darwin's argument in *On the Origin of Species*. Much less have I followed the tangle of debates that lead up to the present version of the theory. Many imagine that the story of divine creation is intrinsically less plausible than evolution. They claim to find in the idea of one-celled primeval slime gradually evolving into complex forms of life under the directionless pressure of natural selection a virtually self-evident truth. I am not persuaded. The compelling quality they attribute to the idea of natural selection itself, I would attribute instead to the institutional arrangements that have succeeded in making belief in evolution a recognized badge of intelligence and educational attainment in our culture. We nonfundamentalists who are not trained in biology believe in evolution, not because we are more rational than biblical literalists, not because we can recite the "good reasons" that a fully rational judgment would require, and not because we have in mind the evidence and experience it would take to envision the process and grasp it in the way biologists do. We believe because we trust biologists.[26]

Our trust is not blind, of course. We willingly defer to the judgment of biologists in large part because we feel sure they have good reasons for their beliefs and could display those reasons to us if we were willing to take the time. But my confidence that good reasons exist does not alter the plain fact that my present acceptance of the theory of evolution is based not on those uninspected reasons but on deference to authority. What shapes my belief is as much psychological and sociological as logical. And although I think the thought process that leads me to my belief is far sounder than the one that leads the creationist to his, the difference is not a matter of his clinging to authority while I rely on reason: we both submit to authority, but to different authorities. For this no apologies are needed. Up to a point, we are better off for our willingness to defer to experts. Even though deference to authority short-circuits the quintessentially rational processes of personally weighing the evidence and following out a chain of logic to one's own inner satisfaction, deferring to experts brings real advantages insofar as it enables us to gain vicariously from others' experience and compensate for the limited range of our own. Sometimes deferring to expert authority is the rational thing to do.

If, as I have been arguing, academic freedom was the capstone of an effort to establish authority by fostering the development of communities of the competent, we should expect to find evidence supporting that claim in the AAUP's charter document, the 1915 Report on Academic Freedom and Tenure. The expectation is amply borne out. As we shall see, Seligman and Lovejoy in writing that document addressed themselves most explicitly to the rights of scholars, the duties of trustees, and the needs of the lay public—the nuts and bolts, as it were, of academic freedom—but at every stage they self-consciously advocated deference to expert authority and took for granted the epistemological efficacy of disciplinary communities. Notice that in doing so they were already moving far beyond any simple correspondence theory of truth. However much they may differ from us, the late Victorians were not epistemologically naive. After all, the first "crisis of historicism" occurred during their watch, and no one since has plumbed the depths of the crisis any more deeply than that renegade Victorian, Friedrich Nietzsche. The generation of the 1890s, of which the founders of the modern university were a part, was already energetically embarked on what H. Stuart Hughes has called a "revolt against positivism." The lessons of fallibilism and the unavoidable subjectivity of perception were widely appreciated at the turn of the century. The insight that truth was a collective, communal enterprise, rather than a solitary, culturally unmediated one—the enabling idea behind the community of the competent—was itself one of the products of the Victorians' struggle to come to terms with the uncertainties that historicism notoriously breeds.[27] The words of the AAUP's 1915 report testify to greater confidence in the power of reason than is commonly acknowledged today and may seem to some readers quaint. But it remains to be seen whether the radical forms of historicism in circulation today will prove as durable as the more moderate varieties that were already firmly in place at the beginning of the century.

In drafting the 1915 report, Lovejoy and Seligman most certainly did not proceed on the Foucauldian premise that power and knowledge were two sides of a single coin. They took the possibilities of disinterestedness and objectivity with utmost seriousness, not as results easily attained but as ideals well worth pursuing. The university, they said, should be an "intellectual experiment station" and an "inviolable refuge" against the equally dangerous tyrannies of public opinion and political autocracy. If scholars were to solve the problems of society, "the disinterestedness and impartiality of their inquiries and their conclusions [would have to be], so far as it is humanly possible, beyond the reach of suspicion."[28] Warding off suspicion meant that the line between authentic scholarship and political propaganda would have to be sharp and clear (the implication again being "so far as it is humanly possible"). They warned against teachers who would take "unfair advantage of the student's immaturity by indoctrinating him with the teacher's own opinions." They associated the right of academic freedom with a duty on the part of the academic profession to police its ranks and rigorously uphold standards. "If this profession," they wrote, "should prove itself unwilling to purge its ranks of the incompetent and unworthy, or to prevent the freedom it claims in the name of science from being used as a shelter for inefficiency, for superficiality, for uncritical and intemperate partisanship, it is certain that the task will be performed by others." Although they specifically moved beyond the German model of academic freedom by claiming protection for extramural as well as intramural utterances, they never doubted the desirability of teachers having "minds untrammeled by party loyalties, unexcited by party enthusiasms, and unbiased by personal political ambitions."[29]

The first section of the 1915 report bears a revealing title: "The Basis of Academic Authority." The section is in its entirety organized around a distinction between real universities, engaged in the pursuit of truth, and "proprietary school[s] . . . designed for the propagation of specific doctrines." The latter are bound by their founders "to a propagandist duty." Seligman and Lovejoy grudgingly acknowledged the legitimacy of proprietary schools (usually religious), but only for the sake of relegating them and their propagandistic function to the lowest ranks of postsecondary education. "Any university which lays restrictions upon the intellectual freedom of its professors," they asserted, "proclaims itself a proprietary institution, and should be so described when it makes a general appeal for funds." By their standard, any institution that withheld from its faculty the rights of academic freedom in the interest of serving a propagandistic function could not claim the authority of a true university and would deserve the support only of fellow sectarians, not that of the general public.[30]

The central thrust of the 1915 report was to displace trustees as sole interpreters of the public interest and put forth a strong claim for the corporate authority of professional communities. As Seligman and Lovejoy put it, "the responsibility of the university teacher is primarily to the public itself, and to the judgment of his own profession."[31] In a nutshell, they were defining the university as a loose-knit family of specialized disciplinary communities and making the family's integrity conditional on the degree of self-governance attained both by the whole and by its constituent parts. The role of the community looms largest in the second section of the report, titled "The Nature of the Academic Profession," where they spelled out the "distinctive and important function" of the professional scholar:

> That function is to deal at first hand, after prolonged and specialized technical training, with the sources of knowledge; and to impart the results of their own and of their fellow-specialists' investigations and reflection, both to stu-

dents and the general public, without fear or favor. The proper discharge of this function requires (among other things) that the university teacher shall be exempt from pecuniary motive or inducement to hold, or to express, any conclusion which is not the genuine and uncolored product of his own study or that of fellow-specialists. Indeed, the proper fulfillment of the work of the professorate [*sic*] requires that our universities shall be so free that no fair-minded person shall find any excuse for even a suspicion that the utterances of university teachers are shaped or restricted by the judgment, not of professional scholars, but of inexpert and possibly not wholly disinterested persons outside their ranks.[32]

Notice that the authors of the 1915 report did not imagine that the problem of intellectual authority was to be solved merely by appeals to disinterestedness. In common with other members of their generation they did of course take it for granted that scholars would display a large measure of that self-denying quality of asceticism that Nietzsche so merrily skewered in the third essay of *The Genealogy of Morals*. But if scholars were to speak without "fear or favor"—and, equally important, be *seen* as speaking thus, so as to earn the deference of the general public—they would not only have to purge themselves of interest, insofar as possible, but generally distance themselves from all influences extrinsic to their work. The latter task was understood by Seligman and Lovejoy as inherently collective: accomplishing it required the existence of a community so energized that its internal relations would overshadow external influences, as members strove above all to earn and retain one another's respect according to standards specifically tailored to the work at hand. Their vision of the ideal community differs little from that of Jürgen Habermas, who defines the "ideal speech situation" as one in which "no force except that of the better argument is exercised; and, . . . as a result, all motives except that of the cooperative search for truth are excluded."[33]

Thus Seligman and Lovejoy's discussion of "The Nature of the Academic Profession" continues:

The lay public is under no compulsion to accept or act upon the opinions of the scientific experts whom, through the universities, it employs. But it is highly needful, in the interest of society at large, that what purport to be the conclusions of men trained for, and dedicated to, the quest for truth, shall in fact be the conclusions of such men, and not echoes of the opinions of the lay public, or of the individuals who endow or manage universities. To the degree that professional scholars, in the formation and promulgation of their opinions, are, or by the character of their tenure, appear to be, subject to any motive other than their own scientific conscience and a desire for the respect of their fellow-experts, to that degree the university teaching profession is corrupted; its proper influence upon public opinion is diminished and vitiated; and society at large fails to get from its scholars, in an unadulterated form, the peculiar and necessary service which it is the office of the professional scholar to furnish.[34]

In the vision set forth by Seligman and Lovejoy, the psychological, institutional, and legal dimensions of the problem of intellectual authority fit together and reinforce one another like the nested boxes of a Chinese puzzle. To speak with authority one must visibly enjoy the respect of one's peers, organized as a self-governing community. In order for the community to exist and be self-governing, its members must, in the work at hand, defer only to one another and be ready to resist the influence of nonpractitioners in matters intrinsic to the community's domain. The legal rights of academic freedom stake out the vital boundary between matters intrinsic and extrinsic, distinguishing those who are competent to judge a practitioner's work from those who are not. In the words of Seligman and Lovejoy, it would be "inadmissible that the power of determining when departures from the requirements of the scientific spirit and method have occurred, should be vested in bodies not composed of the members of the academic profession. Such bodies necessarily lack full competency to judge of those requirements." The proper relationship, then, between professors and trustees is not that of employees to employers. The relation should instead be analogous to that of federal judges and the chief executive who appoints them but then has no authority over their decisions. Leaving unchallenged the power of trustees and administrators to appoint faculty, Seligman and Lovejoy denied that those exercising that power could properly retain any control over the intellectual productions of those whom they appointed, and insisted that appointment itself be based on criteria established within the community, by the candidate's peers.[35]

There is no single author who can be said to have exhaustively conceptualized the widespread assumptions about truth and inquiry that Seligman and Lovejoy were trying to distill in their 1915 report. But Charles Sanders Peirce, arguably the most original of the Pragmatists and the author of the strongest claims for a communal theory of truth ever written, did more than anyone else of his generation to articulate the presuppositions that I believe underlay Victorian reform. My claim is not that his philosophical writings influenced any large number of people or served as a blueprint for action. Peirce's writings on community and the social basis of scientific endeavor were, as a matter of fact, influential among Harvard philosophers while Lovejoy was a graduate student there, but professionalization was a social process with great momentum in late-nineteenth-century life: it did not wait upon theoretical articulation. It is, I believe, no coincidence that Charles Peirce was the son of one of the foremost professionalizers of science in the antebellum period, the eminent Harvard astronomer and mathematician Benjamin Peirce. Member of a self-selected elite of scientists known as the Lazzaroni, the elder Peirce helped organize the Lawrence Scientific School at Harvard, helped write the constitution of the American Association for the Advancement of Science, and helped push through Congress the bill creating the National Academy of Sciences.[36] Charles Peirce's communitarian theory of truth must ultimately stand or fall on its own philosophical legs, but for my purposes it would suffice to regard it as an idealized extrapolation from the practical processes of professionalization that were transforming society during his lifetime. Peirce's theory suits my purposes especially well because it invites comparison with the communitarian theorizing of recent writers such as Thomas Kuhn, Richard Rorty, and Stanley Fish.[37] These three authors share Peirce's basic conviction that communal solidarity among inquirers can function epistemologically, and thus their differences with him—substantial, as we shall see—give us a way of gauging the gap between the Victorians and ourselves.[38]

Charles Peirce believed that the very possibility of attaining truth depended on transcending one's self and entering into intensely communal relations with other competent investigators. As if to repudiate Ralph Waldo Emerson's advice to "trust thyself," Peirce contended that no individual, least of all one's self, could ever be worthy of trust. "The individual man, since his separate existence is manifested only by ignorance and error . . . is only a negation."[39] Peirce's advice was to trust instead the community of inquirers. "What anything really is," argued Peirce, "is what it may finally come to be known to be in the ideal state of complete information." Since information cannot be complete in my lifetime or yours, our best conceptions are riddled with error, and the truth can only be known by the last survivors of a community of inquirers that includes the yet-to-be-born as well as the living and extends indefinitely far into the future. "The real, then," said Peirce in a famous passage, "is that which, sooner or later, information and reasoning would finally result in, and which is independent of the vagaries of me and you. Thus, the very origin of the conception of reality shows that this conception essentially involves the notion of a COMMUNITY, without definite limits, and capable of a definite increase in knowledge."[40]

It may have been his prickly personality and status as an outsider who never found permanent employment in the academic world that sensitized Peirce to the social, consensual quality of all that passes for truth among human beings. Yet in his conception there is no trace of cynicism. The ultimate consensus to be reached by his community of inquiry is of a very special kind, and his theory of reality, though indubitably social, is not at all relativistic, as twentieth-century analogs have tended to be. Like Kuhn, Rorty, and Fish, modern thinkers who have advanced arguments that sound quite Peircean, Peirce himself clearly regarded science and scholarship as the practical accomplishment not of individuals but of a community of re-searchers. Unlike Kuhn, Rorty, and Fish, however, Peirce was a philosophi-cal realist: he supposed that the universe was so made that an ultimate con-vergence of opinion was virtually predestined and that the reality toward which opinion converged was utterly independent, not of thought in gen-eral, but of what any finite number of human beings thought about it. For him reality was socially discovered but not socially constructed. When pressed by a critic, he allowed that the ultimate convergence of opinion might be incomplete in some matters and that convergence was a "hope" rather than an inevitability. But he insisted that the hope was of the same indispensable character as the expectation of survival that a person struggling for his life must feel. To live is to hope; similarly, to inquire is to suppose that opinions ultimately converge toward the real. The following passage catches the spirit of Peirce's discussion of the community better than any other I know:

> This activity of thought by which we are carried, not where we wish, but to a fore-ordained goal, is like the operation of destiny. No modification of the point of view taken, no selection of other facts for study, no natural bent of mind even, can enable a man to escape the predestinate opinion. This great hope [originally he wrote "law"] is embodied in the conception of truth and reality. The opinion which is fated to be agreed to by all who investigate, is what we mean by the truth, and the object represented in this opinion is the real. That is the way I would explain reality.[41]

Peirce was no ideologue. He had no intention whatsoever of supplying existing communities of inquiry in physics, chemistry, or biology with a philosophical warrant for their authority. Much less did he intend to buttress the claims of quasi-sciences like law, medicine, or historical studies. He expressly rejected the "method of authority" as a means of fixing belief, and he equated that method with the claims of priesthoods, aristocracies, guilds, and other "association[s] . . . of men whose interests depend . . . on certain propositions."[42] As long as we interpret Peirce's words strictly, as he no doubt wished us to do, his theory bundles truth off into an infinite progression where it is too remote to serve *any* interest or strengthen any particular claim to knowledge. But if his theory undermines all existing authorities and courts radical skepticism when strictly interpreted—offering no guidance at all when we ask "Which present claim is true?" or "What belief shall I now act on?"—it performs the opposite function of building bulwarks against skepticism when loosely interpreted. And how can we resist interpreting it loosely? As the philosopher John E. Smith has said, "reality in the end for Peirce is future experience, and this is not enough."[43] Peirce conceived of the truth in such a way as to make it literally useless, for no one can claim to know the truth, once it has been defined as the final opinion of a community that extends indefinitely into the future. However, once we accept Peirce's identification of truth as the outcome of a community's striving, then, if a community of inquiry exists in a field that interests us, it is difficult to resist the implication that its *current best opinion* is, in practice, the closest approach to the truth we can possibly hope for. Given a choice between these two interpretations, it may well be that the strict one is closest to Peirce's own intentions. But even if this is so, the most important thing to observe about Peirce's communal theory of reality may be that the more persuasive we find it, the more likely we are to live by the loose interpretation of it. Identifying truth with the community, but lacking the community's final opinion, we are bound to prefer its current best opinion to a chaos of indistinguishable truth claims, which is the only alternative Peirce's line of reasoning leaves us.

No writer today would dare attribute to the community of inquiry quite the same truth-finding power that Peirce assigned it. Of the writers I mentioned above, Kuhn comes closest to Peirce. Certainly in Kuhn's world there is no standard higher than the current best opinion of the relevant scientific community. If one asks "Why should taxpayers foot the bill for professors who devote more time to research than to teaching?" or "Why should trustees tolerate the expression of views they loathe?" Kuhn supplies us with a compelling answer: The community is epistemologically efficacious. Without it, our grasp of reality would be immeasurably weaker. Yet

Kuhn's community is not nearly as efficacious as Peirce's, for Kuhn is not nearly the realist Peirce was. The relationship between the community's current best opinion and anything that deserves the name "truth" becomes problematic in Kuhn's treatment. He retains a trace of realism by holding that the sequence of conceptions espoused by a scientific community takes the shape of an irreversible branching tree. A kind of development not altogether different from progress is, therefore, involved—but this is "progress" away from confusion, rather than toward any antecedent reality existing "out there," independent of human consciousness, awaiting our apprehension of it. How much epistemological comfort we are entitled to draw from this sort of development, especially in fields other than natural science, is an open question.[44]

If the Peircean rationale for disciplinary autonomy is left looking a bit frayed around the edges by Kuhn, it is left in tatters by others who have been inspired by Kuhn's writings. Rorty and Fish both pay homage to Kuhn, but their own posture is that of uncompromising antirealism. Unlike Kuhn, who is ambivalent and who frankly confesses that, although he is disenchanted with the realist view, no existing alternative seems an adequate replacement for it, Rorty and Fish flatly deny that there is any important sense in which ideas can be said to converge on, approximate, correspond with, or be adequate to the real. For them, the real is socially and linguistically constructed, through and through. Rorty declares the entire enterprise of epistemology to be wrongheaded. He joins Derrida in recommending that we overcome our nostalgic longing for "foundations" and throw overboard the entire "metaphysics of presence." Even Derrida's most notorious antirealist sally, "There is nothing outside the text," wins from Rorty a blithe nod of approval. Rorty asks us to believe that the tradition inaugurated by Plato and called "philosophy" has quite simply lost its usefulness and ought to be discontinued in favor of conversations that aim at nothing more than "edification." "The notion of 'accurate representation,'" he says, "is simply an automatic and empty compliment which we pay to those beliefs which are successful in helping us do what we want to do."[45]

The immediate target of Rorty's campaign on behalf of edifying conversation is none other than Arthur Lovejoy, one of the heroes of the Ross case and a founder of the AAUP. It was Lovejoy who, in his presidential address to the American Philosophical Association in 1916, called upon philosophers to choose between edification and verification, hoping they would choose the latter. In picking up the banner of edification, Rorty seeks to turn Lovejoy's Victorian project upside down. Lovejoy epitomizes for Rorty the anti-Pragmatic disciplinarian, who spurns the gentle delights of edification and makes a fetish of rigor and circumspection. "Echoing what was being said simultaneously by Russell in England and Husserl in Germany, Lovejoy urged the sixteenth annual meeting of the APA to aim at making philosophy into a science," reports Rorty. "Lovejoy insisted that philosophy could either be edifying and visionary *or* could produce 'objective, verifiable, and clearly communicable truths,' but not both." William James agreed that the two aims were incompatible, Rorty observes, but wisely preferred edification to science. To Rorty's dismay, "Lovejoy . . . won this battle." The mainstream of the philosophical profession chose the analytical path over edification.[46]

There is no denying that Lovejoy was a devotee of rigor. His belief that philosophy's family quarrels were a "standing scandal" that threatened to bring "discredit upon the entire business" seems to me misguided, and his plan for the production of a catalogue raisonné of "considerations" pertaining to all important issues in philosophy—a modern *Summa Metaphysica,* as he himself called it—seems both misguided and grandiose.[47] I readily confess that if I were choosing books for a year's sojourn on a desert island, Rorty's *Philosophy and the Mirror of Nature* would be a more likely choice than Lovejoy's *Great Chain of Being,* important though the latter is.

These things said, there remains room to argue that Lovejoy was not the Dr. Strangelove that Rorty makes him out to be. In calling for philosophy to become a science, Lovejoy meant only that it should be a *Wissenschaft,* an "organized body of knowledge," not that it should mindlessly imitate physics or chemistry.[48] Lovejoy's essays on Pragmatism are, in my view, the sort of close, respectful criticism that any school of thought should count itself lucky to receive. One of them, titled "William James as a Philosopher," is as warm, generous, and open-minded a tribute as any scholar ever rendered to a rival.[49] Lovejoy's point about edification was not that it was an unworthy goal but that philosophy may not be the best way to achieve it. He acknowledged that "the philosopher's reasonings" may only be his "peculiar way of uttering the burden of his soul and of edifying the like-minded," but, he continued, if edification is the goal, "poetry is surely a happier medium."[50]

Convinced, just as Peirce was, that "philosophizing is a collective process," Lovejoy thought philosophers should never concede the incommensurability of rival positions at the start of an argument, but should instead obstinately hold out the "possibility of unanimity" as a regulative ideal. After all, he observed, the prospect of really achieving unanimity was "scarcely so imminent as to justify alarm." As these words suggest, Lovejoy was not naive about the likelihood of convergence. His aim was to strengthen the community of inquiry by making communication between its members more complete and harder to evade, thus intensifying the half-competitive, half-cooperative exchange of opinions that constitutes the life process of such communities. He shared Walter Bagehot's admiration for a "polity of discussion," in which the obligation to talk things over and seek agreement would always act as a check on precipitate action. Like most Victorians, including Peirce (whose essay "Evolutionary Love" is a sermon on the subject), Lovejoy blamed human ignorance largely on "subjective sources of error" and looked to socialization for the cure. We guard against the snares of subjectivity, he wrote, by

> seeking the complementary and correcting action of other minds upon our own; and not of dead men's minds, alone, but of contemporaries with whose thoughts ours may establish genuine and vital contact, to whom we may explain and re-explain our own thoughts, who will patiently "follow the argument" with us, who will drive their meanings into our consciousness with friendly violence if necessary, and will gladly submit to like violence in return.[51]

Rorty has little use for either Peirce's communal theory of truth or Lovejoy's "friendly violence." The problem with both, apparently, is that by holding out the possibility of rational convergence, they breed confrontation. Unlike the Victorians, who prized criticism and accepted the need for confrontation, Rorty looks forward to a culture devoted to edifying conversation, which he specifically likens to Kuhn's "abnormal" or "revolutionary" science and associates with the perpetual incommensurability of rival vantage points. Since the contributors to Rorty's conversation would by definition share few common presuppositions, their contributions would be largely incommensurable, leading no doubt to an abundance of divergent opinions but seldom to confrontation in the classic sense of a rigorous encounter from which only the truth can emerge unscathed. Everyone's views would be different; no one's would be right or wrong. Most important, no view would qualify even potentially as "normal." Lacking foundations, absent any hope of rational convergence or correspondence with the real, confrontation loses its point and becomes difficult to distinguish from aimless aggression.

Rorty's aversion to convergence-oriented confrontation (perfectly compatible with polemical brilliance, as we shall see) most often manifests itself in his frustrating habit of sidestepping bothersome questions. As Stefan

Collini has remarked, Rorty frequently announces "with a studied off-handedness that some find exhilarating and others infuriating, that a large number of time-honoured questions just are not interesting questions any more." Granting the exceptional range and brilliance of Rorty's contribution, Collini nonetheless complains that "the range of questions which 'we pragmatists' would say there is no point in asking threatens to shrink the horizons of intellectual inquiry," possibly encouraging a kind of "anti-intellectualism."[52]

Rorty assigns top priority not to the characteristically Victorian task of pruning back error in hopes of expanding the domain of reliable knowledge, but instead to the distinctively post-Holocaust task of encouraging respect for otherness and cultivating sensitivity to the lush multiplicity of human perspectives. Rorty's priorities are eminently decent and readily understandable in view of the ethnic clashes and seemingly endless dilemmas of difference that beset the world today. I have no quarrel with those priorities, except insofar as they block historical understanding and tempt us to think we can get away without having any adequate justification for academic freedom. Rorty evidently believes that we academicians have it in our power to help reduce bloodshed and brutality in the world at large simply by adopting a kinder and gentler mode of intellectual exchange within the academy. I demur because I doubt that the academy's influence takes quite that form and because I feel that the intellectual price Rorty is prepared to pay is too high. If I read Lovejoy correctly, he understood full well that many of the great debates in philosophy originate in incommensurable premises and are unlikely ever to yield consensus. What he opposed was a premature abandonment of consensus as an *ideal,* a target one aims at without expecting to reach. That ideal is as indispensable as ever, for the community of the competent cannot do its work of cultivating and authorizing sound opinion unless its members confront one another and engage in mutual criticism. Unless I miss my guess, Lovejoy could have said about philosophy what Clifford Geertz said of anthropology: that it is "a science whose progress is marked less by a perfection of consensus than by a refinement of debate. What gets better is the precision with which we vex each other."[53] Still, Lovejoy would have added, Peirce was right: to inquire at all is to hold out the *possibility* of convergence.

Although Rorty (unlike Fish, as we shall see) is not the sort of person to treat ideals dismissively, this particular ideal gets short shrift in his "conversation of the West." Conversation and consensus figure prominently in his thinking, but their role is therapeutic rather than rigorous, remissive rather than exacting. Conversation he recommends not as a means of exposing error, but rather as an opportunity to savor the kaleidoscopic variety of the human experience. He values consensus less as a regulative ideal, the pursuit of which may provoke confrontation and inflame passion, than as our last hope of solace in a world that lacks foundations. Threatened as we all are by the eruption of violence, he judges the sacrifice of rigor a small price to pay for greater solidarity.

Given Rorty's aversion to confrontation, we should not be surprised that his revival of Pragmatism, unlike those of Richard Bernstein, Hilary Putnam, or Jürgen Habermas, pointedly excludes Peirce from the front ranks of the tradition.[54] A "tendency to overpraise Peirce," he says, is the first symptom of a mistaken conception of what pragmatism is all about.[55] One might think that Peirce's perpetually postponed truth, never accessible in any human "present," would be sufficiently remote and impractical to at least seem harmless, but Rorty detects within it the bitter seeds of tyranny. "The pragmatist must avoid saying, with Peirce, that truth is *fated* to win. He must even avoid saying that the truth *will* win." So deep is Rorty's distaste for this aspect of Peirce's thinking that he appears to sympathize even with an imaginary anti-Pragmatic interlocutor of his own devising, the "traditional philosopher," who asks rhetorically, "When tyrants employ Lenin's blood-curdling sense of 'objective' to describe their lies as 'objectively true,' what is to prevent them from citing Peirce in Lenin's defense?"[56]

At first glance, arguments like these seem to sound a death knell for the dream of epistemological efficacy that Charles Peirce articulated at the dawn of the modern American university system. If convergence is unacceptable, even as an ideal, the disciplinary community cannot serve as a crucible of criticism and so cannot claim any special authority for the ideas it sponsors. Indeed, if Rorty really believes that the very idea of "truth" is dangerous because of the encouragement it gives tyrants, then it is not just Peirce we need to renounce but the university itself, for the university has always been and is likely to remain a hotbed of aspirations for truth, sound opinion, and other invidious distinctions between better and worse ways of thinking. In the words of John Dewey, whom of course Rorty holds in very high regard, and whose conception of truth was not naive, "the university function is the truth function."[57] Dewey published these words in 1902, two years after Ross's dismissal from Stanford and thirteen before taking office as the founding President of the AAUP. In his AAUP inaugural address in 1915, Dewey spoke in the same vein, calling for the "judgment, the courage, and the self sacrifice commensurate with reverence for our calling, which is none other than the discovery and diffusion of truth."[58]

Rorty's conflation of Peircean fallibilism with Leninist objectivism need not be taken as his last word on the subject. Clearly, Peirce's theory of truth is not acceptable to him, and the community of the competent does not, as such, play a prominent role in his thinking. Still, there are important similarities. The philosopher whom William James credited with founding Pragmatism and who wanted to write on every wall of the city of philosophy, "Do not block the way of inquiry," cannot truly be a dangerous man in Rorty's eyes.[59]

One might argue that the two Pragmatists differ more sharply at the level of tactics than ultimate goals. Both want to substitute persuasion for force. Whether to aim at that goal directly and try to extend its benefits to an entire society at once, or to approach it obliquely, relying for the foreseeable future on an elite vanguard of inquirers, is where they seem to differ most concretely. Rorty's "conversation of the West" is conceived in an inclusive spirit of Romantic egalitarianism that embraces an entire ethnos and all who partake of it, leaving no specified role for intellectual elites or disciplinary institutions. In effect, Rorty's vision of the ideal liberal society tacitly anticipates the extension to everyone of the life of inquiry and persuasion that Peirce assigned to a scholarly elite. Rorty's utopia, in short, looks rather like Peirce's community of inquiry writ large—larger than Peirce would have thought appropriate or feasible.[60] Having given up all foundationalist hopes, and having expanded the circle of the "we" to embrace all willing recruits, Rorty's version of the good society presumably would downplay degrees of competence, extending to all citizens the opportunity of engaging as equals in the "conversation" through which reality is socially constructed. Rorty's utopia could even acknowledge a pale surrogate for Peirce's objectivity, defining it as that which wins "unforced agreement."[61] And although Rorty's liberal utopia would most assuredly not be devoted to the pursuit of Truth, he assures us that it would honor "truth," decapitalized and safely quarantined within quotation marks:

> It is central to the idea of liberal society that, in respect to words as opposed to deeds, persuasion as opposed to force, anything goes. This openmindedness should not be fostered because, as Scripture teaches, Truth is great and will prevail, nor because, as Milton suggests, Truth will always win in a free and open encounter. It should be fostered for its own sake. A liberal society is one which is content to call "true" whatever the upshot of such encounters turns out to be.[62]

Here it is tempting to think that Rorty and Peirce come within hailing distance, for Peirce, too, was content (at least on the "loose" interpretation of his doctrine) to call "true" the upshot of the community's debates—

true for now, anyway. Yet the differences remain fundamental. The reality-discovering task that Peirce assigned to the community of the competent, Rorty assigns to liberal society as a whole, and he adds the antirealist proviso—fatal, from Peirce's standpoint—that reality is something we construct, not discover. For much the same reason, relaxed "conversation" replaces confrontational debate. The disciplinary function disappears; the free expression of ideas no longer serves as a means of winnowing truth, for Rorty redefines it as an end in itself. Intellect is dethroned and takes its cue from sociability. In the last analysis, our choice between the two visions is likely to hinge on our estimate of the feasibility and desirability of Rorty's effort to extend to everyone the essential features of a form of life thus far inhabited only by scholars.[63] Not only is it uncertain that all aspire to such a life, many are not well suited for it, making their opportunity to contribute to the conversation merely formal. The history of professionalization over the past century and a half suggests that dense, fast-paced scholarly "conversations" of the sort Rorty admires have greater momentum and will be more difficult for novices to break into than he acknowledges. Indeed, they have proved to be formidable sources of privilege and authority for those who possess the skills to excel in them: democratizing them would be no easy matter.

The most intractable difference between Peirce and Rorty appears to lie in the question of realism. There are of course many versions of realism, and it is not inconceivable that a version making the right sort of concessions to history, perspective, and social convention might earn Rorty's grudging acceptance. But as long as there is no respectable sense (not even a largely social and conventional one) in which we are entitled to say that there is a "nature of things" for inquirers to "get right," then one cannot help wondering what the community of inquiry is for.[64] If nothing at all constrains inquiry, apart from the will of the inquirers and whatever value they may assign to the traditions of their *ethnos,* why should anyone defer to the community's judgment, pay its expenses, or bend over backwards to tolerate its "findings" when they are unsettling? Peirce's fallibilistic realism had ready answers to such questions, because it acknowledged other constraints, clinging fiercely to the possibility of truth even as it admitted truth's elusiveness and hammered home the lesson of fallibility. Antirealism, even Rorty's comparatively domesticated version of it, necessarily annihilates error along with its opposite, truth, making fallibilism an untenable posture: Where no opinions can be right, neither can any be wrong.

Disregard for the moment the deep questions of ontology and epistemology. Even focusing on the rhetorical consequences alone, the death of fallibilism has ominous implications, for it narrows the number of argumentative positions available to us, threatening to reduce all intellectual exchanges to a naked clash of wills. If there is no such thing as truth but only a variety of incommensurable perspectives in criterionless competition with one another, then force and persuasion become indistinguishable, cutting the ground out from under any politics based on consent and representation. If nothing is true, then giving up one's own initial perspective and adopting that of an interlocutor can signify nothing more than submission. The honorable option of bowing to reason and willingly renouncing error for the sake of impersonal truth drops out, leaving only *me v. you*, or *us v. them*. Down this path lies Nietzsche's world, where not only power and knowledge blur together but might and right as well.

It is seldom recognized that, three quarters of a century ago, when William Butler Yeats wondered what new thing "slouches toward Bethlehem" and warned of a time when the best would "lack all conviction, while the worst are full of passionate intensity," the state of the debate was very different than it is today. Nietzsche's influence was slight; no one of consequence contended that there is nothing outside language. The relativism that worried Yeats in "The Second Coming" was a comparatively mild variety that stemmed from the excesses of fallibilism. Fallibilists took the reality of the world for granted but acknowledged that it perpetually eludes our grasp, leaving us with tokens, fragments, and intimations of the real rather than its substance. The danger, as Yeats saw it, was that those with refined intellects, being most likely to acknowledge the frailty of their knowledge, were also likely to be paralyzed by doubt and uncertainty. Meanwhile, the mean and opinionated, taking their own perspective to be the only one possible, would be full of conviction and rule the world with the passionate intensity that only conviction can sustain.

The first lesson of fallibilism is indeed humility. Although it need not be carried to excess, fallibilists must be suspicious of their own convictions. Why? Because those convictions may turn out to be inadequate to the real. Take away the very idea of the real, as Rorty's antirepresentational stance does, and the lesson ceases to be humility and becomes very nearly its opposite. If there is nothing real for one's convictions to represent, then they cannot be inadequate and may as well be asserted with all the force one can muster. The question is no longer whether they are right, or even how they stack up against other people's convictions, but simply whose will prevail, for everyone's convictions are understood to be equally arbitrary. On this model convictions differ not in intrinsic merit or in the degree of their correspondence with the real, but only in the degree of influence they achieve by extrinsic means: the power exerted in their behalf. The characteristic danger that will be perceived by the denizens of an antirepresentationalist era is not the paralyzing excess of humility that alarmed Yeats, but an acute shortage of the brute force needed to make sure things go one's own way.

Thus when push comes to shove, antirepresentationalism cannot help but promote escalation of conflict—just the opposite of the virtue commonly claimed for it. Fallibilism, in sharp contrast, authentically promotes de-escalation. If there is a reality and we possess some ability to "get it right"—but can only hope to do so fallibly and thus are never entitled to feel *certain* we are right—then all of us, friends and foes alike, are equal in our deprivation, similar in our ignorance. The reality that eludes us all dwarfs us all; we share our inferiority to it even when we share nothing else. But if nothing is real, if there is nothing to "get right," then there is nothing of which we are equally ignorant; nothing greater than ourselves; nothing that all acknowledge but none can claim fully to possess. In the absence of anything real, we have little choice but to march under the belligerent banner "Don't tread on me." In contrast, the fallibilist's banner, "Let's talk," presupposes an option not available on antirepresentational premises: the possibility of convergence, not on the home territory of either party (which would represent defeat for the other) but on the common ground of reason and reality. In the absence of anything real, there is no hope of common ground. Convergence becomes capitulation to some "other."

The consequences of doing away with truth (or shrinking it to a vestigial synonym for whatever we want to believe, which comes to the same thing) do not all point in the same direction. The problem is not simply that the rhetorical consequences are escalatory; nor is it simply that Rorty has retreated too far from Peircean claims of epistemological efficacy and thus called into question the cognitive raison d'être of the community of the competent. As Stanley Fish has seen as clearly as anyone, there is a curious sense in which the historicist standpoint, if carried far enough, also makes it possible to impute to such communities an authority more august than Peirce would have dared to claim even in his most extravagant moments. For in keeping with the "linguistic turn" one can argue that if there is no reality with a capital R, then the conversation of inquirers can be regarded not merely as approximating knowledge of the real, but as actually *constituting* the only small *r* socially constructed reality that human beings can ever hope to know. Thus antirealism points paradoxically in two opposed directions, neither reassuring. It is not easy to say which we should think more worrisome: the retreat from Peircean claims of epistemological efficacy or the imperious claim that academic conversations actually constitute reality.[65] Either way, we lack any adequate rationale for the autonomy academic freedom is meant to defend. If we take the modest tack, admitting that our communities aim at nothing more than edification, it becomes unclear why anyone should defer to our judgment. Alternatively, if reality comes to be seen as entirely a social construction, incapable of representing or corresponding to anything outside language, the lay public would have to be incredibly trusting, even gullible, to let us academics retain the disproportionate voice we now have in the language games that are said to make the world what it is.

Whether the greater danger is timidity or hubris, the question we must face about academic freedom today is why, on antirealist premises, trustees and legislators should ever consent to the propagation of a reality not to their taste. Indeed, in the hands of antirealists more radical than Rorty, the pertinent question becomes: *How in good political conscience could anyone who has the resources to shape the very construction of reality—say, by changing the curriculum or influencing the selection of teachers or regulating the discourse of students about gender, ethnicity, or other sensitive issues—pass up such an opportunity? Is not abstention from the use of power on behalf of the good an abdication of responsibility?* The fate of academic freedom cannot be disentangled from prevailing conceptions of the good and the real. Insofar as reality is understood to be a malleable collective construction, political at its core, no person or group in a democratic society could be entitled to any sort of privileged voice—that is, an autonomous and authoritative voice—in its definition. We have seen that the founders of the modern university were not wedded to a naive correspondence theory of truth and made important concessions to truth's historicity, to its conventionality, and occasionally even to its cultural variability. Fallibility they accepted. But they did not doubt that some interpretations were better than others, better in a strong sense that did not necessarily depend on correspondence and yet was not reducible to perspective. If they were wrong about this—if "truth" is so much a matter of perspective that it belongs always inside quotation marks, as befits a claim made only half-seriously—must not the "rights of academic freedom" be enclosed within quotation marks too?[66]

Here we must step back from Rorty's rhetorical posture and begin taking into account his practice, for although he has delivered powerful blows against the assumptions that have traditionally been used to justify the rights of academic freedom, anyone familiar with the whole tenor and spirit of his writings will know perfectly well that he means no harm to the university or to the disciplinary communities it harbors. If push came to shove, he is among the first I would expect to find in the foxholes, risking his own safety in defense of academic freedom. The point of my discussion has not been to indict Rorty as a reckless nihilist, which he most certainly is not, but to highlight the tendency of his antirealist rhetoric to generate implications that spill beyond the limits he evidently intends. Between his words and his intentions a touch of hyperbole often intrudes. There is, for example, room to suspect that, as a recent president of the American Philosophical Association (APA), he may not be altogether serious about doing away with philosophy. His writings, after all, are from a layman's point of view not something other than philosophy but a delightfully lucid example of it, and one which could never have been produced were he not the member of a thriving and well-disciplined community of the competent. His pages bristle with all the tell-tale name-dropping, alliance-building, and allusive arm-wrestling of a scholar whose every thought is conditioned by the network of rivalrous relationships in which the professional community inserts him. Against confrontation? Why, Rorty thrives on it, even as he impugns the epistemological assumptions that would distinguish it from aimless aggression. Like the biblical David with his sling, Rorty has taken on the entire analytical mainstream of his profession at once, as if to prove how fruitful confrontation can be. His own words to the contrary notwithstanding, Rorty is too much the virtuoso of the community of the competent to knowingly contemplate any reduction in its authority.

What, then, are we to make of his antiprofessional posture? A useful corrective to Rorty's underestimation of the role that disciplinary influences play in shaping the way we think can be found in Stanley Fish's witty and perverse defense of professionalism. As will become clear, I have grave reservations about Fish's conception of the professional community, but no one has displayed a keener awareness of the ways in which the community defines the life-world of its members. Drawing on Kuhn's portrait of revolutionary science as a clash between rival groups whose professional worldviews are defined by the paradigmatic, world-making assumptions of their members, Fish argues that in an era of illimitable interpretation such as ours it is the professional community that prevents opinion from becoming merely arbitrary. To be sure, not even the professional community can provide a firm foundation for interpretation. Fish would be the last to suggest that membership in the community enables anyone to transcend time and place, or attain Truth. Still, the current state of opinion within the professional community, even though ultimately a matter of fashion, is all he thinks we need for intelligibility. Just how impressed the public should be with the level of intelligibility currently being sustained in the academy is debatable, but in any event Fish accords to the disciplinary community an important and at least quasi-epistemological function in fixing collective opinion.[67]

Fish sees in antiprofessionalism a posture that serves distinctly professional ends. The relationship he has in mind between individuals and institutions appears to be broadly Freudian. Just as civilization breeds discontent by thwarting instinctual gratification, so on Fish's conception the disciplinary community unavoidably breeds resentment among its members in the course of defining their life-world. The result is a state of consciousness that is not only "false," but inverted, as the community's members conceal from themselves their utter dependence on it by indulging in fantasies of solitude and self-sufficiency, all the while complaining about the shallowness and parochialism of communal life. Far from suggesting the imminent breakdown of the community, these complaints and escapist fantasies can signify that a healthy balance has been achieved between individual initiative and communal constraint. Fish construes his own profession of literary criticism as one that depends vitally on imagining itself to be something other than it is. "Anti-professionalism," he says, "is a form of professional behavior engaged in for the purpose of furthering some professional project." That is how Fish would explain what he calls the "virulence" of antiprofessionalism among literary critics: "While most professions are criticized for betraying their ideals," Fish observes, "this profession betrays its ideals by being practiced at all, by being, as a professor of medicine once put it to me, 'a parasite on the carcass of literature.'"[68] Thus it becomes obligatory within some academic circles to present oneself to the world as a free spirit, spontaneous to the point of idiosyncrasy, who disdains everything that smacks of calculation and self-advancement and lives only for the love of art and justice. Successfully managing such a self-presentation can be the key to professional advancement, precisely because it prominently displays a disposition to subordinate self-advancement to other, higher values.

Fish's point, however, is not simply that conspicuous renunciation of careerist aims can be an effective strategy for their attainment. The larger and less cynical point is that in order for such a community to function effectively, it may be necessary for its members to imagine that they are boldly improvising, even when they are playing roles the community defines for them. Antiprofessionalism in this largest sense, says Fish, is the "founding gesture of the profession," in that it supplies members with a "vocabulary of transcendence" and enables them to ward off fears of heteronomy. "A professional must find a way to operate in the context of purposes, motivations, and possibilities that precede and even define him and yet maintain the conviction that he is 'essentially the proprietor of his own person and capacities.' *The way he finds is anti-professionalism.*" "To be a professional," says Fish, "is to think of oneself as motivated by something larger than market conditions." From this standpoint the community not only can tolerate a high level of antiprofessionalism, but needs it to offset the pressures for consensus and rigor (and perhaps also scholasticism and conformity) that are bred by communal life. Antiprofessionalism of the sort that Rorty displays thus becomes an ironic but integral part of the ideology of professionalism. At the end of his essay titled "Anti-Professionalism," Fish admits that "in my efforts to rehabilitate professionalism, I have come full circle and have ended up by rehabilitating anti-professionalism too." [69]

Alas, Fish's admirable insight that the community must, for its own good, leave a niche for personal autonomy is squandered by his insistence that this niche can never be anything more than a mirage. Freedom for Fish is a myth to which we cling out of hunger for self-esteem. If Rorty's view of the professional scholar is "undersocialized" in its failure to acknowledge the immensity of the intellectual debt each of us owes to the disciplinary matrix within which we work, Fish's view is, in the last analysis, "oversocialized," for in the end his professionals turn out to be nothing more than passive reflexes of their professional surroundings, incapable of voicing any opinion not prefabricated by the community. Taking thought; putting one's affairs in a larger perspective; heightening one's awareness of one's place in the world; attaining higher stages of self-consciousness—all these inward operations performed by the thinking self he dismisses as illusory. "The demand for self-consciousness," he says, "is a demand for a state of consciousness in which nothing has yet been settled and choices can therefore be truly rational." No such state of mind exists. "If you are a finite being, and therefore situated, you are wholly situated, and no part of you or your experience is asituational; your every capability is positive, a reflection and extension of the system of belief that bespeaks you and your possibilities, and there is nothing negative (detached, independent, free) to nurture." Careening over the edge, Fish concludes that "freedom, in whatever shape it appears, is another name for constraint." [70]

Surely this goes too far. It does not follow that since we are situated (constrained by circumstance) we must be "wholly situated" (fated, incapable of authentic choice). The idea of freedom is riddled with paradox and there is plenty of room to criticize commonsense understandings of it, but our vivid everyday experience of choice and decision has to be taken more seriously than this. Nor is it enough to add, as Fish so characteristically does, that perceptions of freedom, although illusory, are built into the human condition and so cannot finally be doubted or set aside, any more than mortality itself.[71] Fish's own doubts about the authenticity of freedom are on record, and he carries them out in practice. Caught up in the exuberance of his own rhetoric, he is not content to describe scholars as independent agents or even as participating members of a community whose every thought bears traces of its corporate origins. Instead, they are mere "extensions" and "reflections" coughed up by a soulless socio-cognitive machine that "bespeaks" them and their possibilities—not a promising place to begin if one is trying to justify academic or any other variety of freedom.

What if the customary rights and privileges of academic freedom were to come under attack: Would Fish defend them? I have no doubt that he would, but only because he is utterly fearless when it comes to incurring charges of inconsistency and expediency. As a self-identified member of the species *homo rhetoricus* who is used to being accused of a morally paralyzing relativism, Fish is quick to insist that we are *always* entitled to assert our interests and resist actions that have deplorable consequences.[72] The adequacy of our justification would not concern him: we defend academic freedom because it is in our interest to do so, and the justificatory rhetoric we employ is adequate insofar as it carries the day—no internal or logical criterion of adequacy applies. Some readers may wonder how anyone who sees so little difference between freedom and unfreedom, and who has so much disdain for the "vocabulary of transcendence," could defend academic freedom with a good intellectual conscience, but from Fish's perspective this is not only a tender-minded response but also an obfuscating one, because of its easy distinction between those who act on conscience and those who do not. This being a Darwinian world, motives unmindful of the self promise extinction. *Us v. them, me v. you:* that's life. Nietzsche's slippery slope holds no terror for Fish. We have been there all along; there is no other place to be.

In a recent essay impishly titled "There's No Such Thing as Free Speech and It's a Good Thing Too," Fish shrugs aside the conventional wisdom that free speech is a right of "independent value"—that is, a value we should uphold for its long-term benefits regardless of whose speech is in question and how well our own immediate interests and preferences are served by it. The alternative, one gathers, is to regard free speech as a *dependent* value, and what it most depends on is whether or not it serves one's own personal or political interests. Fish observes, accurately enough, that no society ever has or ever could protect all speech whatsoever, that a limit must always be set somewhere. From this familiar and uncontroversial fact he brings forth the astonishing non sequitur that, all pretenses aside, free speech has never been anything more than a dependent value and therefore we would be fools to honor the right of free speech when it does not serve our interests. If, in a particular instance, acknowledging a right of free speech would be inconvenient, or suit the other fellow's interests better than your own, well then, says Fish, just don't acknowledge it. In the essay's introductory paragraph he lays out its lesson without a trace of embarrassment:

> Free speech is not an independent value but a political prize, and if that prize has been captured by a politics opposed to yours, it can no longer be invoked in ways that further your purposes for it is now an obstacle to those purposes. This is something that the liberal left has yet to understand and what follows is an attempt to pry its members loose from a vocabulary that may now be a disservice to them.[73]

Fish spells out the lesson again near the essay's end. "My counsel is therefore pragmatic rather than draconian: so long as so-called 'free speech principles' have been fashioned by your enemies, contest their relevance to the issue at hand; but if you manage to refashion them in line with your purposes, urge them with a vengeance."[74] In short, free speech, being a privilege, is best reserved for oneself and one's allies. When in the presence of those who mistake free speech for an independent value, demand it as a right; but do not be so naive as to extend reciprocal rights to them, or anyone else, as long as you can get away without doing so. Fish's Machiavellian advice transforms free speech from a matter of obligation that may constrain us to act against our own wishes into a rhetorical ruse that liberates us to take advantage of suckers, including all who believe in such ephemeral things as independent value. Here the message is delivered in a soothing context of concern about the harmful effects of hate speech, but Fish has delivered similar messages on other occasions and, whatever the occasion, his basic assumptions remain the same. These assumptions, widely shared in the era of power/knowledge, are not hard to enumerate: It's a jungle out there. Politics is the only game in town, all appearances to the contrary notwithstanding. Playing politics means being rhetorical, at least until the violence begins. Only the tender-minded take ideals, principles, and procedural scruples to be actual rules of conduct; everyone else knows them to be nothing more than masks, means of persuasion, moves in a struggle that aims always at dominance. The only operative rules are catch-as-catch-can, winner take all, dupe or be duped.

Given these assumptions, all the agonizing complexities posed by hate speech evaporate into thin air:

> When someone observes, as someone surely will, that anti-harassment codes chill speech, one could reply that since speech only becomes intelligible against the background of what isn't being said, the background of what has already been silenced, *the only question is the political one of which speech is going to be chilled,* and all things considered, it seems like a good thing to chill speech like "nigger," "cunt," "kike," and "faggot." And if someone then says, "But what happened to free speech principles?" one could say what I have now said a dozen times, free speech principles don't exist except as a component in a bad argument in which such principles are invoked to mask motives that would not stand close scrutiny.[75]

Although the raw examples Fish lists would seem potentially to qualify as "fighting words," and thus to be actionable under the principle adopted by the Supreme Court in *Chaplinsky v. New Hampshire* (1942), not even that principle carries any weight with him, for "every idea is an incitement to somebody."[76] Against the dangers of the jungle, principle is powerless, the resort to force inescapable.

It is not hard to imagine what would become of academic freedom if trustees took to heart Fish's lesson that free speech is inescapably a dependent value, to be honored or ignored depending on how well it serves one's own interests. I argued above that academic freedom could not be fully assimilated to free speech protections without grave loss, but the two obviously overlap extensively and the fate of academic freedom can no more be disentangled from free speech protections than it can from epistemological assumptions. If free speech is not an independent value, then neither is academic freedom. Fish claims merely to be refining our understanding of free speech conventions, which he admits usefully "channel" political debate and "protect society against over-hasty outcomes," but in truth widespread adoption of his "refinements" would reduce those conventions to rubble.[77] Insofar as free speech and academic freedom are selectively applied and made dependent on political consequences, they lose their independent status as values and become incapable of channeling debate. Deprived of independence they exert no force of their own and merely augment whatever political interest has overpowered them.

Defining academic freedom as a dependent value would carry us back to the state of affairs that existed in the 1890s, at the time of Edward A. Ross's dismissal. By Fish's Orwellian standard, Mrs. Stanford committed no sin against academic freedom; she just construed it realistically, as a dependent value. Her decision to fire Ross depended on his politics, which Fish recognizes as a good and sufficient reason for withholding free speech protections. Of course Fish might disapprove of her politics and therefore accuse her of violating Ross's rights, but only as a theatrical ploy on behalf of his own politics. The goal of the Victorian project that was brought to completion by the founding of the AAUP in 1915 was to insure that politics and other influences deemed extrinsic to intellectual work would not be the sole, the primary, or even the major determinants of scholarly expression. For Fish such a project can be one of two things: an exercise in futility (if the projectors are sincere about their intentions) or deception (if not). Not that deception would be out of bounds. "The only question," as he says, "is the political one of which speech is going to be chilled."

> People cling to First Amendment pieties because they do not wish to face what they correctly take to be the alternative. That alternative is *politics,* the realization . . . that decisions about what is and is not protected in the realm of expression will rest not on principle or firm doctrine, but on the ability of some persons to interpret—recharacterize or rewrite—principle and doctrine in ways that lead to the protection of speech they want heard and the regulation of speech they want silenced. (That is how George Bush can argue *for* flag-burning statutes and *against* campus hate-speech codes.) When the First Amendment is successfully invoked the result is not a victory for free speech in the face of a challenge from politics, but a *political victory* won by the party that has managed to wrap its agenda in the mantle of free speech. . . . In short, the name of the game has always been politics, even when (indeed, especially when) it is played by stigmatizing politics as the area to be avoided.[78]

The primacy of the political: Here is an article of faith so rich in implications as to be virtually constitutive of the era of power/knowledge. It is deeply inimical to academic freedom, presumably another of the "pieties" like free speech to which Fish says the timid "cling." For those who subscribe to this web of assumptions, politics extends seamlessly into every nook and cranny of life, making unthinkable the very ideas of the unpolitical and the nonpartisan (not to mention the disinterested). Even the thought that politics is a matter of degree, that some decisions or motives are *less* political than others, is taken by the faithful to be an evasion of this all-revealing truth about the universal sway of political motivation. The pervasiveness of the political is commonly presented as a plain and palpable fact of the sort that only fools or knaves could deny, but in fact it is the predictable outcome of a hermeneutics of suspicion to which all of us resort in our most cynical moments, when we are eager to project our own aggression outward into the world. The presumption that everything is political reproduces at the level of policy the character ideal specific to a "therapeutic" culture, in which the goal of personal autonomy has resolved itself into the crass problem of knowing how to use others without being used by them. Just as the inhabitants of a therapeutic culture, in Philip Rieff's words, "cannot conceive of an action that is not self-serving, however it may be disguised or transformed," neither can they imagine anything standing outside the struggle for political advantage. "This is a culture in which each views the other, in the fullness of his self-knowledge, as 'trash.'"[79] One's guard instinctively goes up in the presence of those who mutter "It's a jungle out there!" and for good reason. One never knows whether this incantation is, as it pretends, the prayer of innocents, who fear becoming prey, or instead the curse of predators, eager to dilute their guilt by universalizing it.

The "politics" that is said to be so ubiquitous is a thin, one-dimensional affair, bearing little resemblance either to the bookish subject taught by political science or to the turbulent panorama of horse-trading, arm-twisting, rule-making, and rule-bending—by turns ennobling and degrading—that is on display daily in legislatures, court houses, and town councils across the land. "Politics" stands simply for the lawlessness of the jungle. It is a nightmare vision, devoid of empirical substance and animated by bruised innocence. There is little room in it for the rich assortment of institutions, devices, and strategies by which wise statesmen have tried to deflect power, defuse antagonisms, outwait confrontations, and set baffles in the way of force, for from the vantage point Fish occupies all these measures (like academic freedom) smack of otherworldliness, of the *flight* from the political, of vain attempts to make of ourselves something more than creatures of the jungle.

Thus in the long passage quoted above Fish characteristically identifies politics with the stark "realization" (no mere "supposition" or "hypothesis," contingent on the facts of the case) that our principles and doctrines count for nothing, that the only important question is who gets to *interpret* them. He thereby obscures the elementary political lesson that principles and doctrines can usefully narrow an officeholder's range of personal discretion; that

personality, principle, and doctrine all have a hand in shaping political outcomes; that neither the interpreter nor that which is interpreted determines
everything. In the same vein, he dismisses the argument that the short-run
benefits of silencing haters might be offset by the detrimental long-term
consequences of chilling free expression. He does so archly, on the grounds
that such an argument "could be seen" as the mask that hate wears. Even
when not a mask, he contends, the argument is just the secular residue of
the "Puritan celebration of millenarian hopes," plausible only to those who
put their faith in the "Holy Spirit" and the indefinite future, instead of this
world and the present.[80] When it comes to regulative ideals, Fish simply has
a tin ear. He would no more pursue a goal that he knew in advance could
only be imperfectly attained than go shopping in a museum. Shopping is
for malls, where dollars count and consumers get what they ask for. Why
want something that eludes your grasp, that you cannot wrap up and take
home with you?

Some of the premises underlying academic freedom are open to serious
objections, but the Victorians were not wrong to distinguish between motives more and less political. Those who see ominous political implications
lurking beneath every bed and hiding behind every door do so not because
"that is the way the world is"—an impermissible formulation on their own
premises, after all—but because of assumptions they deploy as a matter of
choice. The skillful deployment of these assumptions is a game. Foucault
was pastmaster and Fish a world-class practitioner, but anyone can play.
Here's how: First, acknowledge no limits to interpretation. Second, acknowledge no difference between intended and unintended consequences.
Third, disregard all distinctions between acts of commission and omission.
Fourth, firmly embrace (as if true) the logical fallacy of supposing that whoever is not for your cause is against it.

These axioms constitute a blank check for tendentiousness. Adopt them
and you, too, will find that politics has expanded to fill your entire universe.
Threatening agendas and scandalous breaches of responsibility will rear up
on all sides; masks will fall away and sordid motives leap into view. Advocates of speech codes will be revealed (in the eyes of their opponents) as
stealthy Stalinists; advocates of free speech will be revealed (in the eyes of
their opponents) as covert bigots. Actions and inactions, words and silences,
choices and accidents, things done and things left undone—all acts and
omissions to act will testify to the universality of self-aggrandizement and
the pervasiveness of political machination. Anyone who rebuffs your idea
of a proper solution will be "part of the problem"; anyone who argues for

an understanding of events more complicated than your own will be guilty of "blaming the victim." Once these strategic premises are in place, responsibility will have been transformed from a concrete relation into a diffuse quality that floats freely through all relations, ready to be imputed to anyone, anytime. If it suits your needs, you can find fault with the person who sends his annual charitable donation to Amnesty International for not caring enough about world hunger, while simultaneously accusing the person who sends her contribution to Oxfam of being indifferent to torture—for from this standpoint nothing evil "just happens." Remember: good acts omitted are no less incriminating than evils committed; the indirect consequences of a person's acts signify unconscious wishes, even if not conscious intention; moral liability extends as far as interpretation can carry it. And interpretation knows no bounds.[81]

Once this perspective is adopted, Fish's description is undeniable: politics floods the world, leaving, as he says, "no safe place."[82] It is a perspective from which academic freedom can be seen as an enviable political prize, well worth hanging on to, but also one from which all efforts at justification have to be interpreted as self-serving rhetoric. Illogical though the assumptions underlying this perspective plainly are, their appeal today is great. Rieff may be right; we may already live in a culture that cannot conceive of acts that are not self-serving and can only define autonomy as the opportunity to use without being used. If so, the "safe place" the Victorian founders of the university tried to create under the banner of academic freedom is beyond any possibility of justification. One can only hope and trust that this is not the case.

NOTES

I am indebted to more people for advice about this essay than I can mention here. Special pains were taken by Steven Crowell, Sanford Levinson, Randall McGowen, Louis Menand, Walter Metzger, Robert Post, and Carol Quillen. Advice sometimes took the form of vigorous dissent, so no one is to be blamed for the final product but me. Various versions of the paper were presented at a conference on "Paradoxes of Rights" at Amherst College in November 1992, at the History Department of the University of Oregon in October 1993, and at the Swedish Collegium for Advanced Study in the Social Sciences and the History Department of Rice University in September 1994. A longer version of the essay appears in *Legal Rights: Historical and Philosophical Perspectives,* ed. Austin Sarat and Thomas R. Kearns (Ann Arbor: University of Michigan Press, 1996), 113–76.

1. College attendance ratios appear in Fritz Machlup, *The Production and Distribution of Knowledge in the United States* (Princeton, N.J.: Princeton University Press, 1962), p.

78. On the development of the modern American university, see Richard Hofstadter and Walter Metzger, *The Development of Academic Freedom in the United States* (New York: Columbia University Press, 1955); Laurence R. Veysey, *The Emergence of the American University* (Chicago: University of Chicago Press, 1965); Hugh Hawkins, *Pioneer: A History of the Johns Hopkins University, 1874–1889* (Ithaca, N.Y.: Cornell University Press, 1960); Thomas Bender, *Intellect and Public Life: Essays on the Social History of Academic Intellectuals in the United States* (Baltimore: Johns Hopkins University Press, 1993); Dorothy Ross, *Origins of American Social Science* (Cambridge: Cambridge University Press, 1991); Burton J. Bledstein, *The Culture of Professionalism: The Middle Class and the Development of Higher Education in America* (New York: Norton, 1976); and Thomas L. Haskell, *The Emergence of Professional Social Science: The American Social Science Association and the Nineteenth-Century Crisis of Authority* (Urbana: University of Illinois Press, 1977).

2. Lorraine Daston, "The Ideal and the Reality of the Republic of Letters in the Enlightenment," *Science in Context* 4 (Autumn 1991): 367–86.

3. The reforms of the nineteenth century were made possible by a long and rich tradition of academic freedom, carefully developed in the classic work by Hofstadter and Metzger, *Development of Academic Freedom.*

4. The term "community of the competent" is that of Francis E. Abbot, who was a member of the "Metaphysical Club" where Charles Peirce and William James worked out the basic ideas of Pragmatism in the 1870s. Stow Persons, *Free Religion: An American Faith* (New Haven, Conn.: Yale University Press, 1947), pp. 31, 125–29; Philip P. Wiener, *Evolution and the Founders of Pragmatism* (New York: Harper and Row, 1965), pp. 41–48.

5. Karl-Otto Apel, *Charles S. Peirce: From Pragmatism to Pragmaticism,* trans. J. M. Krois (Amherst: University of Massachusetts Press, 1981), p. xvi; and Apel, *Toward a Transformation of Philosophy,* trans. G. Adey and D. Frisby (London: Routledge and Kegan Paul, 1980).

6. An early pioneer was Friedrich August Wolf, founder of a famous seminar in classical studies at Halle in the 1780s, who borrowed the ideology of cultivation (*Bildung*) from Humboldt and used it, paradoxically, to elevate research above teaching so as to achieve a level of authority that pedagogy alone could not supply. See Anthony J. La Vopa, "Specialists against Specialization: Hellenism as Professional Ideology in German Classical Studies," in *German Professions, 1800–1950,* ed. Geoffrey Cocks and Konrad H. Jarausch (New York and Oxford: Oxford University Press, 1990), pp. 27–45.

7. The inadequacies of the economic monopoly model are developed more fully in my "Professionalism *versus* Capitalism: R. H. Tawney, Emile Durkheim, and C. S. Peirce on the Disinterestedness of Professional Communities," in *The Authority of Experts: Studies in History and Theory,* ed. Thomas L. Haskell (Bloomington: Indiana University Press, 1984), pp. 180–225. On the "culture of critical discourse" fostered by these communities, see Alvin Gouldner, *The Future of the Intellectuals and the Rise of the New Class* (New York: Continuum, 1979).

8. William Brennan, quoted in William W. Van Alstyne, "Academic Freedom and the First Amendment in the Supreme Court of the United States: An Unhurried Historical Review," in *Freedom and Tenure in the Academy: The Fiftieth Anniversary of the 1940 Statement of Principles,* William Van Alstyne, special editor, *Law and Contemporary Problems* 53 (Summer 1990): 114.

9. Michel Foucault, *Power/Knowledge: Selected Interviews and Other Writings, 1972–1977,* ed. Colin Gordon (New York: Pantheon, 1980). In *Discipline and Punish,* Foucault's formulation took this practical form: "Instead of treating the history of penal law and the history of the human sciences as two separate series [that merely have effects on one another, my aim is to] see whether there is some common matrix or . . . single process of 'epistemological-juridical' formation; in short, [to] make the technology of power the very principle both of the humanization of the penal system and of the knowledge of man." The problem is that in making the "technology of power" the "very principle" of humanitarian reform and knowledge of man, one reduces knowledge and justice to power. Or, to take him at his word, Foucault does not *reduce* one to the other, but argues for their simultaneous production in a "single process," which blurs the opposition between them just as surely as reduction would. Blurring that opposition means obscuring the difference between education and indoctrination, scholarship and propaganda, history and fiction, right and might, consent and coercion, and so on, tending to make these and other classic oppositions, as I put it above, "two sides of a single coin." Michel Foucault, *Discipline and Punish: The Birth of the Prison,* trans. A. Sheridan (New York: Pantheon, 1977), p. 23.

10. Committed Foucauldians will remind us that distinguishing between power and disinterested knowledge can itself be construed as an exercise in power. Indeed it can. Once one accepts the proposition that power is the only game in town, power relations can and will be teased out of anything at all. The same could be said for sex, religion, or any number of other grand obsessions. Any master key, once subscribed to, will seem to open all locks. The dangers of reducing everything to power relations are twofold. First, making power the master category obscures a vital distinction between force and persuasion that is constitutive for liberal politics. Second, unlike sex, religion, and other interpretive obsessions, the presumption that power is the master motive is a classic example of the self-fulfilling prophecy. He who insists upon construing dancing as sex by other means is merely a bore; but he who construes scholarship as politics by other means provokes in others the very motives he imputes to them, no matter how unjust the original imputation.

11. Mary O. Furner, *Advocacy and Objectivity: A Crisis in the Professionalization of American Social Science, 1865–1905* (Lexington: University Press of Kentucky, 1975), p. 234.

12. Ibid.

13. Ibid., p. 235.

14. Ibid., pp. 235–36.

15. James C. Mohr, "Academic Turmoil and Public Opinion: The Ross Case at Stanford," *Pacific Historical Review* 39 (February 1970): 39–61; Furner, *Advocacy and Objectivity,* p. 238.

16. Ross, quoted in Furner, *Advocacy and Objectivity,* p. 238.

17. Ibid., pp. 239–41.

18. Ibid., p. 245; Hofstadter and Metzger, *Development of Academic Freedom,* pp. 442–43.

19. Furner, *Advocacy and Objectivity,* pp. 246, 251, 252–53.

20. Albion Small, quoted in Hofstadter and Metzger, *Development of Academic Freedom,* p. 443.

21. Oliver Wendell Holmes, quoted in William W. Van Alstyne, "Academic Freedom and the First Amendment," pp. 98, 84. Even today, of course, the legal protections

of the First Amendment extend only to public institutions, but I assume that that has been far enough to decisively influence the culture of the private sphere as well.

22. The kinship of professors and professionals was especially close in the case of the social science disciplines, which received unprecedented prominence in the modern American university and provided the most frequent setting for academic freedom controversies. The pioneering members of the American Social Science Association, which began meeting in 1865 and spawned the AHA in 1884 and the AEA in 1885, were forward looking professional men and women. In their eyes the social sciences were elaborations of a professional division of labor that extended far beyond the university and defined the wisdom and knowledge necessary for exercising leadership in a merit-based liberal democracy. See my *Emergence of Professional Social Science,* pp. 100–110. Stephen Bann brings out the intimate dependence of the historians' mode of discourse on that deployed by physicians, lawyers, and ministers. See Bann, "History and Her Siblings: Law, Medicine, and Theology," *The Inventions of History: Essays on the Representation of the Past* (Manchester: Manchester University Press, 1990), pp. 12–32.

23. These words appear in the three-page brochure sent out by the "committee on organization" in November 1914, announcing the founding session to be held in January. The passage continues as follows: "The general purposes of such an Association would be to facilitate a more effective cooperation among the members of the profession in the discharge of their special responsibilities as custodians of the interests of higher education and research in America; to promote a more general and methodical discussion of problems related to education in higher institutions of learning; to create means for the authoritative expression of the public opinion of college and university teachers; and to maintain and advance the standards and ideals of the profession." AAUP Archives, file marked "A. O. Lovejoy 1914"; also published in *Bulletin of the AAUP* 2 (March 1916): 11–13.

24. I follow the lead of Walter Metzger in stressing the tension between two definitions of academic freedom, the "professional" and the "constitutional" (the latter deriving from the First Amendment): see Metzger, "Profession and Constitution: Two Definitions of Academic Freedom in America," *Texas Law Review* 66 (June 1988): 1265–1322. For a somewhat divergent view, see David M. Rabban, "A Functional Analysis of 'Individual' and 'Institutional' Academic Freedom under the First Amendment," in Van Alstyne, *Law and Contemporary Problems,* pp. 227–301.

25. On this point the charter document of the AAUP, the 1915 Report on Academic Freedom and Tenure, is explicit: "It is, in short, not the absolute freedom of utterance of the individual scholar, but the absolute freedom of thought, of inquiry, of discussion and of teaching, of the academic profession, that is asserted by this declaration of principles." AAUP, "General Report of the Committee on Academic Freedom and Academic Tenure (1915)," included as Appendix A in Van Alstyne, *Law and Contemporary Problems,* pp. 404–5 (hereafter referred to as AAUP, "The 1915 Report on Academic Freedom and Tenure").

26. This and the next paragraph borrow from the introduction to my *Authority of Experts,* pp. x–xi.

27. H. Stuart Hughes, *Consciousness and Society: The Reorientation of European Social Thought, 1890–1930* (New York: Knopf, 1958), chap. 2; James Kloppenberg, *Uncertain Victory: Social Democracy and Progressivism in European and American Thought, 1870–1920* (New York and Oxford: Oxford University Press, 1986).

28. AAUP, "The 1915 Report on Academic Freedom and Tenure," p. 399.

29. Ibid., pp. 400, 402, 404.

30. Ibid., pp. 394–95.

31. Ibid., p. 397. The 1915 report also presented "practical proposals" calling for faculty representation on committees considering reappointment; judicial hearings and formulation of explicit grounds in cases of dismissal; and permanent tenure for all positions above the grade of instructor after ten (not seven) years of service. The practical nuts and bolts underpinning academic freedom were further developed in a second landmark AAUP document that continues to enjoy something approaching constitutional status today, the "1940 Statement of Principles on Academic Freedom and Tenure." By that date, although as many as half of all colleges and universities may have still been appointing faculty on an annual basis, hiring practices had become sufficiently uniform at the leading institutions that the AAUP made a bid to install tenure as the keystone of academic freedom. It called for permanent tenure for all academics after a probationary period normally not exceeding seven years, and allowed for termination only at retirement, upon demonstration of adequate cause, or because of extraordinary financial exigencies. The 1940 statement, which of course does not have the force of law, was a compromise jointly authored by teachers in the AAUP and administrators in the American Association of Colleges. The premier association of administrators, the American Association of Universities, has never endorsed the 1940 principles, although its member institutions probably uphold them at least as scrupulously as other schools. See Walter P. Metzger, "The 1940 Statement of Principles on Academic Freedom and Tenure," in Van Alstyne, *Law and Contemporary Problems*, pp. 1–77.

32. AAUP, "The 1915 Report on Academic Freedom and Tenure," pp. 396–97.

33. Jürgen Habermas, *Legitimation Crisis* (Boston: Beacon Press, 1975), pp. 107–8.

34. AAUP, "The 1915 Report on Academic Freedom and Tenure," pp. 396–97.

35. Ibid., pp. 402, 397.

36. For a fuller discussion of the two Peirces and the theme of professionalization, see my *Emergence of Professional Social Science* and "Professionalization *versus* Capitalism," p. 208. On Peirce's influence at Harvard, see Bruce Kuklick, *The Rise of American Philosophy: Cambridge, Massachusetts, 1860–1930* (New Haven, Conn.: Yale University Press, 1977).

37. Thomas Kuhn, *The Structure of Scientific Revolutions*, 2d ed. (Chicago: University of Chicago Press, 1970); Richard Rorty, *Philosophy and the Mirror of Nature* (Princeton, N.J.: Princeton University Press, 1979); Stanley Fish, *Is There a Text in This Class? The Authority of Interpretive Communities* (Cambridge, Mass.: Harvard University Press, 1980), and "Anti-Professionalism," in Fish, *Doing What Comes Naturally: Change, Rhetoric, and the Place of Theory in Literary and Legal Studies* (Durham, N.C.: Duke University Press, 1989), chap. 11.

38. Stephen Toulmin never mentions Charles Peirce, but presents an account of knowledge that is comparably community oriented, in his *Human Understanding: The Collective Use and Evolution of Concepts* (Princeton, N.J.: Princeton University Press, 1972). An explosion of interest in Peirce is underway today; among many recent publications, most relevant is C. J. Misak, *Truth and the End of Inquiry* (Oxford: Oxford University Press, 1991).

39. Charles S. Peirce, *Collected Papers,* ed. Charles Hartshorne and Paul Weiss (Cambridge, Mass.: Harvard University Press, 1931–60), V-317 (reference is to volume and

paragraph). This and the next five paragraphs are based on my essay "Professionalism *versus* Capitalism"; the essay is an extension and revision of my comments on Peirce in *The Emergence of Professional Social Science.*

40. Peirce, *Collected Papers,* V-316, 311; emphasis in the original.

41. Ibid., V-407, 408; VI-610.

42. Ibid., V-379.

43. John E. Smith, "Community and Reality," in *Perspectives on Peirce,* ed. Richard J. Bernstein (New Haven, Conn.: Yale University Press, 1965), p. 118.

44. Kuhn, *Structure of Scientific Revolutions,* pp. 205–6, 170–72.

45. For Kuhn's ambivalence, see ibid., pp. 121, 126, 170–73. Rorty, *Philosophy and the Mirror of Nature,* p. 10; Rorty, *Consequences of Pragmatism: Essays, 1972–1980* (Minneapolis: University of Minnesota Press, 1982), xiv, pp. 96–98. In an unpublished 1984 paper titled "Rhetoric and Liberation," Kuhn, commenting on a paper by Rorty titled "Solidarity or Objectivity?" expressed his dissent from Rorty's sweeping rejection of objectivity and warm embrace of solidarity as an adequate standard of correct belief. Kuhn warned of a "profound misconception of the human condition, a misconception here manifest in an insufficient respect for the intrinsic authority of language. . . . I said I would speak as Cassandra, and I have been doing so. What I fear are attempts to separate language or discourse from the real and to do so in the name of freedom." Rorty's paper was published in *Post-Analytic Philosophy,* ed. John Rajchman and Cornel West (New York: Columbia University Press, 1985).

46. Rorty, *Consequences of Pragmatism,* 169–70; emphasis in the original. On the issue of edification versus verification, see A. O. Lovejoy, "On Some Conditions of Progress in Philosophical Inquiry," *Philosophical Review* 26 (March 1917): 131–38, and Daniel J. Wilson, *Arthur O. Lovejoy and the Quest for Intelligibility* (Chapel Hill: University of North Carolina Press, 1980), p. 92.

47. Lovejoy, "On Some Conditions of Progress," pp. 130, 159–60.

48. Ibid., p. 160.

49. A. O. Lovejoy, "William James as a Philosopher," *The Thirteen Pragmatisms and Other Essays* (Baltimore: Johns Hopkins University Press, 1963).

50. Lovejoy, "On Some Conditions of Progress," p. 131.

51. Lovejoy, "On Some Conditions of Progress," pp. 150, 133, 132, 151–52.

52. Stefan Collini, ed., *Interpretation and Overinterpretation: Umberto Eco with Richard Rorty, Jonathan Culler, Christine Brooke-Rose* (Cambridge: Cambridge University Press, 1992), pp. 12, 19.

53. Clifford Geertz, *The Interpretation of Cultures* (New York: Basic Books, 1973), p. 29.

54. See, for examples, Richard J. Bernstein, *Beyond Objectivism and Relativism: Science, Hermeneutics, and Praxis* (Philadelphia: University of Pennsylvania Press, 1988), pp. 36, 69, 71; Hilary Putnam, *Realism with a Human Face,* ed. James Conant (Cambridge, Mass.: Harvard University Press, 1990), pp. 21–22; and Jürgen Habermas, *Postmetaphysical Thinking: Philosophical Essays,* trans. William Mark Hehengarten (Cambridge, Mass.: MIT Press, 1992), chap. 5, "Peirce and Communication."

55. Rorty, *Consequences of Pragmatism,* p. 160.

56. Ibid., p. 173; emphasis in the original. The order of the quoted passages has been altered. See other comments about Peirce, in ibid., pp. 160–61, xlv.

57. The passage is worth quoting at greater length. Notice that neither literally nor in spirit did Dewey put the word "truth" in quotation marks. Rorty's proto-Nietzschean Dewey is not easily detected in passages such as this. "It is clear that . . . any attack, or even any restriction, upon academic freedom is directed against the university itself. To investigate truth; critically to verify fact; to reach conclusions by means of the best methods at command, untrammeled by external fear or favor, to communicate this truth to the student; to interpret to him its bearing on the questions he will have to face in life— this is precisely the aim and object of the university. To aim a blow at any one of these operations is to deal a vital wound to the university itself. The university function is the truth function. At one time it may be more concerned with the tradition or transmission of truth, and at another time with its discovery. . . . The one thing that is inherent and essential is the idea of truth." John Dewey, "Academic Freedom," *Educational Review* 23 (1902): 3; reprinted in *The American Concept of Academic Freedom in Formation: A Collection of Essays and Reports,* ed. Walter P. Metzger (New York: Arno Press, 1977).

58. Dewey's speech appears in *Science,* n.s. 41 (29 January 1915): 150.

59. This famous line of Peirce's is given a place of honor in a recent ringing defense of free speech by Jonathan Rauch, *Kindly Inquisitors: The New Attacks on Free Thought* (Chicago: University of Chicago Press, 1993), p. vii.

60. Rorty sometimes uses the term "community of inquiry" as a near synonym for culture or society: "We can always enlarge the scope of 'us' by regarding other people, or cultures, as members of the same community of inquiry as ourselves—by treating them as part of the group among whom unforced agreement is to be sought." Richard Rorty, *Objectivity, Relativism, and Truth: Philosophical Papers* (Cambridge: Cambridge University Press, 1991), 1:38.

61. Ibid., 1:38, 41, 88.

62. Richard Rorty, *Contingency, Irony, and Solidarity* (Cambridge: Cambridge University Press, 1989), pp. 51–52.

63. Rorty is not the first to see in the values of the academic community a way of life suitable for the larger society. For similar gestures at the turn of the century by R. H. Tawney and Emile Durkheim, see my essay "Professionalism *versus* Capitalism."

64. What I have in mind is something corresponding roughly to the "moderate realism" Mary Hesse proposes for science, which steers a middle course between instrumentalism and the "strong realism" of, say, Plato. "Such a moderate realism of scientific knowledge turns out to be particular rather than general, local rather than universal, approximate rather than exact, immediately describable and verifiable rather than theoretically deep and reductive. It is not the theoretical frameworks as such that validate the claim of science to be a distinctive and reliable body of knowledge, but rather the way they are used to further the feedback method of successful prediction and control." Mary B. Hesse, "Models, Metaphors and Truth," in *Knowledge and Language,* vol. 3 of *Metaphor and Knowledge,* ed. F. R. Ankersmit and J. J. A. Mooij (Dordrecht: Kluwer, 1993), pp. 49–66. Along similar lines, one thinks of Stephen Toulmin's comment that "Questions of 'rationality' are concerned, precisely, not with the particular intellectual doctrines that a man—or a professional group—adopts at any given time, but rather with the conditions on which, and the manner in which, he is prepared to criticize and change those doctrines as time goes on." Stephen Toulmin, *Human Understanding,* p. 84.

65. For an amusing and trenchant response to this imperial prospect, see David A.

Hollinger, "Giving at the Office in the Age of Power/Knowledge," *Michigan Quarterly Review* 29 (Winter 1990).

66. I am obliged to David Rabban for this succinct formulation of the problem.

67. Fish, *Is There a Text in This Class?*

68. Stanley Fish, *Doing What Comes Naturally*, pp. 207, 201.

69. Ibid., pp. 179, 201–2, 244, 177, 246; emphasis in the original.

70. Ibid., pp. 394, 430, 459. These three quotations, all concerned with the Critical Legal Studies movement, come from three different articles. The immediate context of the first is a discussion of the work of Mark Kelman, of the last two a discussion of the work of Roberto Unger. Since Kelman and Unger are members of the same movement, bringing the passages together does not, I think, deprive them of an appropriate context.

71. Ibid., p. 246.

72. Ibid., pp. 482–83.

73. Fish, "There's No Such Thing As Free Speech and It's a Good Thing Too," *Boston Review* 17 (February 1992): 3; also published in *Debating PC: The Controversy over Political Correctness on College Campuses*, ed. Paul Berman (New York: Dell, 1992), and reprinted in Stanley Fish, *There's No Such Thing as Free Speech and It's a Good Thing, Too* (New York: Oxford University Press, 1994).

74. Ibid., p. 26.

75. Ibid., p. 25; emphasis added.

76. Ibid., p. 23. Fish presents his own position as an alternative to "First Amendment absolutism," but his dismissive attitude toward the "fighting words" test puts him in opposition to many nonabsolutists, such as myself, who are worried about the growing censoriousness of the academic Left but who also believe that the most abusive and persistent hate speech should be punished.

77. Ibid., p. 26.

78. Ibid., p. 25; emphasis in the original.

79. Philip Rieff, *The Triumph of the Therapeutic: Uses of Faith after Freud* (Chicago: University of Chicago Press, 1987), p. 61.

80. Fish, "There's No Such Thing," p. 25.

81. This is not the place to spell out the way these assumptions operate in the work of Foucault and other recent writers, but many readers will recognize them as the foundational assumptions, as it were, of antifoundationalism. Even so sympathetic a reader as Charles Taylor rejects what he calls Foucault's "case for the invasion of everyday understanding by relations of power," formidable though he admits it is. "Only if we could show that relations of domination, and the strategies which create and sustain them, have totally invaded the world of everyday self-understanding could we adopt the narrow, neo-Clausewitzian interpretation [according to which intellectual debate is war by other means] and make all dominant ideas the outcome of conflicts which center on war and the struggle for power." Taylor, "The Hermeneutics of Conflict," in *Meaning and Context: Quentin Skinner and His Critics,* ed. James Tully (Princeton, N.J.: Princeton University Press, 1988), p. 226. For telling second thoughts about the supposed boundlessness of interpretation (by an influential early advocate of the reader's power to "produce" the meaning of a text), see Umberto Eco's contribution to Stefan Collini, *Interpretation and Overinterpretation*.

82. Fish, "There's No Such Thing," p. 26.

FOUR

Academic Freedom and Law: Liberalism, Speech Codes, and Related Problems

Cass R. Sunstein

The law has rarely been at odds with academic freedom.[1] In recent years, however, the development of campus speech codes has created a range of new controversies. In these remarks, one of my purposes is to defend the constitutionality of narrowly drawn restrictions on hate speech, arguing in the process against some broader versions that have become popular in some institutions. My most general goal is to set the dispute over speech codes in the broader context of the liberal commitment to freedom of speech and academic pluralism. Through this approach it may be possible to overcome the "all or nothing" tone that has dominated much of public and even academic discussion. In the process of defending some narrow restrictions on hate speech, it will be necessary to say a good deal about the principle of neutrality in constitutional law, academic life, and perhaps elsewhere.

The discussion will obviously bear on the subject of academic freedom. The subject is complex in part because no academic institution can avoid making certain controversial substantive judgments; because those judgments will intrude on some forms of freedom; and because those intrusions will interfere with speech. If we understand the hate speech controversy in this light, we will be pushed away from an attractive and commonly held vision of academic freedom—what might be called a neutral or skeptical vision in which all comers are accepted. We might be led to endorse instead a nonneutral, substantive view that embodies three defining commitments: 93

political equality; a mild version of liberal perfectionism; and an insistence on exposure to a wide range of conceptions of the good and the right, so long as all of these are supported by reasons. I will offer some preliminary remarks on the relationship between the speech code controversy and these commitments.

I. LIBERAL POLITICS AND FREE EXPRESSION

The ideal of academic freedom is an important part of liberal institutions. I begin with a brief discussion of those institutions, with particular reference to American constitutional law. A theory of academic freedom is an aspect of a theory of democracy.

A. Defining Ideals

What underlies a system of politics in a liberal democracy? This is of course a large and complex question. I suggest that in the American legal order, such a system is closely connected to the central constitutional goal of creating a deliberative democracy.[2] In such a system, politics is not supposed merely to protect preexisting private rights or to reflect the outcomes of interest-group pressures. It is not intended to aggregate existing private preferences, or to produce compromises among various affected groups with self-interested stakes in the outcome. Instead it is designed to have an important deliberative feature, in which new information and perspectives influence social judgments about possible courses of action. Through exposure to such information and perspectives, both collective and individual decisions can be shaped and improved.

The system of free expression is the foundation of this process. One of its basic goals is to ensure broad communication about matters of public concern among the citizenry at large and between citizens and representatives. Indeed, we might even define political truth as the outcome of this deliberative process, assuming that the process can approach or meet the appropriate conditions. Those conditions include adequate information; a norm of political equality, in which arguments matter but power and authority do not; an absence of strategic manipulation of information, perspective, processes, or outcomes in general; and a broad public orientation toward reaching right answers rather than serving self-interest, narrowly defined. It is not necessary to claim that the result of any such deliberative process will be unanimity or even consensus. Sometimes people genuinely disagree, and discussion will not bring them together. It may even tear them apart. We should also acknowledge that real-world processes do not conform to these conditions. But under the right circumstances, the system of public discussion should improve outcomes and help move judgments in appropriate directions.

In this system of "government by discussion,"[3] private preferences and beliefs are not taken as fixed and static. What people now prefer and believe may be a product of insufficient information, limited opportunities, legal constraints, or unjust background conditions. People may think as they do simply because they have not been provided with sufficient information and opportunities. It is not paternalistic, or an illegitimate interference with competing conceptions of the good, for a democracy to promote scrutiny and testing of preferences and beliefs through deliberative processes. (Of course there must be rights-based constraints on what might occur in or as a result of those processes.) Politics itself has an educative function, at least when things are working well.

In this way the commitment to liberal politics might be seen as embodying a modest form of perfectionism—a belief that a well-functioning policy should encourage the development of certain salutary characteristics. In Justice Brandeis's words, the greatest menace to liberty is an "inert people." Part of the point of liberal politics is to encourage a certain set of characteristics—activity rather than passivity; curiosity; a capacity to form, scrutinize, and follow a plan of life with diverse features; an ability to discuss and evaluate competing conceptions of the good; interest in and empathetic understanding of other people as well as in oneself; and others.[4] These are the characteristics of liberal citizenship. On this view, a system of liberal politics is not entirely neutral on competing conceptions of the good. It takes a stand.

Moreover, the system of deliberative democracy is premised on and even defined by reference to the commitment to political equality. At least in the public sphere, every person counts as no more and no less than one. In markets, "votes" are measured by dollars, which of course vary from rich to poor. In public life, a different norm of equality plays a key role. The constitutional principle of one person–one vote is simply the most recent effort to concretize the traditional constitutional commitment to political equality. It follows that in the deliberative process, arguments are to count if good reasons are offered on their behalf. The identity, the resources, and the power of the speaker do not matter. To institutionalize the idea that the force of an argument is independent of the person who makes it, the system of deliberative democracy must incorporate this principle of political equality.

A system of liberal politics sharply constrains the public sphere. It says that government may not regulate ideas because they are (a) offensive or (b) persuasive. When we are dealing with political speech, it says that government may not regulate speech unless the relevant harms are likely to occur, intended by the speaker, and imminent. Otherwise the appropriate remedy—as Justice Brandeis wrote in the most distinguished judicial contribution to thought about free expression—is "more speech, not enforced silence."[5]

This "counterspeech" principle is supported by the democratic emphasis on the exchange of reasons within the public sphere. If government can regulate speech merely because it may be dangerous, that exchange cannot occur. The counterspeech principle is also supported by a commitment to respecting the autonomy of people who listen to speech. This commitment protects listeners by forbidding government to regulate speech because listeners might be influenced by it.[6] On this view, government cannot insult the moral autonomy of its citizens by stopping them from hearing what other people have to say—especially if the reason that government acts is its fear that citizens will be influenced or persuaded by what is said. This is a unique invasion into each individual's moral and deliberative capacities. As we will soon see, these considerations bear directly on the subject of academic freedom.

B. *Low Value and High Value Speech*

If the system of free expression is rooted in ideas of this sort, it will be necessary to distinguish between different forms of speech in terms of their relationship to those ideals. Current constitutional law does indeed make such distinctions, asking whether speech qualifies as "low value" or "high value." Some speech lies at the free speech "core." Such speech may be regulated, if at all, only on the strongest showing of harm. Other speech lies at the periphery or outside of the Constitution altogether. This low value speech may be regulated if the government can show a legitimate, plausible justification.

Much of this framework follows naturally from the account I have offered thus far. Ordinary political speech, dealing with governmental matters, unquestionably belongs at the core. Such speech may not be regulated unless there is a clear and present danger, or, in the Supreme Court's words, unless it is "directed to inciting or producing imminent lawless action and is likely to incite or produce such action."[7] Under this standard, a speech containing racial hatred, offered by a member of the Ku Klux Klan, is usually protected; so too with a speech by a member of the Black Panthers, or by Nazis during a march in Skokie, Illinois, the home of many survivors of concentration camps.

But much speech falls into the periphery of constitutional concern. Commercial speech, for example, receives some constitutional protection, in the sense that it qualifies as speech within the meaning of the First Amendment. Truthful, nondeceptive advertising is generally protected from regulation. But government may regulate commercial advertising it if it is false or misleading. There are many other kinds of low value speech. Consider threats, attempted bribes, perjury, criminal conspiracy, price-fixing, criminal solicitation, private libel, unlicensed medical and legal advice, sexual and racial harassment. All these can be regulated without meeting the ordinary, highly speech-protective standards.

The Supreme Court has not set out anything like a clear theory to explain why and when speech qualifies for the top tier. At times the Court has indicated that speech belongs in the top tier if it is part of the exchange of ideas, or if it bears on the political process.[8] But apart from these ambiguous hints, it has failed to tell us much about its basis for deciding that some forms of expression are different from others.

Is a two-tier First Amendment inevitable or desirable? Some people claim to be free speech absolutists—they think they believe that all speech is protected, or that speech can be regulated only if the government can show overwhelming harm. But it does seem that any well-functioning system of free expression must ultimately distinguish between different kinds of speech by reference to their centrality to the First Amendment guarantee.

Begin with a truly absolutist position: Anyone may say anything at all at any time. A moment's reflection should show that this position could not be seriously maintained. It would not make sense to forbid government from regulating perjury, bribes, threats, fraudulent real estate deals, unlicensed medical and legal advice, willfully false advertising, and many other forms of expression. Realistically speaking, our choices are a range of non-absolutist approaches.

It is tempting to resist this conclusion by proposing that the speech that is unprotected is "really" not speech at all, but merely action. When someone attempts to bribe a government official, perhaps he is "acting," or perhaps the regulation of criminal solicitation is ancillary or incidental to the regulation of conduct. But as stated, I think that this suggestion is unhelpful. Criminal solicitation and attempted bribes are speech, not action. They may lead to action; but by themselves they are simply words. If I tell you that I want you to help me to commit an assault, I have spoken words; if I say that I will give you $10,000 if you vote for me, I have merely talked; if I say "Kill!" to a trained attack dog, I have done something regulable, but I have still just spoken. If these things are to be treated as action—that is, if they are not to be protected as speech—it is because of their distinctive features. This is what must be discussed. The word "action" is simply a placeholder for that unprovided discussion.

So much for the speech-conduct distinction. The only nonabsolutist alternative to an approach that looks at free speech value would be this: All speech stands on basically the same footing. We will not look at value at all. The only relevant issue is one of *harm*. Speech may be regulated if government can make a demonstration that the speech at issue will produce sufficiently bad consequences. Would it not be possible, and desirable, to have a single-tier First Amendment, in the sense that all speech is presumed protected, but we allow government to regulate speech in those rare cases where the harm is very great?

The answer is that it would not be plausible to say that all speech stands on the same footing. For example, courts should not test regulation of campaign speeches under the same standards applied to misleading commercial speech, child pornography, conspiracies, libel of private persons, and threats. If the same standards were applied, one of two results would follow, and both are unacceptable.

The first possible result would be to lower the burden of justification for governmental regulation as a whole, so as to allow for restrictions on misleading commercial speech, private libel, and so forth. If this were the consequence, there would be an unacceptably high threat to political expression. Upon a reasonably persuasive showing of harm, government could regulate misleading campaign statements, just as it can now regulate misleading proxy statements. A generally lowered burden of justification would therefore be intolerable.

The second possible result is that courts would apply the properly stringent standards for regulation of political speech to (for example) conspiracies, criminal solicitation, commercial speech, private libel, and child pornography. The central problem with this approach is that it would ensure that government could not control speech that should be regulated. A system in which the most stringent standards were applied across the board would ensure that government could not regulate criminal solicitation, child pornography, private libel, and false or misleading commercial speech, among others. The harms that justify such regulation are real, but they are insufficient to permit government controls under the extremely high standards applied to regulation of political speech.

If courts are to be honest about the matter, an insistence that "all speech is speech" would mean that they must eliminate many currently unobjectionable and even necessary controls—or more likely that judgments about value, because unavoidable, would continue to be made, but covertly. We will soon see that this claim bears directly on the questions raised by speech codes and by academic freedom generally.

C. Political Speech at the Core

Thus far I have suggested that a workable system of free expression ought to make distinctions between different sorts of speech; but it remains to decide by what standard courts might accomplish this task. To support an emphasis on politics, we need to define the category of political speech. For present purposes I will treat speech as political *when it is both intended and received as a contribution to public deliberation about some issue.* By requiring intent, I do not mean to require a trial on the question of subjective motivation. Generally this issue can be resolved simply on the basis of the nature of the speech at issue. By requiring that the speech be received as a contribution to public deliberation, I do not mean that all listeners or readers must see the substantive content. It is sufficient if some do.

An approach that affords special protection to political speech, thus defined, is justified on numerous grounds. Such an approach receives firm support from history—not only from the constitutional framers' theory of free expression but also from the development of that principle through the history of American law. There can be little doubt that suppression by the government of political ideas that it disapproved of, or found threatening, was the central motivation for the clause. The worst examples of unacceptable censorship involve efforts by government to insulate itself from criticism. Judicial interpretations over the course of time also support a political conception of the First Amendment.

This approach also seems likely to accord fairly well with our initial or considered judgments about particular free speech problems. Any approach to the First Amendment will have to take substantial account of those judgments and adjust itself accordingly. Of course we are not unanimous in our considered judgments. But it seems clear that such forms of speech as perjury, bribery, threats, misleading or false commercial advertising, criminal solicitation, and libel of private persons—or at least most of these—are not entitled to the highest degree of constitutional protection. No other general approach unifies initial or preliminary judgments about these matters as well as a political conception of the First Amendment.

In addition, an insistence that government's burden is greatest when political speech is at issue responds well to the fact that here government is most likely to be biased. The premise of distrust of government is strongest when politics are at issue. It is far weaker when government is regulating (say) commercial speech, bribery, private libel, or obscenity. In such cases there is less reason to suppose that it is insulating itself from criticism.

Finally, this approach protects speech when regulation is most likely to be harmful. Restrictions on political speech have the distinctive feature of impairing the ordinary channels for political change; such restrictions are especially dangerous. If there are controls on commercial advertising, it always remains possible to argue that such controls should be lifted. If the government bans violent pornography, citizens can continue to argue against the ban. But if the government forecloses political argument, the democratic corrective is unavailable. Controls on nonpolitical speech do not have this uniquely damaging feature.

Taken in concert, these considerations suggest that in a liberal democracy, government should be under a special burden of justification when it seeks to control speech intended and received as a contribution to public deliberation. This does not mean that government is unconstrained when it attempts to regulate other speech. Recall that government cannot regulate speech because it is persuasive; recall too that offense at ideas is an illegitimate ground for legal controls. Always the government must be able to make a strong showing of harm. For this reason art, literature, and scientific speech will generally be protected from government controls even if some of these fall within the second tier. Of course these statements will leave ambiguities in hard intermediate cases.

II. LIBERALISM AND SPEECH ON CAMPUS

I have tried thus far to set out some of the features of a well-functioning system of free expression. In that system, political speech belongs in the top tier; more speech, not censorship, is the remedy for speech that threatens harm; only an emergency can support suppression. Nonpolitical speech is also protected, but it can be regulated on the basis of a lesser showing of harm. Here too the government must point to something other than persuasiveness or offense at the content of ideas.

We can use this discussion as a basis for exploring the complex problems resulting from recent efforts to regulate hate speech on campus. Some regulations are often associated with alleged efforts to impose an ideological orthodoxy on students and faculty, under the rubric of "political correctness." Perhaps radical left-wing campuses, under pressure from well-organized groups, are silencing people who disagree. Are the campus speech codes constitutional? I emphasize that I am exploring the legal issue; in general, I think that codes are a bad idea, and that any problems of hate speech should be handled not through codes but in an informal manner. Let us deal, however, with the Constitution.

To the extent that we are dealing with private universities, the Constitution is not implicated at all, and hence all such restrictions are permissible. This is an exceptionally important point. Private universities can do whatever they like. They can ban all speech by Republicans, by Democrats, or by anyone they want to silence. But many private universities like to follow the Constitution even if they are not required to do so. In any case, public universities are subject to the Constitution, and so it is important to try to establish what the First Amendment means for them.

A. A Provisional Thesis

On the approach provided thus far, we can offer an important provisional conclusion: If campus speech restrictions at public universities cover not merely epithets but speech that is part of social deliberation, they might well be seen as unconstitutional for that very reason.[9] At least as a presumption, speech that is intended and received as a contribution to social deliberation is constitutionally protected even if it amounts to what is sometimes classified as hate speech—even if it is racist and sexist.

Consider, for example, the University of Michigan's judicially invalidated ban on "any behavior, verbal or physical, that stigmatizes or victimizes an individual on the basis of race, ethnicity, religion, sex, sexual orientation, creed, national origin, ancestry, age, marital status, handicap, or Vietnam-era veteran status, and that . . . creates an intimidating, hostile, or demeaning environment for educational pursuits." This broad ban forbids a wide range of statements that are part of the exchange of ideas. It also fails to give people sufficient notice of what statements are allowed. For both reasons, it seems invalid.

In a famous case, Justice Frankfurter, speaking for a 5–4 majority of the Supreme Court, rejected this view. *Beauharnais v. Illinois*[10] upheld an Illinois law making it unlawful to publish or exhibit any publication which "portrays depravity, criminality, unchastity, or lack of virtue of a class of citizens, which [publication] exposes the citizens of any race, color, creed or religion to contempt, derision, or obloquy or which is productive of breach of the peace or riots." The law was applied to ban circulation of a petition urging "the need to prevent the white race from becoming mongrelized by the negro," and complaining of the "aggressions, rapes, robberies, knives, guns and marijuana of the negro."

In upholding the law, Justice Frankfurter referred to a range of factors. He point to the historical exclusion of libel from free speech protection; to the risks to social cohesion created by racial hate speech; and to the need for judicial deference to legislative judgments on these complex matters. Many countries in Europe accept the same analysis and do not afford protection to racial and ethnic hate speech. But most people think that after *New York Times Co. v. Sullivan,*[11] *Beauharnais* is no longer the law. In *New York Times,* the Court indicated that the law of libel must be evaluated in accordance with the constitutional commitment to robust debate on public issues. The conventional view—which the Supreme Court has not directly addressed—is that racial hate speech contains highly political ideas, that it belongs in the free speech "core," and that it may not be suppressed merely because it is offensive or otherwise harmful.

There are real complexities here. In its strongest form, the defense of *Beauharnais* would point toward the contribution of hate speech to the maintenance of a caste system based on race and gender. A principal point here would be the effect of such speech on the self-respect of its victims and also the relationship between such speech and fears of racially motivated violence.[12] I cannot fully discuss this issue here; but I think that *Beauharnais* was incorrect. No one should deny that distinctive harms are produced by racial hate speech, especially when it is directed against members of minority groups. It is only obtuseness—a failure of perception or empathetic identification—that would enable someone to say that the word "fascist" or "pig" or "communist," or even "honky," produces the same feelings as the word "nigger." In view of our history, invective directed against minority groups, and racist speech in general, create fears of violence and subordination—of second-class citizenship—that are not plausibly described as mere offense. As I have noted, most European countries, including flourishing democracies committed to free speech, make exceptions for such expression. In many countries, including our own, it is possible to think that racial and ethnic hate speech is really sui generis, and that it is properly treated differently.

But there are strong counterarguments. If we were to excise all of what is described as hate speech from political debate, we would severely truncate our discussion of such important matters as civil rights, foreign policy, crime, conscription, abortion, and social welfare policy. Even if speech produces anger or resentment on the basis of race, it might well be thought a legitimate part of the deliberative process, and it bears directly on politics. Foreclosure of such speech would probably accomplish little good, and by stopping people from hearing certain ideas, it could bring about a great deal of harm. These are the most conventional Millian arguments for the protection of speech.

From all this it seems that the University of Michigan ban was far too broad. On the other hand, it should be permissible for colleges and universities to build on the basic case of the epithet in order to regulate certain narrowly defined categories of hate speech. Standing by themselves, or accompanied by little else, epithets are not intended and received as contributions to social deliberation about anything. We are therefore dealing with lower tier speech. The injury to dignity and self-respect is a sufficient harm to allow regulation. (See my discussion of the Stanford regulation below.)

It is now possible to offer a provisional conclusion. A public university should be allowed to regulate hate speech in the form of epithets. But it should be prohibited from reaching very far beyond epithets to forbid the expression of views on public issues, whatever those views may be. I will qualify this conclusion shortly, but it seems like a good place to start.

B. *The Question of Neutrality*

But are restrictions on hate speech impermissibly selective? In *R.A.V. v. St. Paul,* the Court invalidated a law directed against a certain kind of hate speech, principally on the ground that it discriminated on the basis of subject matter. The case involved an act of cross-burning on a private yard. All the justices agreed that the content-neutral trespass law could be applied against that act; the question was whether a special "hate speech" law was constitutional as applied to that act.

As interpreted by the Minnesota Supreme Court, the relevant law banned any so-called fighting words that produced anger or resentment on the basis of race, religion, or gender. In invalidating the act, the *R.A.V.* Court emphasized that the law at issue was not a broad or general proscription of fighting words. It reflects a decision to single out a certain category of fighting words, defined in terms of audience reactions to speech about certain topics. Is this illegitimate? The point bears on almost all efforts to regulate hate speech, on campus and elsewhere.

The Supreme Court's basic idea is this: Whether or not we are dealing with high value speech, government cannot draw lines on a partisan basis. It cannot say, for example, that libel of Democrats will be punished more severely than libel of Republicans, or that obscenity will be regulated only if it makes fun of the president. A law of this sort would be "viewpoint based," that is, it makes the viewpoint of the speaker the basis for regulation. To that extent it is invalid. Moreover, the government is sharply constrained in its ability to limit speech on certain subjects. It could not, for example, ban speech about AIDS. "Subject-matter" restrictions are more neutral than viewpoint-based restrictions. They are not per se invalid, but they are treated with considerable skepticism. For the Supreme Court, the major problem with the Minnesota law was that it was an impermissible subject-matter restriction.

To the distinction between low value and high value speech, then, we must add that the First Amendment limits the government's line-drawing power. The government must not be impermissibly selective, even if it is regulating low value speech. Hence in the *R.A.V.* case, the Court concluded that St. Paul had violated the First Amendment, not because it had regulated constitutionally protected speech but because it had chosen to regulate only fighting words of a certain, governmentally disapproved sort, and allowed the rest to flourish.

In his dissenting opinion, Justice Stevens argued that St. Paul had not made an impermissible distinction, since the harms underlying the regulated speech were sufficiently distinctive. He wrote that "race based threats may cause more harm to society and to individuals than other threats. Just as the statute prohibiting threats against the President is justifiable because of the place of the President in our social and political order, so a statute prohibiting race based threats is justifiable because of the place of race in our social and political order." In his view, "threatening someone because of her race or religious beliefs may cause particularly severe trauma or touch off a riot . . . ; such threats may be punished more severely than threats against someone based on, for example, his support of a particular athletic team." Thus there were "legitimate, reasonable, and neutral justifications" for the special rule. But Justice Stevens spoke only for himself, and his view was firmly rejected by the majority.

The question then becomes whether university restrictions on hate speech are impermissibly selective. A university might well, post-*R.A.V.*, be forbidden from singling out for punishment speech that many universities want to control, such as (a) a narrowly defined category of insults toward such specifically enumerated groups as blacks, women, and homosexuals, or (b) a narrowly defined category of insults directed at individuals involving race, sex, and sexual orientation. How would restrictions of this kind be treated?

Under current law, a restriction that involves (a) is viewpoint based, and to that extent even worse than the restriction in *R.A.V.* itself. On the analysis of the *R.A.V.* Court, restriction (a) tries to silence one side in a debate. A restriction that involves (b) is a subject-matter restriction, not based on viewpoint. But it too is impermissibly selective in exactly the same sense as the restriction invalidated in the *R.A.V.* case.

It is possible to say that the conclusions in *R.A.V.* are incorrect in principle, because there are sufficiently neutral grounds for restrictions (a) and (b).[13] Perhaps a university could neutrally decide that epithets directed against blacks, women, and homosexuals cause distinctive harms. But this conclusion is hard to reconcile with the *R.A.V.* decision.

C. The Special Place of the University

Colleges and universities do, however, have some arguments that were unavailable to St. Paul, Minnesota. In order to make the conclusions to this point more than provisional, we have to address those arguments. If *R.A.V.* does not apply to the campus, it might be because public universities can claim a large degree of insulation from judicial supervision. That claim to insulation is closely connected to the idea of academic freedom.

1. *In general.* The largest point here is that colleges and universities are often in the business of controlling speech, and their controls are hardly ever thought to raise free speech problems. Indeed, controlling speech is, in one sense, a defining characteristic of the university. There are at least four different ways in which such controls occur.

First, universities impose major limits on the topics that can be discussed in the classroom. Subject-matter restrictions are part of education. Irrelevant discussion is banned. Students cannot discuss the presidential election, or Marx and Mill, if the subject is math. Schools are allowed to impose subject-matter restrictions that would be plainly unacceptable if enacted by states or localities.

Second, a teacher can require students to treat each other with at least a minimum of basic respect. It would certainly be legitimate to suspend a student for using consistently abusive or profane language in the classroom. This is so even if that language would receive firm constitutional protection on the street corner. The educational process requires at least a measure of civility. Perhaps it would be unacceptable for universities to ban expressions of anger or intense feeling; the notion of civility should not be a disguise for forbidding irreverence or disagreement. But so long as requirements of civility are both reasonable and neutral with respect to viewpoint, a university may limit abusive or profane comments within the classroom.

The problem goes deeper, for—and this is the third kind of academic control on speech—judgments about quality are pervasive. Such judgments affect admissions, evaluation of students in class and on paper, and evaluation of prospective and actual faculty as well. Academic decisions about quality will of course be based on a conception of appropriate standards of argument and justification. These standards involve judgments about merit or excellence that would be unacceptable in the setting of criminal punishment or civil fine, but that are a perfectly and nearly inescapable legitimate part of the educational function. At least this is so if there is no discrimination on the basis of viewpoint, that is, if the person involved in making the assessment offers judgments on the basis of standards of quality that are applied neutrally to everyone (an ambitious aspiration, and one that is conceptually complex).

But there is a fourth and more troublesome way in which universities control speech, and this involves the fact that many academic judgments are viewpoint based, certainly in practice. In many places, a student who defends fascism or communism is unlikely to receive a good grade. In many economics departments, sharp deviation from the views of Adam Smith may well be punished. History and literature departments have their own conceptions of what sorts of arguments are retrograde or beyond the pale. Viewpoint discrimination is undoubtedly present in practice, and even if we object to it in principle, it is impossible and perhaps undesirable for outsiders to attempt to police it.

Thus far I have been discussing students; but much the same is true for faculty members. Universities can impose on their faculty restrictive rules of decorum and civic participation. A teacher who refuses to teach the subject, fails to allow counterarguments, treats students contemptuously, or vilifies them in class, can be penalized without offense to the Constitution. The job performance of teachers consists mostly of speech. When that performance is found wanting, it is almost always because of content, including judgments about subject matter and quality, and sometimes because of viewpoint.

It is worthwhile pausing over this point. Initial hirings, tenure, and promotion all involve subject-matter restrictions, and sometimes viewpoint discrimination in practice. All this suggests that universities are engaged in regulating speech through content discrimination and at least implicit viewpoint discrimination. The evaluation of students and colleagues cannot occur without resort to content, and it would be most surprising if viewpoint discrimination did not affect many evaluations.

These examples do not by any means compel the conclusion that any and all censorship is acceptable in an academic setting. A university can have a good deal of power over what happens in the classroom, so as to promote the educational enterprise, without also being allowed to decree a political orthodoxy by discriminating on the basis of viewpoint. If a public university were to ban students from defending (say) conservative or liberal causes in political science classes, a serious free speech issue would be raised. There are therefore real limits to permissible viewpoint discrimination within the classroom, even if it is hard to police the relevant boundaries. Certainly the university's permissible limits over the classroom do not extend to the campus in general. We could not allow major restrictions on what students and faculty may say when they are not in class. A university could not say that outside of class, students can talk only about subjects of the university's choice.

From these various propositions, we might adopt a principle: *The university can impose subject-matter or other restrictions on speech only to the extent that the restrictions are closely related to its educational mission.* This proposition contains both an authorization to the university and sharp limitations on what it may do. There is a close parallel here with decisions about what to include or exclude from libraries and about how to fund the arts; in all these contexts, certain forms of content discrimination are inescapable. But in cases in which the educational mission is not reasonably at stake, restrictions on speech should be invalidated. Certainly this would be true in most cases in which a university attempts to impose a political orthodoxy, whether inside or outside the classroom. We might react to the existence of implicit viewpoint discrimination by saying that although it is hard for courts to police, it is nonetheless a real offense to both academic aspirations and free speech principles.

2. *Educational requirements and hate speech.* How does this proposition bear on the hate speech issue? Perhaps a university could use its frequently exercised power over speech in order to argue for certain kinds of hate speech codes. Perhaps it could say that when it legitimately controls speech, it does so in order to promote its educational mission, which inevitably entails limits on who may say what. Perhaps a university could be allowed to conclude that its educational mission requires unusually firm controls on hate speech, so as not to compromise the values of education itself.

The university might emphasize in this regard that it has a special obligation to protect all of its students as equal members of the community. This obligation calls for restrictions on what faculty members may say. The university might believe that certain narrowly defined forms of hate speech are highly destructive to the students' chance to learn. It might think that black students and women can be effectively excluded by certain forms of hate speech. Probably a university should be given more leeway to restrict hate speech than a state or locality, precisely because it ought to receive the benefit of the doubt when it invokes concerns of this kind. Surely the educational mission ought to grant the university somewhat greater room to maneuver, especially in light of the complexity and delicacy of the relevant policy questions. Courts might also hesitate before finding viewpoint discrimination or impermissible selectivity. Perhaps there should be a presumption in favor of a university's judgment that narrowly defined hate speech directed at blacks or women produces harm that is especially threatening to the educational enterprise.

This conclusion is buttressed by two additional factors. First, there are numerous colleges and universities. Many students can choose among a range of alternatives, and a restriction in one, two, or more imposes an extremely small incursion into the system of free expression. Colleges that restrict a large amount of speech may find themselves with few students, and in any case other institutions will be available. Second, the Constitution is itself committed to the elimination of second-class citizenship, and this commitment makes it hard to say that an educational judgment opposed to certain forms of hate speech is impermissibly partisan.

3. *Details.* I think that an analysis of this kind would justify two different sorts of approaches to the general issue of hate speech on campus. First, a university might regulate hate speech, narrowly defined, as simply a part of its general class of restrictions on speech that is incompatible with the educational mission. On this approach, there would be no restriction specifically directed against hate speech—no campus "speech code"—but a general, suitably defined requirement of decency and civility, and this requirement would regulate hate speech as well as other forms of abuse. Just as a university might ban the use of profanity in class, or personally abusive behavior on campus, so it might stop racial epithets and similar expressions of hatred or contempt. This is not to say that students and teachers who violate this ban must be expelled or suspended. Generally informal sanctions, involving conversations rather than punishment, are much to be preferred. Hate speech restrictions usually cause more harm than they are worth. But the Constitution should not stand as a barrier to approaches of this sort, so long as the university is neutral in this way.

Second, courts should allow narrowly defined hate speech restrictions even if those restrictions are not part of general proscriptions on indecent or uncivil behavior. For example, Stanford now forbids speech that amounts to "harassment by personal vilification." (Stanford is a private university, free from constitutional restraint; but it has chosen to comply with its understanding of what the First Amendment means as applied to public universities.) Under the Stanford rule, speech qualifies as regulable "harassment" if it (1) is intended to insult or stigmatize an individual or a small number of individuals on the basis of their sex, race, color, handicap, religion, sexual orientation, or national and ethnic origin, (2) is addressed directly to the individual or individuals whom it insults or stigmatizes, and (3) makes use of insulting or fighting words or nonverbal symbols. To qualify under (3), the speech must by its "very utterance inflict injury or tend to incite to an immediate breach of the peace," and must be "commonly understood to convey direct and visceral hatred and contempt for human beings on the basis of" one of the grounds enumerated in (1).

The Stanford regulation should not be faulted for excessive breadth. It is quite narrowly defined. If a public university adopted it, the major constitutional problem, fueled by the outcome in *R.A.V.,* would not be breadth but unacceptable selectivity. Why has the university not controlled other forms of fighting words, like the word "fascist," or "commie," or "bastard"? Does its selectivity show an impermissible motivation? Shouldn't we find its selectivity to be impermissibly partisan? I do not think that we should. A university could reasonably and neutrally decide that the harms caused by the regulated fighting words are, at least in the university setting, more severe than the harms caused by other kinds of fighting words. I conclude that public universities may regulate speech of the sort controlled by the Stanford regulation and probably go somewhat further, and that such restrictions should not be invalidated as impermissibly selective.

We can also use this discussion as a basis for exploring the question of the university's power over employees, arising out of the highly publicized decision of the City University of New York to remove Dr. Leonard Jeffries as chair of the black studies department at City College. Jeffries had reportedly made a range of apparently anti-Semitic remarks, blaming rich Jews for the black slave trade, complaining that Russian Jews and "their financial partners, the Mafia, put together a financial system of destruction of black people," and claiming that Jews and Italians had "planned, plotted, and programmed out of Hollywood" to denigrate blacks in films. Could the City University take these remarks as a reason to remove Jeffries from his position as department chair? (We should agree that removal could be justified if, as some say, it was a response to an inadequate record of publication, to poor research, or to low-quality work.)

The answer depends on whether the removal was based on an effort neutrally to promote educational goals, or whether it was instead an effort to punish the expression of a controversial point of view. In the abstract this question is hard to answer, but it can be clarified through examples. Under the First Amendment, a public university could not fire a mathematics professor because he is a Republican, extremely conservative, or a sharp critic of the Supreme Court; such a discharge could not plausibly be connected with legitimate concerns about job performance. Even if the mathematics professor was a department chair, these political convictions are unrelated to job performance.

On the other hand, a university could surely fire the head of an admissions committee who persisted in making invidiously derogatory comments about blacks, women, and Jews. It would be reasonable for the university to say that someone who makes such comments cannot perform his job, which includes attracting good students, male and female, and of various races and religions. The discharge of the admissions head would not really be based on viewpoint; it would be part of a viewpoint-neutral effort to ensure that the head can do what he is supposed to do. Much the same could be said of a university president or many other high-visibility public employees. Consider the fact that the president, or a governor, is freely permitted to fire high level officials who make statements that compromise job performance, even if those statements are political in nature; if the secretary of state says publicly that the president is a fool, or even that the president's policy toward Russia is senseless, the president can tell the secretary to seek employment elsewhere.

It seems to follow that a university could remove a department chair if his comments make him unable successfully to undertake his ordinary duties as chair. The governing principle seems to be this: *A university can penalize speech if and only if it can show that the relevant speech makes it very difficult or impossible for the employee adequately to perform his job.* Whenever a university seeks to punish speech, it should face a large burden to show that it is behaving neutrally and not trying to punish a disfavored point of view. On this approach, teachers and researchers will almost always be protected. Controversial political statements will not be a sufficient basis for punishment or discharge. A political science professor may criticize (or endorse) the president without becoming less able to perform the job, and most teachers will be able to say whatever they like without subjecting themselves to the possibility of discipline. It follows that City College could not punish (as it tried to do) a philosophy professor for publishing the view that blacks are, on average, intellectually inferior to whites. It also follows that City College could remove Professor Jeffries from his tenured position merely because of actually or apparently anti-Semitic statements.

But we can imagine a range of statements that might make job performance quite difficult, at least for someone in a high-level administrative position—statements, for example, expressing general contempt for students and colleagues, a refusal to participate in the academic enterprise, or hatred directed against people who are part of the university community. Perhaps such statements would not be sufficient to allow discharge from a faculty position; but they could make it hard for the relevant speakers to perform as deans, as admissions officers, or as chairs of departments. In the Jeffries case, the best argument in favor of the City University of New York would be that it is difficult for someone to succeed as chair of a prominent black studies department if he has made sharply derogatory statements about members of other groups defined in racial, religious, or ethnic terms. This argument would not allow Jeffries to be discharged from his position as professor, but it should allow him to be removed from the position of department chair, which involves a range of distinctive tasks. It follows that on the facts I have assumed, City College did not violate Jeffries' First Amendment rights. Of course the case would be different if Jeffries could prove that City College was reacting not to impaired job performance but to its own disapproval of Jeffries' point of view.

An opposing principle would take the following form: *A university should not be permitted to burden or to deny benefits to an employee on the basis of the employee's point of view, even if the point of view does damage job performance.* On this view, people who disapprove of the point of view of others—students, other faculty, potential contributors—should not be permitted to enshrine their own views by affecting the university's decisions about employees. We might argue for this principle on the ground that there should no "heckler's veto" against unpopular opinions. We should not have a system in which people who dislike a certain point of view can stop dissenters from assuming prominent positions in the university.

This argument is not without force, but I do not think that it should be adopted. Everyone seems to agree that the president and the governor may make hiring decisions on the basis of viewpoint; it would not make sense to disable the president from ensuring that high level employees do not try, through speech, to undermine the president's program. Any resulting interference with the system of free expression seems minimal, and the president has a strong need for a loyal staff. Similarly, universities have powerful and legitimate reasons to expect their employees to perform their jobs, especially if those employees are engaged in highly public administrative tasks, and especially if professors who are not performing administrative tasks are realistically not threatened. At least under ordinary circumstances, there will be no substantial interference with the system of free expression if universities are given the narrow authority for which I have argued. I conclude that outside of legitimate judgments about quality and subject matter, universities may punish employees for their speech only in a narrow set of circumstances—almost always involving highly public, administrative positions—in which the relevant speech makes it difficult or impossible for employees to perform their jobs.

It follows from all this that the national government should abandon its efforts to subject private universities to the constraints of the First Amendment. This is an area in which national authorities should proceed with caution. Of course we could imagine experiments that we might deplore. But there is no reason for the federal government to require uniformity on this complex matter.

III. LIBERAL EDUCATION

Thus far I have outlined the commitments of a well-functioning system of liberal politics and described how these commitments might relate to freedom of speech in the educational setting. These remarks, though founded on current legal debates, bear on the general subject of liberal education— a subject that has become especially controversial in prominent attacks on "autonomy" and on "liberalism." In some work on academic freedom and liberty of expression, it has become popular to doubt the relevance of the governing ideals—to say that because speech is always a cultural construct, and freedom a function of contextual constraint, the ideals must themselves be thrown into severe question. I will conclude with some brief and impressionistic comments on this subject.

Some current writings about the politics of knowledge and academic freedom are reminiscent of a very striking part of Judge Robert Bork's *The Tempting of America*[14]—Bork's treatment of *Brown v. Board of Education,* the case in which the Supreme Court invalidated school segregation. Bork's argument may seem far afield, but it bears on questions involving academic freedom and even the canon itself. Bork is of course an "originalist," someone who believes that the meaning of the Constitution is settled by the understanding of those who ratified it. Of course Bork knows that the framers of the Fourteenth Amendment did not specifically intend the federal courts to eliminate segregation. On Bork's own method, *Brown* seems pretty easy—and wrong. But Bork did not reach this conclusion. Instead he struggled mightily to explain why *Brown* was right after all.

What is interesting for present purposes is not the details of Bork's argument, but the fact that Bork found it necessary to make it. Now what are we to make of this state of affairs? We could understand this situation in two very different ways. First:

1. Lawyers have lost sight of the fact that *Brown* was very much a human creation, very controversial (to say the least) in its time. Bizarrely, they take this human outcome as an absolutely fixed point for an analysis, when they should understand it as a contingent product of distinctive social forces. Lawyers have really committed an act of idolatry. As part of the legal canon, *Brown* stops thought. Our principal interests should instead be in genealogy—in how things got to be this way. What gave *Brown* its special status?

Now here is a second and different response to what has happened with Judge Bork and *Brown*:

2. Lawyers take *Brown* as correct for good reasons. Lawyers think that a constitutional order that allowed apartheid would not be worthy of respect. Lawyers think that any system of constitutional interpretation must ensure that our constitutional order is worthy of respect. They have reasons for their conclusion; these reasons have to do with the purposes and effects of racial caste systems for the people subject to those systems.

I am an outsider to the literary and historical debate over the political or social nature of knowledge and the canon, and what I am about to say may be inadequately informed; but in that debate, it seems to me that many people accept some version of response (1). They emphasize that the canon is socially constructed, is a product of social forces, and could have been otherwise. They believe that these claims make it hard or impossible to offer response (2), which suggests that there are good reasons for giving special status to some practices and texts, for claiming them as authorities. In the end, they think that the availability of response (1) casts doubt on certain ideals associated with liberal education, including the commitment to truth and objectivity.

I believe that all this is a mistake.[15] The mistake takes the following form. If we do not have wholly external or transcendent foundations for something—if all we have is produced through human filters—we really have nothing at all. If the self is a social artifact, or a social product, the concept of freedom itself is jeopardized. Our belief in liberty is an illusion simply because mental powers and commitments are shaped and constrained by external influence; free speech, as conventionally understood, is an illusion too.

I have said that there is a mistake here. Now let me suggest why. From the absence of external or transcendental foundations, it does not follow that everything is up for grabs, or that all we have is conventions, or power, or play. (I refer here, respectively, to Fish, Foucault, and Derrida.) It is right to say that there is no wholly external perspective on human endeavors, that canonization cannot be grounded without language or culture. But this does not mean that good reasons cannot be offered on behalf of one view rather than another. The alleged choice—between transcendental foundations on the one hand and power, conventions, or play on the other—is entirely unnecessary. Instead we need to think about what sorts of approaches will serve what sorts of things we, in our diversity and our commonality, really value. We do not need transcendental foundations to say that a regime of academic freedom is different from a regime of tyranny.

The fact that people are influenced in what they have to say does not impugn freedom, or free speech, or liberalism. Both freedom and lack of freedom are socially constructed; they are an outcome of human practices. We can imagine a system in which people are exposed only to a narrow set of ideas, or to an official orthodoxy; we can also imagine a system in which certain groups are given little information and little opportunity. Any such system would be socially constructed. A system in which people are given a good deal of information, opportunity, and choice—or exposed to a wide range of ideas—is one of freedom. Its origins in society and in cultural practices or even "conditioning" do not impugn this fact.

All this has been quite abstract. Now let me offer a few notations about academic freedom and the canon. Some people—we might call them traditionalists—contend that the existing canon has a special claim on us. On their view, any proposal for change or revision reflects a kind of cheap faddishness, disrespect for real quality, or hubris. On the traditionalist view, we really should take our canon as given rather than chosen. If we do not, we will be giving into a kind of strident, standardless relativism in which political interest, rather than reason, governs intellectual life. This is an illiberal position because it does not allow critical scrutiny of what has been handed down. It is inconsistent with the most attractive conceptions of liberal politics and liberal education.

Another group—I will call them "postmodernists," recognizing the large ambiguity of the category—think that canons in general reflect the interests of certain groups (whites, or males, or heterosexuals, or Europeans) and that a recognition of this fact will point the way to a form of plurality that better serves socially diverse interests. So far, very plausibly, so good. But for some people who hold this sort of view, most or all forms of ranking or valuation or judgment are perniciously hierarchical, or disabled in some way by virtue of the fact that they come from human beings. There are no common standards—only diverse interests, power, and conventions. On this view, the notion of academic freedom is made extremely problematic by virtue of the human origins of what academics think. Thus it is said that there is no such thing as truth, but only interest; that norms of objectivity are pernicious; that knowledge is political.

Both of these positions seem to me to contain important truths. It does not much matter whether Kant and Milton got into the canon for some bad reasons; they belong. At the same time, there are undoubted biases in existing approaches. But these important truths notwithstanding, I think that what I am calling traditionalism and postmodernism are both inadequate for most of the questions that face the academy and those who are concerned about academic freedom. They are each other's flip sides; they reflect the same kind of belief in the necessity for wholly external foundations.

The traditionalist approach is inadequate because there is no sufficient reason to think that any existing canon adequately serves educational goals. If what we want is good learning, and a good appreciation of what intellectual life has to offer, we should say that the virtues of wisdom, clarity, and good argumentation are not limited to particular periods, genders, races, and countries. And this fact means that some current approaches must be revisited. The commitment to liberal education itself entails this conclusion.

But despite its currency, the postmodern position is little better.[16] At least in some forms, that position makes it very hard to explain why we should engage in intellectual life at all; if political power and political interest are all that is at stake, discussion of texts is hardly a good path to follow. Moreover, what underlies some of the most plausible claims of those who attack the current canon is the belief that the canon *should* include works of certain kinds. This belief—this use of "should"—makes sense only to the extent that it is based on generally acceptable reasons, not on political interest. This belief depends on a set of claims about bias and partiality, and those claims would be unintelligible unless the relevant antonym—objectivity, understood in a human rather than metaphysical or transcendental sense—was also a conceptual possibility.

Against both traditionalism and postmodernism, I suggest that we oppose a third alternative, which might well be understood as a version of the commitment to liberal education. I will not be able to say much about that commitment here; but it should be clear that liberal education is not neutral. It embodies conceptions of both the good and the right. At a minimum, the commitment requires us to try to impart deep and wide understanding—to counteract ignorance, bias, and parochialism, and to promote choice among a set of acceptable alternatives. It requires all approaches to be supported by reasons, not by reference to authority. History and "nature" are themselves inadequate unless these can be made part of a reasoned argument.

From this perspective, the purpose of liberal education is associated with the production of certain valuable human characteristics, including a capacity for activity, the ability to develop, pursue, and evaluate a plan of life, and much more—a project connecting Mill, Dewey, and many others. On this view, the acquisition of knowledge may be political, broadly speaking, in the sense that it is a human product, and inevitably associated with some conception of the good or the right for human beings. But this conception of politics does not reduce that term to narrow interest, or power, or perspective. An adequate account would have to say much more. But perhaps we can see how a commitment to liberal education, understood in this general way, may well help inform the conception of liberal politics and the best view of the principle of freedom of expression.

CONCLUSION

In this essay, I have tried to discuss the issue of academic freedom in the context of the commitment to liberal politics. A system of free expression should be designed to safeguard the exchange of ideas. This understanding calls for protection of much of what might be considered hate speech; but it also allows restrictions on speech that amounts to epithets. There are some additional complexities in the academic setting. Universities are pervasively and necessarily engaged in regulation of speech, and this fact complicates many existing claims about hate speech codes. In the end I suggest that the test is whether the restriction on speech is a legitimate part of the institution's educational mission, understanding that ideal by reference to the commitment to liberal education. This mission is not neutral among different conceptions of the good. It embodies a substantive project (though the project is one that allows exposure to a wide range of competing conceptions). This understanding would allow for somewhat broader restrictions than would be acceptable for states and localities.

I have used this discussion as the basis for some preliminary remarks on the general subject of academic freedom. Academic freedom is not a neutral commitment. It can be taken as part of a belief in a modest form of liberal perfectionism, designed to exemplify and to promote individual autonomy. Most or even all knowledge may be political, broadly speaking, if the contested word "political" is taken to embody some stand on issues of the right or the good. But we should not identify that word with narrow power or interest, much less with arbitrary whim. It may be that academic life can embody conceptions of politics that are defensible by reference to reasons, or by reference to an understanding of what is contained in an autonomous life. The ideal of liberal education, and even of academic freedom, is best understood by reference to some such understanding.

NOTES

I draw here on some work published elsewhere: Cass R. Sunstein, *The Partial Constitution* (Cambridge, Mass.: Harvard University Press, 1993); Cass R. Sunstein, *Democracy and the Problem of Free Speech* (New York: Free Press, 1993). Some of the issues discussed here are treated in more detail in these places.

1. I do not discuss here the issues raised by the claim that academic freedom forbids certain governmental intrusions into the affairs of the university, though some of what I say does bear on those issues.

2. On deliberative democracy, see Joseph Bessette, "Deliberative Democracy: The Majority Principle in Republican Government," in *How Democratic Is the Constitution?* ed. Robert Goldwin and William Schambra (Washington, D.C.: American Enterprise Institute for Public Policy Research, 1980); Sunstein, *The Partial Constitution,* chaps. 5 and 6.

3. See Samuel H. Beer, *To Make a Nation: The Rediscovery of American Federalism* (Cambridge, Mass.: Harvard University Press, 1993); Stephen Holmes, *Passions and Constraint: On the Theory of Liberal Democracy* (Chicago: University of Chicago Press, 1995).

4. This is Mill's version of liberalism, associated with Dewey as well; it is of course contested by many liberals.

5. *Whitney v. California,* 274 U.S. 357 (1927).

6. T. M. Scanlon, "A Theory of Free Expression," *Philosophy and Public Affairs* 1 (1972): 204.

7. *Brandenburg v. Ohio,* 395 U.S. 444 (1969).

8. *New York Times v. Sullivan,* 376 U.S. 254 (1964) (invoking democratic goals); *Chaplinsky v. New Hampshire,* 315 U.S. 568 (1942) (invoking exchange of ideas).

9. See *Doe v. University of Michigan,* 721 F. Supp. 852 (E.D. Mich. 1989); *UWM Post, Inc. v. Bd. of Regents,* 774 F. Supp. 1163 (E.D. Wis. 1991).

10. 343 U.S. 250 (1952).

11. 376 US 254 (1964).

12. See Charles R. Lawrence, "If He Hollers Let Him Go," *Duke Law Journal* (1990): 431; Mari Matsuda, "Public Response to Racist Speech," *Michigan Law Review* 87 (1989): 2320; Richard Delgado, "Words That Wound," *Harvard Civil Rights–Civil Liberties Law Review* 17 (1982): 133.

13. I offer an argument to this effect in Sunstein, *Democracy and the Problem of Free Speech*.

14. Robert Bork, *The Tempting of America: The Political Seduction of the Law* (New York: Free Press, 1990).

15. Relevant discussion can be found in Hilary Putnam, *Renewing Philosophy* (Cambridge, Mass.: Harvard University Press, 1992), and in Martha Nussbaum, "Sophistry about Conventions," *Love's Knowledge: Essays on Philosophy and Literature* (New York: Oxford University Press, 1990).

16. I draw in this and the following paragraph from the valuable discussion in Amy Gutmann, "Introduction," in Charles Taylor, *Multiculturalism and the Politics of Recognition,* ed. Amy Gutmann (Princeton: Princeton University Press, 1991).

FIVE

Critical Race Theory and Freedom of Speech

Henry Louis Gates Jr.

> As a thumbnail summary of the last two or three decades
> of speech issues in the Supreme Court, we may come to
> see the Negro as winning back for us the freedoms the
> Communists seemed to have lost for us.
>
> —Harry Kalven Jr.,
> *The Negro and the First Amendment* (1965)

I

Writing in the heyday of the civil rights era, the great First Amendment scholar Harry Kalven Jr. was confident that civil rights and civil liberties were marching in unison, that their mutual expansion represented, for a nation in a time of tumult, an intertwined destiny. He might have been surprised had he lived to witness the shifting nature of their relations. For today, the partnership named in the title of his classic study seems in hopeless disrepair: civil liberties are regarded by many as a chief obstacle to civil rights. To be sure, blacks are still on the front lines of First Amendment jurisprudence, only this time we soldier on the other side. The byword among many black activists and intellectuals is no longer the political imperative to protect free speech but the moral imperative to suppress hate speech. And therein hangs a tale.

Like such phrases as "prochoice" and "prolife," the phrase "hate speech" is ideology in capsule form. It is the term-of-art of a movement—most active on college campuses and in liberal municipalities—that has caused many civil rights activists to rethink their allegiance to the First Amendment, the amendment that licensed the protests, rallies, organizing, *119* and agitation that so galvanized the nation in a bygone era. Addressing the concerns of a very different era, the hate speech movement has enlisted the energies of some of our most engaged and interesting legal scholars. The result has been the proliferation of campus speech codes as well as municipal ordinances enhancing penalties for bias crimes. Of course, the relation between the internal governance of the academy and the larger issues of constitutional jurisprudence is itself a contested one: certainly few argue that the boundaries of discourse in the academy must mirror those prescribed for public forums. And yet the ethos established by jurisprudence of speech is of profound importance to such institutions, which are neither wholly public nor wholly private.

Equally important, the hate speech movement has provided an opportunity for scholars and citizens who are outside it to clarify and rethink the meaning of their commitment to freedom of expression. It is an opportunity few have taken up. What makes this ironic is that if America has a civic religion today, the First Amendment may be its central credo. "It's a free country," we shrug, and what we usually mean is: you can say what you please. "Sticks and stones can break my bones," we are taught to chant as children, "but words can never hurt me." Americans "are taught this view by about the fourth grade and continue to absorb it through osmosis from everything around them for the rest of their lives," Catharine MacKinnon writes with no little asperity in *Only Words,* her latest and most accessible book, "to the point that those who embrace it think it is their own personal faith, their own original view, and trot it out like something learned from their own personal lives every time a problem is denominated one of 'speech,' whether it really fits or not."[1]

The strongest argument for regulating hate speech is the unreflective stupidity of most of the arguments you hear on the other side. I do not refer to the debate as it has proceeded in the law reviews: there you find qualities of caution, clarity, and tentativeness largely missing from the larger public discourse. Regrettably enough, those law professors who offer the best analysis of public discourse exert very little influence *within* public discourse. And that leaves us with a now familiar stalemate. On the one hand are those who speak of "hate speech," a phrase which alludes to an argument without revealing anything much about it; to insist on probing further is to admit, fearsomely, that you just "don't get it." On the other hand are their opponents, who invoke the First Amendment like a mantra and seem immediately to fall into a trance, so oblivious are they to further argumentation and evidence. A small number of anecdotes, either about racism on campus or about "PC" inquisitions on campus, are endlessly recycled; and a University of Pennsylvania undergraduate named Eden Jacobowitz—he of "water buffalo" fame—becomes a Dreyfus *de nos jours*.

There's a practical reason to worry about how impoverished the national discourse on free speech has become. For if we keep losing the arguments, in time we may lose our grip on the liberties they were meant to defend. We may come to think that our bad arguments are the only arguments to be made, and when someone finally disabuses us of them, we may switch sides without ever considering other and better arguments for staying put.

To get an appreciation of these arguments, though, we must be prepared to go beyond where the water buffalo roam. For all the pleasures of demonology, the burgeoning literature urging the regulation of racist speech has a serious claim on our attention. The time has come to accord these arguments the full consideration they deserve. Conveniently enough, *Words That Wound: Critical Race Theory, Assaultive Speech, and the First Amendment* has collected for the first time the three most widely cited and influential papers to make the case for the regulation of racist speech. These three papers—which originally appeared in law reviews over the past several years, only to circulate even more widely through the samizdat of the photocopier—complement each other surprisingly well. Though each makes larger arguments as well, one proposal focuses on criminal law, another focuses on civil law, and a third focuses on campus speech codes.

The authors of these proposals are minority law professors who teach at mainstream institutions—Mari J. Matsuda and Charles R. Lawrence III at Georgetown, Richard Delgado at the University of Colorado—and who write vigorous and accessible prose. They are, one can fairly say, the legal eagles of the crusade against racist hate speech. But they are also the principal architects of "critical race theory." In their jointly written introduction, the authors trace the social origins of critical race theory to a 1981 student boycott of a Harvard Law School course on "Race, Racism, and American Law." Organizing an informal alternative course, students invited lawyers and law professors of color to lecture weekly on the topic. Kimberlè Williams Crenshaw, another contributor to *Words That Wound,* was one of the student organizers of the alternative course; Matsuda was one of its participants; Delgado and Lawrence were among its guest lecturers. And thus was formed the nucleus of "a small but growing group of scholars committed to finding new ways to think about and act in pursuit of racial justice."[2]

The intellectual ancestry of the movement is complex, but its two main progenitors are, on the one hand, the particular brand of feminist theory associated with Catharine MacKinnon (like that of Marx, the name of MacKinnon designates a body of argument that can no longer be distinguished from a political movement) and, on the other, the radical skepticism toward traditional black-letter pieties associated with critical legal studies. Almost invariably, the literature arguing for hate speech regulation cites MacKinnon as an authority and model; almost invariably, the literature takes on one or more of the traditional legal distinctions (such as that between private and public) whose dismantling—though to a considerable extent pioneered by the legal realists of the 1930s—is a staple in the critical legal studies repertory.

So it is no surprise that conservative pundits denounce these theorists of hate speech as faddish foes of freedom. In fact, we would more accurately describe their approach as neotraditional. And those conservatives who dream of turning the cultural clock back to the fifties should realize that the First Amendment law of those years is just what these supposedly faddish scholars wish to revive. That much should suggest something amiss about our rhetoric concerning our First Amendment "traditions." And therein hangs yet another tale.

II

The conventional defense of free speech absolutism—the kind your uncle bangs on about—rests upon three pillars, all pretty thoroughly rotted through. Dr. Johnson thought he could refute Bishop Berkeley by kicking a stone, and armchair absolutists often think they can win debates through the self-evident authority of the First Amendment itself. The invocation is generally folded together with a vague sort of historical argument. The First Amendment, we are told, has stood us in good stead through the more than two centuries of this great republic; quite possibly, our greatness depends on it. The framers knew what they were doing, and—this directed to those inclined to bog down in interpretative quibbles—at the end of the day, *the First Amendment means what it says.*

This is a dependable and well-rehearsed argument, whose only flaw is that it happens to be entirely false. Indeed, the notion that the First Amendment has been a historical mainstay of American liberty is a paradigm instance of invented tradition. To begin with, the First Amendment, conceived as protecting the free speech of citizens, did not exist until 1931. (Cases in 1925 and 1927 are often cited as establishing this development;

but it was in 1931 that the Court first stated explicitly that the First Amendment applies to the states.) Before then, the Court took the amendment at its word: "*Congress* shall make no law . . ." Congress couldn't; states and municipalities could do what they liked. Given this background, it shouldn't surprise us that even after the Supreme Court recognized freedom of expression as a right held by citizens, the interpretation of its scope remained quite narrow (notwithstanding such landmark cases as Learned Hand's opinion in *Masses Publishing Co. v. Patten* in 1917 or the Supreme Court's 1937 decision in *DeJonge v. Oregon*) until after World War II, when the Warren Court gradually opened up a more generous vision of civil liberties. So the expansive First Amendment that people either celebrate or bemoan is really only a few decades old.

And even the Court's most expansive interpretation of First Amendment protection has always come with a list of exceptions, such as libel, invasion of privacy, and obscenity. "Categorization" is the legal buzzword for deciding whether an expression is protected by determining which category the expression falls into—having first determined whether it qualifies as expression at all. While speech may be a species of conduct, much in case law still hangs on whether conduct (say, nude dancing, or flag burning) will be allowed to count as expression for First Amendment purposes. Various refinements on the test have been proposed. To John Hart Ely, for example, the question for judicial scrutiny shouldn't be whether something is expression or conduct, for everything is both, but whether it is the expressive dimension of the speech-conduct amalgam that has provoked its prosecution.[3] One may suspect that this refinement merely defers the difficulty of distinguishing. At the very least, MacKinnon's position—which extends no particular protection to expression over conduct—has the advantage of coherence (more proof that in the real world, theoretical coherence is an overrated virtue).

In their categorizing mode, the courts have also respected a general hierarchy of protected speech, such that political speech is deemed worthy of significant protection while commercial speech is highly subject to regulation. But even political speech is subject to the old clear-and-present danger exception, and a cluster of variants. To venture into murkier waters, the issue of speech management arises in the highly contested matter of the public forum: Where may one exercise these supposedly valuable rights of free speech? How much (if any) access to these forums will we enjoy? And this isn't even to consider the unbounded array of criminal and civil offenses—conspiracy, solicitation of a bribe, perjury, and so on—that are enacted through expression. As Frederick Schauer, Stanton Professor of the First Amendment at Harvard University, has observed, absolute protection would make unconstitutional "all of contract law, most of antitrust law, and much of criminal law."[4] In view of this brambly legal landscape, to invoke the First Amendment as if it settled anything by itself can sound very much like know-nothingism.

When the myth of the self-justifying First Amendment is put aside, the armchair absolutist is left with his two fallback arguments. Dredging up childhood memories, he comes up with that playground chant about sticks and stones. Offensive expression should be protected because it is costless, "only words." But if words really were inert, we wouldn't invest so much in their protection; it is a vacuous conception of expressive liberty that is predicated upon the innocuousness of its exercise. "Every idea is an incitement," Justice Holmes famously wrote, albeit in dissent.[5] In his recent history of obscenity law, Edward de Grazia tells of an especially sad and instructive example of the power of words to cause harm: evidently the heated rhetoric of MacKinnon's 1984 campaign for an antipornography ordinance in Minneapolis moved one young supporter to douse herself with gasoline and set herself afire.

This leaves us with the armchair absolutist's Old Reliable: the slippery-slope argument. Perhaps racist speech is hurtful and without value, he will concede, but tolerating it is the price we must pay to ensure the protection of other, beneficial and valuable speech. The picture here is that if we take one step down from the mountain peak of expressive freedom, we'll slide down to the valley of expressive tyranny. But a more accurate account of where we currently stand is somewhere halfway up the side of the mountain; we already are, and always were, on that slippery slope. And its very slipperiness is why First Amendment jurisprudence is so strenuous, why the struggle for traction is so demanding.

I should be clear. Slippery-slopism isn't worthless as a consideration: because the terrain is slippery we *ought* to step carefully. And there are many examples of "wedge" cases that have led to progressive restrictions in civil liberties. (For example, *Bowers v. Hardwick,* the 1986 case in which the Supreme Court affirmed the constitutionality of statutes prohibiting sodomy, has since been invoked in over one hundred state and federal court decisions denying the right to privacy.) Even so, slippery-slopism sounds better in the abstract than in the particular. For one thing, courts often must balance conflicting rights, as with "hostile environment" cases of workplace harassment. For another, we do not always know immediately if the step taken will ultimately lead us downhill or up—as with William Brennan's decision in *Roth v. United States* (1957), which affirmed Stanley Roth's conviction for publishing an Aubrey Beardsley book and declared obscenity to be utterly without redeeming value. The wording of that decision, however unpromising at first glance, turned out to be a boon for the civil libertarian position: if obscenity was utterly without redeeming value, then anything to which redeeming value could be ascribed was ipso facto not obscene.

III

But the hate speech movement hasn't been content with exposing the sort of weaknesses I've just rehearsed. It has also aligned itself with earlier traditions of jurisprudence, and it is here that the movement's seeming atavism is most clearly displayed. The sort of speech the movement wishes to restrict falls into two expressive categories that the Supreme Court has previously held (and, they argue, correctly so) to be undeserving of First Amendment protection. The categories are those of fighting words and group defamation, as exemplified by two cases decided in 1942 and 1952.

It is out of respect for the prerogative of "categorization" that critical race theorists root their model of assaultive speech in the Supreme Court opinion of *Chaplinsky v. New Hampshire* (1942), which bequeathed us the fighting words doctrine. Chaplinsky was a Jehovah's Witness who was convicted for calling a city marshal a "God damned racketeer" and "a damned Fascist." The statute he violated forbade one to address "any offensive, derisive or annoying word to any other person" in a public place. Affirming the conviction, the Court held that "there are certain well-defined and narrowly limited classes of speech, the prevention and punishment of which have never been thought to raise any Constitutional problem." Among them were "the insulting or 'fighting' words—those which by their very utterance inflict injury or tend to incite an immediate breach of the peace." "Such utterances are no essential part of any exposition of ideas," Justice Murphy wrote for the majority, "and are of such slight social value as a step to truth that any benefit that may be derived from them is clearly outweighed by the social interest in order and morality."[6]

The Court's reference to those words "which by their very utterance inflict injury" is especially cherished by the hate speech movement, for it seems to presage its account of "assaultive speech," or words that wound. In accord with *Chaplinsky,* critical race theorists emphasize the immediate and visceral harms incurred by hate speech. "Many victims of hate propaganda have experienced physiological and emotional symptoms, such as rapid pulse rate and difficulty in breathing," Lawrence writes.[7] Matsuda has even more alarming findings to report: "Victims of vicious hate propaganda experience physiological symptoms and emotional distress ranging from fear in the gut to rapid pulse rate and difficulty in breathing, nightmares, post-traumatic stress disorder, hypertension, psychosis, and suicide." And Delgado further notes that the psychic injuries incurred by racist speech have additional costs down the road: "The person who is timid, withdrawn, bitter, hypertense, or psychotic will almost certainly fare poorly in employment settings."[8] (As a member of the Harvard faculty, I would venture that there are exceptions to this rule.)

But *Chaplinsky* has other useful elements, too. Certainly the approach entailed by the Court's conclusion that such words as the Jehovah's Witness uttered "are no essential part of any exposition of ideas" has been pressed into service. It shows up in the insistence that racist speech has no content, that it is more like a blunt instrument than a vehicle of thought. "The racial invective is experienced as a blow, not a proffered idea," Lawrence writes. By contrast, the "fighting words" prong of the *Chaplinsky* test—specifying words likely to incite an immediate breach of the peace—has been widely condemned for bias: why should those persons (women, for example) who are less likely to strike back physically be less protected from abuse? For this reason, Lawrence in effect urges an expansion of the fighting words doctrine, arguing that racist speech (which may silence its victims, rather than provoking them to violence) should be understood as the "functional equivalent of fighting words," and thus equally unworthy of First Amendment protection.[9]

The hate speech movement's deployment of *Chaplinsky* is certainly within the pale of standard legal argument; indeed, the carefully drafted speech code adopted by Stanford University explicitly extends only to fighting words or symbols, thus wearing its claim to constitutionality on its face. So if *Chaplinsky* can shoulder the legal and ethical burdens placed upon it, the regulationists have a powerful weapon on their side. Can it?

Probably not. To begin with, it is an open question whether *Chaplinsky* remains, as they say, "good law," given that in the fifty years since its promulgation the Supreme Court has never once affirmed a conviction for uttering either fighting words or words that "by their very utterance inflict injury." Indeed, in part because of its functional desuetude, in part because of the male bias of the "breach of the peace" prong, the editors of the *Harvard Law Review* have recently issued a call for the doctrine's explicit interment.[10] So much for the doctrine's judicial value.

But they also note, as others have, that statutes prohibiting fighting words have had discriminatory effects. An apparently not atypical conviction—upheld by the Louisiana state court—was occasioned by the following exchange between a white police officer and the black mother of a young suspect. He: "Get your black ass in the goddamned car." She: "You god damn mother fucking police—I am going to [the Superintendent of Police] about this."[11] No prize for guessing which one was convicted for uttering fighting words. As the legal scholar Kenneth Karst reports, "statutes proscribing abusive words are applied to members of racial and political minorities more frequently than can be wholly explained by any special proclivity of those people to speak abusively."[12] So much for the doctrine's political value.

Nor, finally, does the *Chaplinsky*-derived description of assaultive speech as being devoid of political or other ideational content—"experienced as a blow, not a proffered idea," in Lawrence's compelling formulation—survive closer inspection. Consider the incident that, Lawrence tells us, moved him to take up the hate speech cause in the first place. Two white Stanford freshmen had an argument with a black student about Beethoven's ancestry: he claimed, and they denied, that the Flemish-German composer was really of African descent. The next evening, apparently as a satirical commentary, the white students acquired a poster of Beethoven, colored it in with Sambo-like features, and posted it on the door of the student's dorm room at Ujamaa, Stanford's black theme house. Lawrence "experienced the defacement as representative of the university community's racism and not as an exceptional incident in a community in which the absence of racism is the rule"—and the rest is critical-race-theory history.[13]

Now then, is Lawrence's paradigm example of racist hate speech in fact devoid of ideational or political content, as his analysis would suggest? Evidently not, for in their jointly written manifesto for critical race theory, the authors of *Words That Wound* spell out what they believe its message to have been:

> The message said, "This is you. This is you and all of your African-American brothers and sisters. You are all Sambos. It's a joke to think that you could ever be a Beethoven. It's ridiculous to believe that you could ever be anything other than a caricature of real genius."[14]

The defaced poster also inspired a lengthy and passionate essay by the legal theorist Patricia J. Williams, an essay that extracts an even more elaborated account of its meaning.[15] This was one picture, clearly, that really was worth a thousand words.

The same paradox surfaces in Delgado's groundbreaking proposal for a tort action to redress racist speech. To define this tort, he must distinguish offensive racist speech from offensive political speech; for in *Cohen v. California* (1971), the Supreme Court decided that a jacket emblazoned with the words "Fuck the Draft" and worn in a courthouse would be protected as political speech, despite its patent offensiveness. Delgado argues that a racial insult, by contrast, "is not political speech; its perpetrator intends not to discover truth or advocate social action, but to injure the victim." It's a curious disjunction, this, between advocacy and injury. For if Delgado and his fellow contributors have a central message to impart, it's that racial insults are profoundly political, part of a larger mechanism of social subordination, and thus in contravention of the spirit of the equal protection clause of the Fourteenth Amendment. And the most harmful forms of racist speech are precisely those that combine injury with advocacy—those that are, in short, the most "political." "Are racial insults ideas?" Lawrence asks. "Do they encourage wide-open debate?"[16] He means the question to be rhetorical, but after reading his work and those of his fellow critical race theorists, who could possibly doubt it?

IV

Even if we finally reject the picture of assaultive speech as empty of political content, along with the other tenets of the *Chaplinsky* doctrine, the hate speech movement can still link itself to constitutional precedent through the alternative model of defamation. Indeed, I would argue that the defamation model is more central, more weight-bearing, in these arguments than the assaultive one. And note that these *are* alternatives, not just different ways of describing the same thing. The fighting words/assaultive speech paradigm analogizes racist expression to physical assault: at its simplest, it characterizes an act of aggression between two individuals, victim and victimizer. By contrast, the defamation paradigm analogizes racist speech to libel, a dignitary affront. The harm is essentially social: to be defamed is to be defamed in the eyes of other people.

Here, the guiding precedent is Justice Frankfurter's majority opinion in the 1952 case of *Beauharnais v. Illinois,* in which the Court upheld a conviction under an Illinois group libel ordinance. The ordinance was clumsily written, but it essentially prohibited public expression that "portrays depravity, criminality, unchastity, or lack of virtue in a class of citizens of any race, color, creed, or religion," thereby exposing them to "contempt, derision, or obloquy." Mr. Beauharnais ran afoul of the ordinance when he circulated a leaflet that urged whites to unite against the menace posed by their black fellow citizens.

> Preserve and Protect White Neighborhoods! from the constant and continuous invasion, harassment and encroachment by the Negroes. . . . The white people of Chicago must take advantage of the opportunity to be united. If persuasion and the need to prevent the white race from being mongrelized by the Negro will not unite us, then the aggressions, rapes, robberies, knives, guns, and marijuana of the Negro surely will.

So averred Mr. Beauharnais, and it was the last sentence, specifying the Negro's offenses, that was held to violate the law. In Justice Frankfurter's opinion, "If an utterance directed at an individual may be the object of criminal sanctions we cannot deny to a State power to punish the same utterance directed at a defined group," at least as long as the restriction related to the peace and well-being of the state.[17]

To be sure, *Beauharnais v. Illinois* has since fallen into judicial disrepute, having been reversed in its particulars by subsequent cases like the celebrated *New York Times Co. v. Sullivan* (1964). Indeed, more widely cited than Justice Frankfurter's opinion is Justice Hugo Black's dissent: "If there be minority groups who hail this holding as their victory, they might consider the possible relevancy of this ancient remark: 'Another such victory and I am undone.'"[18] And yet Frankfurter's claim for the congruence of individual and group libel is not, on the face of it, implausible. One could argue (as MacKinnon does) that this precedent is deserving of revival—or, more elaborately (as Lawrence does), that it was never truly reversed, because the notion of group libel tacitly underlies and sponsors more prestigious Supreme Court precedents.

Thus MacKinnon, in *Only Words,* deplores the celebrated *Sullivan* case for undermining the vitality and superior virtue of *Beauharnais v. Illinois.* "This arrangement avoids the rather obvious reality that groups are made up of individuals," she writes. "In reality, libel of groups multiplies rather than avoids the very same damage through reputation which the law of individual libel recognizes when done one at a time, as well as inflicting some of its own. . . . The idea seems to be that injury to one person is legally actionable, but the same injury to thousands of people is protected speech."[19] Where's the justice in that? MacKinnon would thus revive the state's winning argument in *Beauharnais:* "Petitioner cannot gain constitutional protection from the consequence of libel by multiplying victims and identifying them by a collective term."[20] (A similar argument was elaborated in a classic defense of group defamation laws written by none other than David Riesman, during his brief career as a law professor.)[21]

And the plausibility of this simple but powerful idea is what has made it so attractive to theorists of hate speech. As Matsuda writes movingly:

> When the legal mind understands that reputational interests . . . must be balanced against first amendment interests, it recognizes the concrete reality of what happens to people who are defamed. Their lives are changed. Their standing in the community, their opportunities, their self-worth, their free enjoyment of life are limited. Their political capital—their ability to speak and be heard—is diminished. To see this, and yet to fail to see that the very same things happen to the victims of racist speech, is selective vision.[22]

The defamation model plays an even more central role in Lawrence's analysis. He argues that *Brown v. Board of Education,* decided just two years after *Beauharnais,* is best interpreted as a "case about group defamation. The message of segregation was stigmatizing to Black children. . . . *Brown* reflects the understanding that racism is a form of subordination that achieves its purpose through group defamation." Indeed, Lawrence seems to move close to the position that *all* racism is essentially to be understood as defamation. And he protests that "there has not yet been a satisfactory retraction of the government-sponsored defamation in the slavery clauses, the *Dred Scott* decision, the Black codes, the segregation statutes, and countless *other group libels.*"[23] Let's leave aside for the moment Lawrence's intriguing reinterpretation of legal history. What is wrong with the basic claim here, one endorsed by judges and scholars across the ideological spectrum, that group libel is just individual libel multiplied? As I say, we should grant that the claim has prima facie plausibility. And yet the very case of *Beauharnais* illustrates the attendant difficulties. For while Mr. Beauharnais' racism is everywhere in evidence, it's actually unclear what charge is being made in the one sentence of his leaflet that was found to be libelous. That is, the accusation about the "aggressions" and so on of the Negro need not obtain about any particular Negro; and nobody claimed that *no* Negro was guilty of such misdeeds as he enumerated. Since the Sedition Act of 1798, truth has been allowed as a defense in American libel law. But the Illinois ordinance nowhere mentions the question of truth or falsity, and we might think it odd, even insulting, if it did. (At his trial, Mr. Beauharnais offered to prove the truth of his allegations by introducing evidence about the higher incidence of crime in black districts; his offer was declined.) And this points us toward the significant disanalogy between group and individual libel.

Start with the notion that individual libel involves the publication of information about someone that is both damaging and false. Lawrence inadvertently directs us to the source of the problem. The racial epithet, he writes, "is invoked as an assault, not as a statement of fact that may be proven true or false."[24] But that suggests that the evaluative judgments that are characteristic of racial invective do not lend themselves to factual verification, and here the comparison with individual libel breaks down. The same problem emerges when MacKinnon identifies pornography as group defamation whose message is (roughly) that it would be nice if women were available for sexual exploitation; for a proposition of that form may be right or wrong, but it cannot be true or false. The conclusion Lawrence draws is that racist speech is a form of defamation immune from the *Sullivan* rule protecting statements of fact that are later discovered to be erroneous. A more obvious conclusion to reach would be that racist invective isn't best understood as an extension of individual libel at all. You cannot libel someone by saying "I despise you," which seems to be the essential message common to most racial epithets.

Delgado himself offers further reasons to reject the defamation model that colleagues like Lawrence, Matsuda, and MacKinnon find so appealing. As he notes: "A third party who learned that a person was the victim of a racial insult, but did not know the victim, would probably conclude that the victim is a member of a particular racial minority. But if this conclusion is true, the victim cannot recover [under defamation law] because no falsehood has occurred." If you learn that somebody called George a "nigger," you might infer that George is black, but that's about all. "And whether or not the conclusion is true," Delgado continues, "it is not desirable that the law view membership in a racial minority as damaging to a person's reputation, even if some members of society consider it so."[25]

I think we may fairly conclude, then, that *Beauharnais* is best left undisturbed in its slumbers, and that the model of group libel founders on the flawed analogy to individual libel. "Nigger" (used in the vocative) is not helpfully treated as group libel for the same reason it is not helpfully treated as individual libel. On the categorization front, at least, civil libertarians need not cede critical race theory an inch.

V

Critical race theory is at its strongest, however, not when it seeks to establish a bridgehead with constitutional precedent but when it frontally contests what has recently emerged as a central aspect of Supreme Court First Amendment doctrine: the principle of content and viewpoint neutrality.

The principle of content and viewpoint neutrality is meant to serve as a guideline for how speech can permissibly be regulated, ensuring basic fairness by preventing the law from favoring one partisan interest over another. So, for example, a law forbidding the discussion of race would violate the principle of content neutrality, which is held to be a bad thing; a law that forbade the advocacy of black supremacy would violate the principle of viewpoint neutrality, which is held to be a worse thing. When the Minnesota Supreme Court affirmed the content-sensitive hate speech ordinance at issue in *R.A.V. v. St. Paul* (1992), it cited Matsuda's work in reaching its conclusions. When Justice Scalia reversed and invalidated the ordinance on the grounds of viewpoint discrimination, he was implicitly writing against Matsuda's argument. So what we saw was no merely academic conflict of vision; these are arguments with judicial consequences.

In my view, Matsuda's rejection of what she calls the "neutrality trap" is probably the most powerful element of her argument. Rather than trying to fashion neutral laws to further our social objectives, why not put our cards on the table and acknowledge what we know? As an example of where the neutrality trap leads, she cites the antimask statutes that many states passed "in a barely disguised effort to limit Ku Klux Klan activities."

> These statutes purportedly cover the wearing of masks in general, with no specific mention of the intent to control the Klan. Neutral reasons, such as the need to prevent pickpockets from moving unidentified through crowds or the need to unmask burglars or bank robbers are proffered for such statutes. The result of forgetting—or pretending to forget—the real reason for antimask legislation is farcical. Masks are used in protest against terrorist regimes for reasons of both symbolism and personal safety. Iranian students wearing masks and opposing human rights violations by the Shah of Iran, for example, were prosecuted under a California antimask statute.
>
> I call here for an end of such unknowing. We know why state legislatures—those quirkily populist institutions—have passed antimask statutes. It is more honest, and less cynically manipulative of legal doctrine, to legislate openly against the worst forms of racist speech, allowing ourselves to know what we know.[26]

What makes her position particularly attractive is that she offers a pragmatic, pro-civil-liberties argument for such content specificity. "The alternative to recognizing racist speech as qualitatively different because of its content is to continue to stretch existing first amendment exceptions, such as the 'fighting words' doctrine and the 'content/conduct' distinction," she writes. "This stretching ultimately weakens the first amendment fabric, creating neutral holes that remove protection for many forms of speech. Setting aside the worst forms of racist speech for special treatment is a non-neutral, value-laden approach that will better preserve free speech."[27]

Another cogent argument against the notion of neutral principles is the fact that apparently neutral principles are often anything but in practice. "The law, in its infinite majesty, forbids rich and poor alike from sleeping under bridges," Anatole France famously observed. If neutrality is, in the end, a masquerade, why bother with it? Why not abandon neutral principles and permit what Matsuda calls "expanded relevance," allowing courts to take into account the experience of racism, the victim group's conscious-ness, in assessing the harm of racist speech? At the very least, this approach would promise a quick solution to the sorts of abuses of fighting words ordinances we saw. To see how, consider Matsuda's own approach to legal sanctions for racist speech.

By way of distinguishing "the worst, paradigm example of racist hate messages from other forms of racist and nonracist speech," she offers three identifying characteristics:

1. The message is of racial inferiority.
2. The message is directed against a historically oppressed group.
3. The message is persecutory, hateful, and degrading.

The third element, she says, is "related to the 'fighting words' idea"; and the first "is the primary identifier of racist speech"; but it is the second element that "attempts to further define racism by recognizing the connec-tion of racism to power and subordination."[28] And it is the second element that most radically departs from the current requirement that law be neutral as to content and viewpoint. Still, it would seem to forestall some of the abuses to which earlier speech ordinances have been put, simply by requir-ing the victim of the penalized speech to be a member of a "historically oppressed group." And there's something refreshingly straightforward about her call for "an end to unknowing." Is Matsuda on to something? Curiously enough, what trips up the content-specific approach is that it can never be content-specific enough. Take a second look at her three identifying characteristics of paradigm hate speech. First, recall, the message is of racial inferiority. Now, Matsuda makes clear that she wants her definition to encompass, inter alia, anti-Semitic and anti-Asian prejudice: but anti-

Semitism—as the philosopher Laurence Thomas (who is black and Jewish) observes—traditionally imputes to its target not inferiority but iniquity. And anti-Asian prejudice often more closely resembles anti-Semitic prejudice than it does anti-black prejudice. Surely anti-Asian prejudice that depicts Asians as menacingly superior, and therefore a threat to "us," is just as likely, perhaps more likely, to arouse the sort of violence that notoriously claimed the life of Vincent Chin ten years ago in Detroit. More obviously, the test of membership in a "historically oppressed" group is in danger of being either too narrow (just blacks?) or too broad (just about everybody). Are poor Appalachians—a group I knew well from growing up in a West Virginia mill town—"historically oppressed" or "dominant group members"?

If we adopted the "historically oppressed" proviso, I suspect it would just be a matter of time before a group of black women in Chicago are arraigned for calling a policeman a "dumb Polack." Evidence that Poles are a historically oppressed group in Chicago will be in plentiful supply; the policeman's grandmother will offer poignant firsthand testimony to that. Of course, we might—ever mindful that minority groups have been especially vulnerable to statutes forbidding abusive speech—amend the criminal code by exempting members of historically oppressed groups from its sanctions. This would circumvent the risk of authorities employing the rules, perversely, against the very minority groups they were designed to empower. But then the white male student facing disciplinary procedures for calling a black classmate a "nigger" will always have the option of declaring himself to be gay, raising what the military calls a rebuttable presumption. The disciplinary committee would have to decide if it will be satisfied with the defendant's sexual self-ascription, or, more rigorously, require evidence of actual conduct. Matsuda rightly observes that "the legal imagination is a fruitful one," but might we not wish to see it employed at more useful tasks?

My point is one that some recent Pragmatists have been fond of making, since Matsuda wants to abandon not principles or rules but only "neutral" principles and rules; and the sort of complications she decries (the imperfect "fit" between a rule and the cases it must govern) is the sort those Pragmatists find with all principles and rules, neutral or not. Rather than rescuing us from the legal game of Twister, her approach merely provides a differently colored mat. And that mars the practical appeal of her position. Why abandon the notion of content-neutrality—which has a decent, if flawed, track record—if doing so just replaces one set of problems with another?

It's also important to distinguish between a position that advocates abandoning our adherence to general rules and principles and one that says there is nothing to abandon, for we never really had them in the first place: both are plausible positions, but to confuse them is like confusing satanism and atheism. As we saw, Matsuda is no skeptic about rules: what worries her about neutral principles is that they detach themselves from their original contexts and acquire a sometimes destructive measure of autonomy— as when the antimask statute was used against the Iranian protester. From a Pragmatist perspective, a more thoroughgoing skepticism about rule-based accounts of First Amendment law has been offered by Stanley Fish, in a now notorious essay entitled "There's No Such Thing as Free Speech and It's a Good Thing, Too." First, though, a caveat. Despite the arresting title (and some arresting turns of argument), Fish turns out to be no foe of free speech as it is conventionally understood. Indeed, he essentially endorses the balancing approach to First Amendment cases proposed by Judge Learned Hand (in *Dennis v. United States* [1950]), and, in the scheme of history, Judge Learned Hand has come to be regarded as one of the best friends the First Amendment ever had. "My rule of thumb is, 'Don't regulate unless you have to,'" Fish writes, though, as he recognizes, that simply defers the question about when you have to.[29]

Fish's central claim is that there are no final principles that will adjudicate First Amendment disputes, and that there is no avoiding a somewhat ad hoc balancing of interests. This is so because, despite our disclaimers, free speech is always justified in reference to goals (the only alternative would be to refuse to justify it at all) and so we will end up deciding hard cases by an assessment as to how well the contested speech subserves those goals. Moreover, this is so even for those theorists, like Ronald Dworkin, who justify freedom of expression not by its possible long-term benefits (which Dworkin considers to be too much a matter of conjecture to support our firm commitment to expressive freedom), but by a view of these rights (along with, say, the subsuming ideal of moral autonomy) as a constitutive element of a liberal society. Even deontological theories like Dworkin's—in which conformity to rules or rights, not good consequences, is what justifies action—are consequentialist, too, Fish argues: so long as they make exceptions to their vaunted rights for familiar consequentialist reasons (as in the event of clear and present danger), they are as fallen as the rest of us.

You will notice that Fish's argument essentially has the same form as the old and undoubtedly sexist joke (a joke recently adapted into a film starring Demi Moore and Robert Redford) about the man who asks a woman if she would sleep with him for a million dollars. She allows that she probably would. In that case, the man presses, would you sleep with me for $10? "What kind of a woman do you think I am?" she asks, indignant. "We've already established what kind of a woman you are," the retort comes. "Now we're just negotiating over the price."

So, yes, if you raise the stakes enough, it turns out that we are all whores—even the most chaste among us, even Demi Moore. And if you up the stakes enough, we are all consequentialists, too—even the most deontological among us, even Ronald Dworkin. Once Fish has exposed us, he won't allow us to keep our pretensions to chastity, or deontology, for pretensions are all they are. I am less demanding than he. I would allow that rights needn't be infinitely stringent, for they may conflict with other rights, and so in practice the whole affair will, as Fish does not miss, have an air of the ad hoc about it. But that doesn't mean that our principles and rules do not work, that they are merely subterfuge. Maybe there's a useful sense in which we are *not* all whores. Besides, isn't that all-or-nothing rhetoric at odds with the whatever-works eclecticism of Pragmatism at its best? The fact that First Amendment jurisprudence represents a hodgepodge of approaches, some of them at odds with each other, isn't necessarily a weakness.

Fish quotes Frederick Schauer criticizing the First Amendment for being an "ideology." But what's wrong with, and what's the alternative to, ideology? Granted, "ideology" is a pejorative term, somebody else's politics, as another old joke has it; but it's precisely as an ideology, which is only to say as an ideal that commands our public loyalties, that it has the beneficial effect that Fish himself commends: it functions as a brake on the overregulation of speech, even if it cannot present a permanent obstacle to it.

Where legal Pragmatists, mainstream scholars, and critical race theorists converge is in their affirmation of the balancing approach toward the First Amendment and in their corresponding skepticism toward what could be labeled the "Skokie school" of jurisprudence. When the American Civil Liberties Union defended the right of neo-Nazis to march in Skokie, a predominantly Jewish suburb of Chicago where a number of Holocaust survivors lived, they did so to protect and fortify the constitutional right at issue. Indeed, they may have reasoned, if a civil liberty can be tested and upheld in so odious an exercise of it, the precedent will make it that much stronger in all the less obnoxious cases where it may be disputed in the future. Hard cases harden laws.

But the strategy of the Skokie school relies on a number of presuppositions that critical legal theorists and others regard as doubtful. Most importantly, it revolves around the neutral operation of principle in judicial decision making. But what if judges really decided matters in a political, unprincipled way, and invoked principles only by way of window dressing? In cases close enough to require the Supreme Court to decide them, precedent and principle are elastic enough, or complex enough, that justices can often decide either way without brazenly contradicting themselves. And even if the justices want to make principled decisions, it may turn out that the facts of the case—in the real-world cases that come before them—are too various and complicated ever to be overdetermined by the rule of precedent, stare decisis. In either event, it could turn out that defending neo-Nazis was just . . . defending neo-Nazis. Moreover, it may be that the sort of formal liberties vouchsafed by this process aren't the sort of liberties we need most. Maybe we've been overly impressed by the frisson of defending bad people for good causes, when the good consequences may be at best conjectural and the bad ones are real and immediate. Maybe, these critics conclude, it's time to give up the pursuit of abstract principles and defend victims against victimizers, achieving results in the here-and-now, not the sweet hereafter.

Now, there's something to this position, but like the position it is meant to rebuff, it is overstated. Nadine Strossen, president of the American Civil Liberties Union, can show, for example, that the organization's winning First Amendment defense of the racist Father Terminiello in 1949 bore Fourteenth Amendment fruit when it was able to use the landmark *Terminiello* decision to defend the free speech rights of civil rights protestors in the sixties and seventies.[30] Granted, this may not constitute proof, an elusive thing in historical argument, but such cases provide good prima facie reason to think that the Skokie school has pragmatic justification, not just blind faith, on its side.

Another problem with the abandonment of principled adjudication is what it leaves in its wake, which is the case-by-case balancing of interests. My point isn't that "normal" First Amendment jurisprudence can or should completely eschew balancing; but there's a difference between resorting to it in extremis and employing it as the first and only approach. Now, in the case of racist invective, a balancing approach may be especially tempting, because the class of expression to be restricted seems so confined, while the harms with which it is associated can be vividly evoked. As Robert C. Post argues, however, this invitation to balance is best declined, because of what he terms "the fallacy of immaculate isolation."

> There is no shortage of powerful groups contending that uncivil speech within public discourse ought to be "minimally" regulated for highly pressing symbolic reasons. . . . In a large heterogeneous country populated by assertive

and conflicting groups, the logic of circumscribing public discourse to reduce political estrangement is virtually unstoppable.[31]

But there are other reasons to be chary about the application of balancing. For an unfettered regime of balancing simply admits too much to judicial inspection. What we miss when we dwell on the rarefied workings of high court decision making is the way in which laws exert their effects far lower down the legal food chain. It's been pointed out that when police arrest somebody for loitering or disorderly conduct, the experience of arrest—being hauled off to the station and fingerprinted before being released—very often *is* the punishment. Fighting words ordinances have lent themselves to similar abuse. Anthony D'Amato, a law professor at Northwestern University, makes a crucial and often overlooked point when he argues: "In some areas of law we do not want judges to decide cases at all—not justly or any other way. In these areas, the mere possibility of judicial decisionmaking exerts a chilling effect that can undermine what we want the law to achieve."[32]

But what if that chilling effect is precisely what the law is designed for? After all, one person's chill is another person's civility. In any event, it's clear that all manner of punitive speech regulations are meant to have effects far beyond the classic triad of deterrence, reform, and retribution.

VI

In fact, the main appeal of speech codes usually turns out to be primarily expressive or symbolic rather than consequential in nature. That is, their advocates do not depend on the claim that the statute will spare victim groups some foreseeable amount of psychic trauma. They say, rather, that by adopting such a statute, the university *expresses* its opposition to hate-speech and bigotry. More positively, the statute *symbolizes* our commitment to tolerance, to the creation of an educational environment where mutual colloquy and comity are preserved. (Of course, the symbolic dimension may be valued because of *its* consequences. Indeed, the conservative sociologist James Q. Wilson makes a parallel argument for the case of obscenity regulation when he writes of his "belief that human character is, in the long run, affected less by occasional furtive experiences than by whether society does or does not state that there is an important distinction between the loathsome and the decent.")

It is in this spirit that Matsuda writes: "A legal response to racist speech is a *statement* that victims of racism are valued members of our polity," and that "in a society that *expresses* its moral judgments through the law," the "absence of laws against racist speech is telling." It is in this spirit that Delgado suggests that a tort action for racist speech will have the effect of "*communicating* to the perpetrator and to society that such abuse will not be tolerated either by its victims or by the courts."[33] And it is in this spirit that Thomas Grey, the Stanford law professor who helped draft the campus speech regulations, counsels: "Authorities make the most effective statement when they are honestly concerned to do something *beyond* making a statement," thus "putting their money where their mouth is."[34] The punitive function of speech codes is thus enlisted to expressive means, as a means of bolstering the credibility of the antiracist statement.

And yet once we have admitted that the regulation of racist speech is, in part or whole, a symbolic act, we must register the force of the other symbolic considerations that may come into play. So, even if you think that the notion of free speech contains logical inconsistencies, you need to register the symbolic force of its further abridgment. And it is this level of scrutiny that may tip the balance in the other direction. The controversy over flag burning is a good illustration of the double-edged nature of symbolic arguments. Perhaps safeguarding the flag symbolized something nice, but, for many of us, safeguarding our freedom to burn the flag symbolized something nicer.

Note, too, the contradiction in the expressivist position I just reviewed: a university administration that merely condemns hate speech, without mobilizing punitive sanctions, is held to have done little, offering "mere words." Yet this skepticism about the potency of mere words comports oddly with the attempt to regulate mere words that, since they are spoken by those not in a position of authority, would seem to have even less symbolic force. Why is it mere words when a university only condemns racist speech, but not when the student utters the abusive words in the first place? Whose words are "only words"? Why are racist words deeds, but antiracist words just lip service?

Further, is the verbal situation as asymmetric as it first appears? Does the rebuke "racist" have no power to wound on a college campus? One of the cases that arose under the University of Michigan speech code involved a group discussion at the beginning of a dentistry class, in which the teacher, a black woman, sought to "identify concerns of students." A student reported that he had heard, from his roommate, who was a member of a minority group, that minority students had a hard time in the class and were not treated fairly. In response, the outraged teacher lodged a complaint against the student for having accused her (as she perceived it) of racism. For this black woman, at least, even an indirect accusation of racism apparently carried the brunt of racial stigmatization.

Still, I would insist that there is nothing unusual about the movement's emphasis on the expressive aspect of the law. "To listen to something on the assumption of the speaker's right to say it is to legitimate it," the conservative legal philosopher Alexander Bickel told us. "Where nothing is unspeakable, nothing is undoable."[35] And I think there's an important point of convergence there: Bickel's precept that to "listen to something on the assumption of the speaker's right to say it is to legitimate it" underlies much of the contemporary resistance to unregulated expression on campus and elsewhere. For the flip side of the view that hate speech ordinances are necessary to express sincere opposition to hate speech is the view—which recurs in much of the literature on the subject—that to tolerate racist expression is effectively to endorse it: the Bickel principle. Thus "government protection of the right of the Klan to exist publicly and to spread a racist message promotes the role of the Klan as a legitimizer of racism," Matsuda writes. For his part, Lawrence seems to suggest that merely to defend civil liberties on campus may be to "valorize bigotry."[36]

Like many other positions identified with the hate speech movement, the thesis that toleration equals endorsement is not as radical as it first appears. In fact, this is precisely the position elaborated by Lord Patrick Devlin in 1965, in his famous attack on the Wolfenden Report's recommendation to decriminalize homosexual behavior in Britain. "If society has the right to make a judgment," he wrote, "then society may use the law to preserve morality in the same way as it uses it to safeguard anything else that is essential to its existence." On this basis, he argued, "society has a prima facie right to legislate against immorality as such."[37] In Lord Devlin's account, as in Matsuda's, the law expresses the moral judgment of society; to countenance things that affront public morality is thus a betrayal of its purpose.

Of course, Matsuda's belief that the government that protects the rights of the Klan also promotes its views would have many surprising consequences if taken seriously. One might conclude that the government that provided civic services to the 1992 March on Washington was solidly behind the cause of gay rights. Or that in giving police protection to several of the Reverend Sharpton's marches in New York, it was lending its moral support to the cause of black resistance. Or that in providing services to the Wigstock festivities in Tompkins Square Park, it was plumping for transvestism. Or that in policing both rallies in favor of abortion and those opposed, it was somehow supporting both positions. One might, but of course one wouldn't. And since, in the scheme of things, policing Klan marches commands a tiny fraction of the state's resources—less, I would surmise, than do such African-American events as Caribbean Day parades—our worries on this score seem misplaced.

One final paradox fissures the hate speech movement. Because these scholars wish to show that substantial restrictions on racist speech are consistent with the Constitution, they must make the case that racist speech is sui generis among offensive or injurious utterances; otherwise the domain of unprotected speech would mushroom beyond the point of constitutional and political plausibility. The title of Delgado's trailblazing essay and of the collection, "Words That Wound," designates a category that includes but is scarcely exhausted by racist speech. Nor could we maintain that racist insults, which tend to be generic, are necessarily more wounding than an insult tailor-made to hurt someone: being jeered at for your acne, or obesity, may be far more hurtful than being jeered at for your race or religion.

So clearly the level of emotional distress associated with racist abuse cannot be its distinguishing characteristic; what must be distinguishing is its connection to systemic patterns of subordination. (Even so, there are other such patterns of subordination. "Racism is a breach of the ideal of egalitarianism, that 'all men are created equal' and each person is an equal moral agent, an ideal that is a cornerstone of the American moral and legal system," writes Delgado. "A society in which some members regularly are subjected to degradation because of their race hardly exemplifies this ideal."[38] But racism isn't the only reason people are subjected to degradation: what about shortcomings in appearance or intelligence, traits that, like race, we can do little about?)

Scholars like Mari Matsuda, Charles Lawrence, and Richard Delgado argue that racist speech is peculiarly deserving of curtailment precisely because it participates in (and is at least partly constitutive of) the larger structures of racism hegemonic in our society. "Black folks know that no racial incident is 'isolated' in the United States," writes Lawrence. "That is what makes the incidents so horrible, so scary. It is the knowledge that they are *not* the isolated unpopular speech of a dissident few that makes them so frightening. These incidents are manifestations of an ubiquitous and deeply ingrained cultural belief system, an American way of life."[39]

What Matsuda annexes to this consideration is the further argument that what distinguishes racist speech from other forms of unpopular speech is "the universal acceptance of the wrongness of the doctrine of racial supremacy." Unlike Marxist speech, say, racist speech is "universally condemned."[40] At first blush, this is a surprising claim. After all, if it *were* universally rejected, hate speech ordinances would be an exercise in antiquarianism. And yet there is something in what Matsuda says: at the very least, it bespeaks a shared conviction about the weight of the antiracist consensus, the conviction that at least overt racists are an unpopular minority, and that authority is likely to side with *us* against *them*. In truth, this conviction provides the hidden foundation for the hate speech movement. Why would you entrust authority with enlarged powers of regulating the speech of unpopular minorities, unless you were confident the unpopular minorities would be racists, not blacks? Lawrence may know that racial incidents are never "isolated," but he must also believe them to be less than wholly systemic. You don't go to the teacher to complain about the school bully if he's the teacher's son.

Critical race theory's implicit confidence in the antiracist consensus also enables its critique of neutral principles, as becomes clear when one considers the best arguments in favor of such principles. Thus, David Cole, a law professor at Georgetown University, suggests that,

> In a democratic society the only speech government is likely to succeed in regulating will be that of the politically marginalized. If an idea is sufficiently popular, a representative government will lack the political wherewithal to suppress it, irrespective of the First Amendment. But if an idea is unpopular, the only thing that may protect it from the majority is a strong constitutional norm of content neutrality.[41]

Reverse his assumptions about whose speech is marginalized and you can stand this argument on its head. If blatantly racist speech is unpopular and stigmatized, a strong constitutional norm of content neutrality may be its best hope for protection: and for critical race theory, that's a damning argument *against* content neutrality.

Here, then, is the political ambiguity that haunts the new academic activism. "Our colleagues of color, struggling to carry the multiple burdens of token representative, role model, and change agent in increasingly hostile environments, needed to know that the institutions in which they worked stood behind them," the critical race theory manifesto informs us.[42] *Needed to know that the institutions in which they worked stood behind them:* I have difficulty imagining that this sentiment could have been expressed by their activist counterparts in the sixties, who defined themselves through their adversarial relation to authority and its institutions. And that is the crucial difference this time around. Today, the aim is not to resist power but to enlist power.

"Critical race theory challenges ahistoricism and insists on a contextual/ historical analysis of the law," the critical race theory manifesto instructs us.[43] It is not a bad principle. But what it suggests to me is that we get down to cases and consider, as critical race theorists do not, the actual results of various regimes of hate speech regulation.

Matsuda, surveying United Nations conventions urging the criminalization of racist hate speech, bemoans the fact that the United States, out of First Amendment scruple, has declined fully to endorse such resolutions. By contrast, she commends to our attention states such as Canada and the United Kingdom. Canada's appeal to the hate speech movement is obvious. After all, the new Canadian Bill of Rights has not (as she observes) been allowed to interfere with its national statutes governing hate propaganda. What's more, Canada's Supreme Court has recently adopted MacKinnon's statutory definition of pornography as the law of the land.

What you don't hear from the hate speech theorists is that the first casualty of the MacKinnonite anti-obscenity ruling was a gay and lesbian bookshop in Toronto, which was raided by the police because of a lesbian magazine it carried. (Homosexual literature is a frequent target of Canada's restrictions on free expression.) Nor are they likely to mention that just this past June, copies of a book widely assigned in women's studies courses, *Black Looks: Race and Representation,* by the well-known black feminist scholar bell hooks, were confiscated by Canadian authorities as possible "hate literature." Is the Canadian system really our beacon of hope?

Even more perplexing—especially given the stated imperative to challenge ahistoricism and attend to context—is the nomination of Britain as an exemplar of a more enlightened free-speech jurisprudence. Does anyone believe that racism has subsided in Britain since the adoption of the 1965 Race Relations Act forbidding racial defamation? Or that the legal climate in that country is more conducive to searching political debate? Ask any British newspaperman about that. When Harry Evans, then editor of the London *Times,* famously proclaimed that the British press was, by comparison to ours, only "half-free," he was not exaggerating by much. The result of Britain's judicial climate is to make the country a net importer of libel suits launched by tycoons who are displeased with their biographers. By now, everyone knows that a British libel suit offers all the conveniences of a Reno divorce.

Is the British approach to the regulation and punishment of speech really an advance on ours? Ask the editors of the *New Statesman & Observer,* whose continued existence was put in jeopardy after Prime Minister John Major sued the publication for mentioning, though not endorsing, the rumor that he was having an affair with a caterer. (Depending how you interpret the facts in the case, it may be that I, and the publisher of this volume, have just repeated the tortious offense.) Nor (in line with the Canadian example) has the British penchant for singling out gay publications for punishment escaped notice. Ask the editors of *Oz,* who discovered that the lesbian imagery on their cover represented a punishable offense. Ask the editors of the magazine *Gay News,* who were convicted for "blasphemous libel" when they published a poem involving a homosexual fantasy about Christ and received jail sentences (later suspended). Ask the owner of Gay's the Word bookshop in London, found guilty of "conspiring to import indecent and obscene material" in 1984. For that matter, ask Jenny White, who was prosecuted for privately purchasing American-made lesbian videos in 1991. The mordant irony is that American progressives should propose Britain, and its underdeveloped protection of expression, as a model to emulate at a time when many progressives in Britain are agitating for a bill of rights and broader First Amendment-style protections. To be sure, Britain has its attractions—scones, tea, cucumber sandwiches. But the jurisprudence of free speech isn't among them.

Nor is the record of U.K. student groups to be preferred. Nadine Strossen has pointed out the ironic history of a resolution adopted by the British National Union of Students in 1974, to the effect that representatives of "openly racist and fascist organizations" were to be kept from speaking on college campuses by "whatever means necessary (including disruption of the meeting)."[44] It was a measure taken against groups like the National Front. But when, in the wake of the UN resolution, some British students designated Zionism a form of racism, the rule was invoked against Israelis, including Israel's ambassador to the United Kingdom—a turn of events that came much to the delight of the National Front.

To her credit, Matsuda is up front about the sort of difficulties likely to arise in her regime of criminalization. In a section called "Hard Cases," she considers the hard case of Zionism and decides that some forms of Zionist expression—those expressed in "reaction to historical persecution"—are to receive protection, while other forms, which participate in the sort of "white supremacy" that some identify as intrinsic to the Middle East conflict, will not. She adds that "the various subordinated communities" are best equipped to identify such victimizing hate speech.[45] In other words, the Palestinian is best equipped to decide whether and when the Zionist's speech should be criminalized. (It is unclear whether the Zionist can return the favor.)

And what of speech codes on American campuses? The record may surprise some advocates of hate speech regulations. "When the ACLU enters the debate by challenging the University of Michigan's efforts to provide a safe harbor for its Black, Latino, and Asian students," Lawrence writes, "we should not be surprised that nonwhite students feel abandoned."[46] In light of the actual record of enforcement, you may view the situation differently. During the year in which Michigan's speech code was enforced, more than twenty blacks were charged—by whites—with racist speech. As Strossen notes, not a single instance of white racist speech was punished. (Lawrence's talk of a "safe harbor" sounds more wishful than informed.) A full disciplinary hearing was conducted only in the case of a black social work student who was charged with saying, in a class discussion of research projects, that he believed that homosexuality was an illness, and that he was developing a social work approach to move homosexuals toward heterosexuality. ("These charges will haunt me for the rest of my life," the black student claimed in a court affidavit.)

By my lights, this is a good example of how speech codes kill critique. I think that the student's views about homosexuality (which may or may not have been well-intentioned) are both widespread and unlikely to survive close intellectual scrutiny. Regrettably, we have not yet achieved a public consensus in this country on the moral legitimacy (or, more precisely, moral indifference) of homosexuality. Yet it may well be that a class on social work is not an inappropriate forum for a rational discussion of why the disease model of sexual difference has lost credibility among social scientists. (This isn't PC brainwashing, either; in a class on social work, this is simply education.) But you cannot begin to conduct this conversation when you outlaw the expression of the view you would critique.

Critical race theorists are fond of the ideal of conversation. "This chapter attempts to begin a conversation about the first amendment," Matsuda writes toward the end of her contribution. "Most important, we must continue this discussion," Lawrence writes toward the end of his.[47] It is too easy to lose sight of the fact that the conversation to which they're devoted is aimed at limiting conversation; and that if there are costs to speech, there are costs, as well, to curtailing speech, often unpredictable ones.

Our homophobic social work student may have been one of its casualties. As the legal philosopher David A. J. Richards contends: "It is a vicious political fallacy of the right and the left to assume that our contempt for false evaluative opinions may justly be transferred to contempt for the persons who conscientiously hold and express such views. Such persons are not, as it were, beyond the civilizing community of humane discourse."[48] Or as Samuel Johnson, who crafted an art out of words that wound, admonishes, "punishment is able only to silence, not to confute."

We should be clear that speech codes may be far more narrowly tailored, and the Stanford rules—carefully drafted by scholars, like the Stanford law professor Thomas Grey, with civil libertarian sympathies—have, justly, been taken as a model of such careful delimitation. For rather than following the arguments against racist speech to their natural conclusion, the Stanford rules prohibit only insulting expression that conveys "direct and visceral hatred or contempt" for people on the basis of their sex, race, color, handicap, religion, sexual orientation, or national and ethnic origin, and that is "addressed directly to the individual or individuals whom it insults or stigmatizes."

Though the Stanford rules have since been invalidated by a lower-court decision, the chances are that the Stanford rules wouldn't have done much harm, if any. The chances are, too, that they wouldn't have done much good, if any. As long as the eminently reasonable Professor Grey is drafting and enforcing such restrictions, I won't lose much sleep over it either way. But we should also be clear how inadequate the code is as a response to the powerful arguments that were marshaled to support it.

Contrast the following two statements addressed to a black freshman at Stanford.

(A) LeVon, if you find yourself struggling in your classes here, you should realize it isn't your fault. It's simply that you're the beneficiary of a disruptive policy of affirmative action that places underqualified, underprepared, and often undertalented black students in demanding educational environments like this one. The policy's egalitarian aims may be well-intentioned, but given the fact that aptitude tests place African-Americans almost a full standard deviation below the mean, even controlling for socioeconomic disparities, they are also profoundly misguided. The truth is, you probably don't belong here, and your college experience will be a long downhill slide.

(B) Out of my face, jungle bunny.

Surely there is no doubt which is likely to be more "wounding" and alienating to its intended audience. Under the Stanford speech regulations, however, the first is protected speech; the second may well not be, a result that makes a mockery of the words-that-wound rationale. If you really want to penalize such wounding words, it makes no sense to single out gutter epithets—which, on many college campuses, to be candid, are more likely to stigmatize the speaker than their intended victim—and leave the far more painful disquisition alone.

Taking the expressivist tack, Thomas Grey argues that punitive sanctions are useful because they shore up salutary symbolism: "When a university administration backs its antiracist pronouncements with action, it puts its money where its mouth is."[49] It's a punchy metaphor, and the implication is that, by adopting these regulations, his university has put itself on the line, taken measures that may extract real costs from it. In fact, this is a pretty costless trade. It's safe to say that Stanford's faculty and administration, however benighted or enlightened they may be on racial matters, manage nicely without the face-to-face deployment of naughty epithets. In adopting the regulations, therefore, they sacrifice nothing but the occasional drunken undergraduate. "Putting your money where your mouth is" may bolster your credibility; but whose money is it, really?

A rule of thumb: in American society today, the real power commanded by the racist is likely to vary inversely with the vulgarity with which it is expressed. Black professionals soon learn that it is the socially disenfranchised—the lower-class, the homeless—who are most likely to hail them as "niggers." The circles of power have long since switched to a vocabulary of indirection. Unfortunately, those who pit the First Amendment against the Fourteenth invite us to spend more time worrying about speech codes than coded speech.

I suspect that many of those liberals who supported Stanford's restrictions on abusive language did so because they thought it was the civil thing to do. Few imagined that, say, the graduation rates or GPAs of Stanford's blacks (or Asians, gays, etc.) are likely to rise significantly as a result. Few imagined, that is, that the restrictions would lead to substantive rights or minority empowerment. They just believed that gutter epithets violate the sort of civility that ought to prevail on campus. In all likelihood, the considerations that prevailed owed more to Emily Post than to Robert Post. In spirit, then, the new regulations were little different from the rules about curfews, drinking, or the after-hours presence of women in male dormitories that once governed America's campuses and preoccupied their disciplinary committees.

Not that civility rules are without value. Lawrence charges that civil libertarians who disagree with him about speech regulations may be "unconscious racists." I don't doubt this is so; I don't doubt that some of those who *support* speech codes are unconscious racists. What I doubt is that the imputation of racism is the most effective way to advance the debate between civil rights and civil liberties.

IX

"What is ultimately at stake in this debate is our vision for this society,"[50] write the authors of *Words That Wound,* and they are quite right. The risk, in parsing the reasoning of the hate speech movement, is of missing the civic forest for the legal trees. For beyond the wrangling over particular statutes and codes lies an encompassing vision of state and civil society. Moreover, it is one whose wellsprings are to be found not in legal scholarship or theory but in the much more powerful cultural currents identified with the "recovery movement." At the vital center of the hate speech movement is the seductive vision of the therapeutic state.

We can see this vision clearly presaged in the critical race theory manifesto itself:

> Too often victims of hate speech find themselves without the words to articulate what they see, feel, and know. In the absence of theory and analysis that give them a diagnosis and a name for the injury they have suffered, they internalize the injury done them and are rendered silent in the face of continuing injury. Critical race theory names the injury and identifies its origins.[51]

This sounds, of course, like a popular primer on how psychotherapy is supposed to work, and, with a few changes, the passage might be from a book addressed to survivors of toxic parenting. Indeed, "alexathymia"—the inability to name and articulate one's feelings—is a faddish diagnosis within psychiatry these days. Nor is the affinity that critical race theory shares with the currently booming recovery industry a matter of fortuity, for at present the recovery movement is perhaps the principal countertrend to an older and now much-beleaguered American tradition of individualism.

"When ideology is deconstructed and injury is named, subordinated victims find their voices," we are told in the manifesto. "They discover they are not alone in their subordination. They are empowered."[52] Here the recovery/survivor-group paradigm does lead to a puzzling contradiction: we are told that victims of racist speech are cured—that is, empowered—when they learn they are "not alone" in their subordination, but are subordinated as a group. Elsewhere we are told that what makes racist speech peculiarly wounding is that it conveys precisely that content, that you are a member of a subordinated group. How can the message of group subordination be both poison and antidote?

The therapeutic claims made for critical race theory cut against the hate speech offensive in more important ways. For if we took these claims at face value, critical race theory would not buttress speech regulations but obviate the need for them. The problem Lawrence worries about—that racist speech "silences members of those groups who are its targets"[53]—would naturally be addressed not through bureaucratic regulations, but through the sort of deconstruction and critique that critical race theory promises will enable victims to "find their voices." Another painful irony: this all sounds very much like Justice Brandeis's hoary and much-scorned prescription for redressing harmful speech: more speech.

Yet while scholars like Delgado and Matsuda emphasize the adverse psychological effects of racial abuse, the proposed therapeutic regime is no mere talking cure. Delgado writes: "Because they constantly hear racist messages, minority children, not surprisingly, come to question their competence, intelligence, and worth." But in the Republic of Self-Esteem, we are invited to conceive the lawsuit as therapy. "When victimized by racist language, victims must be able to threaten and institute legal action, thereby relieving the sense of helplessness that leads to psychological harm."[54]

A similar therapeutic function could be played by criminal proceedings in Matsuda's view. When the government does nothing about racist speech, she argues, it actually causes a second injury. "The second injury is the pain of knowing that the government provides no remedy and offers no recognition of the dehumanizing experience that victims of hate propaganda are subjected to." In fact, "the government's denial of personhood through its denial of legal recourse may even be more painful than the initial act of hatred."[55] Of course, what this grievance presupposes is that the state is there, in loco parentis, to confer personhood in the first place.

What Matsuda has recourse to, finally, is not an instrumental conception of the state, but rather a conception of the state as the "official embodiment of the society we live in," and, as such, it is rather remote and abstracted from the realities of our heterogeneous populace, with so many conflicting norms and values. Perhaps that is only to say that psychotherapy cannot do the hard work of politics. But a similar therapeutic vision animates the more broad-gauged campus regulations, like those adopted in the late 1980s at the University of Connecticut. Its rules sought to proscribe such behavior as, inter alia:

Treating people differently solely because they are in some way different from the majority.

Imitating stereotypes in speech or mannerisms.

Attributing objections to any of the above actions to "hypersensitivity" of the targeted individual or group.

The last provision was especially cunning. It meant that even if you believed a complainant was overreacting to an innocuous remark, to try to defend yourself in this way would only serve as proof of your guilt. But the rationale of the university's rules was made explicit in its general prohibition on actions that undermined the "security or self-esteem" of persons or groups. (Would awarding low grades count?) Not surprisingly, the university's expressed objective was to provide "a positive environment in which everyone feels comfortable working or living." It was unclear whether any provisions were to be made for those who did not feel "comfortable" working or living under such restrictive regulations; in any event, the regulations were later dropped under threat of legal action.

Still, perhaps the widespread skepticism about any real divide between public and private made it inevitable that the recovery movement would translate into a politics, and that this politics would center on a vocabulary of trauma and abuse, one in which their verbal and physical varieties are seen as equivalent. Perhaps it was inevitable that the Citizen at the center of classical Enlightenment political theory would be replaced by the Infant at the center of modern depth psychology and its popular therapeutic variants. The inner child may hurt and grieve, as we have been advised; is it also to vote?

X

But there are older ideas of civil society in conflict within the hate speech debate. To oversimplify, critical race theory sees a society composed of groups; moral primacy is conferred upon those collectivities whose equal treatment and protection ought to be guaranteed under law. (Having established the primacy of the group, it can then distinguish between dominant and subordinate groups.) The classic civil libertarian view, by contrast, sees a society composed of individuals, who possess rights only as public citizens, whatever other collective allegiances they may entertain privately. Individualism has its weaknesses, to be sure. Part of what we value most about ourselves as individuals often turns out to be a collective attribute—our religious or racial identity, say. And when we are discriminated against, it is as a member of a group. Nor does the implicit model of voluntarism work well for ethnic, sexual, racial, or religious identities, identities about which we may have little say. There is something unsatisfactory in a legal approach that treats being a black woman as analogous to being a stamp collector.

And yet the very importance of these social identities underscores one of the most potent arguments for an individualist approach toward the First Amendment. In a recent book, *Constitutional Domains: Democracy, Community, Management,* Robert C. Post has examined just such issues as they relate to an emerging conception of public discourse. "One is not born a woman," Simone de Beauvoir famously avowed, and her point can be extended: the meaning of all our social identities is mutable and constantly evolving, the product of articulation, contestation, and negotiation.

Indeed, these are circumstances to which critical race theorists ought to be more attuned than most. Thus Lawrence approvingly quotes MacKinnon's observation that "to the extent that pornography succeeds in constructing social reality, it becomes invisible as harm." He concludes: "This truth about gender discrimination is equally true of racism."[56] And yet to speak of the social construction of reality is already to give up the very idea of "getting it right." When Lawrence refers to "the continuing real-life struggle through which we define the community in which we live," he identifies a major function of unfettered debate, but does so, incongruously, by way of proposing to shrink its domain. To remove the very formation of our identities from the messy realm of contestation and debate is an elemental, not incidental, truncation of the ideal of public discourse. And so we must return to MacKinnon's correct insistence on "the rather obvious reality that groups are made up of individuals."[57]

Now, as Post (citing the work of Charles Taylor) has observed, the neutrality of individualism is only relative. The autonomous moral agent of liberal society requires the entrenchment of a political culture conducive to that identity. Even though the strong tendency in legal culture is to overcriminalize and overregulate, the preservation of a broadly democratic polity entails that there will be, and must be, limits, and establishing them will involve political considerations. Thus Post writes, in a penetrating analysis of the Supreme Court decision in *Falwell v. Hustler:* "The ultimate fact of ideological regulation . . . cannot be blinked. In the end, therefore, there can be no final account of the boundaries of the domain of public discourse."[58]

So perhaps the most powerful arguments of all for the regulation of hate speech come from those who maintain that such regulation will really enhance the diversity and range of public discourse. At their boldest, these arguments cast free speech and hate speech as antagonists, such that public discourse is robbed and weakened by the silencing and exclusionary effects of racist speech. Restricting hate speech actually increases the circulation of speech, the argument runs, by defending the speech rights of victim-groups whom such abuse would otherwise silence. And so the purging of racist speech from the body politic is proposed as a curative technique akin to the suction cups and leeches of eighteenth-century medicine, which were meant to strengthen the patient by draining off excessive toxins.

Needless to say, the question of the safety and efficacy of the treatment is an open one. And, as Post points out, the "question of whether public discourse is irretrievably damaged by racist speech must itself ultimately be addressed through the medium of public discourse."

> Because those participating in public discourse will not themselves have been silenced (almost by definition), a heavy, frustrating burden is de facto placed on those who would truncate public discourse in order to save it. They must represent themselves as "speaking for" those who have been deprived of their voice. But the negative space of that silence reigns inscrutable, neither confirming nor denying this claim. And the more eloquent the appeal, the less compelling the claim, for the more accessible public discourse will then appear to exactly the perspectives racist speech is said to repress.[59]

The larger question—the political question—is how we came to decide that our energies were best directed not at strengthening our position in the field of public discourse, but at trying to move its boundary posts.

XI

So I want to return to the puzzling disalignment with which I began. The struggle with racism has traditionally been waged through language, not against it; the tumult of the civil rights era was sponsored by an expansive vision of the First Amendment, a vision to which the struggle against racism in turn lent its moral prestige. And it is this concrete history and context that makes it so perplexing that a new generation of activists—avowedly sensitive to history and context—should choose the First Amendment as a battlefield in their fight for Fourteenth Amendment guarantees.

I detect two motivations for the shift, one that relates to the academy and one that relates to the world outside it. In a trend we've already touched upon, there has been increased attention on the formative power of language in the creation of our social reality—on language as "performative," as itself constituting a "speech act." While these are phrases and ideas that the ordinary language philosopher J. L. Austin developed in midcentury, MacKinnon adds them to her argumentative arsenal in her latest book. The notion of the speech act has new force when the act in question is rape.

Now MacKinnon's emphasis on the realness, the act-like nature, of expression receives an interesting twist in the attempt by some hate speech theorists to "textualize" the Fourteenth Amendment. For if expression is act, then act must be expression. If the First Amendment is about speech, so, too, is the Fourteenth Amendment. It is in line with this reasoning that Lawrence has proposed—in an influential and admired reinterpretation of legal history—that *Brown v. Board of Education* and, on analogy, all subsequent civil rights decisions and legislation are in fact prohibitions on expressive behavior, forbidding not racism per se but the expression of racism. In line with this argument, he tells us that "discriminatory conduct is not racist unless it also conveys the message of white supremacy," thus contributing to the social construction of racism.[60]

This is a bold and unsettling claim, which commits Lawrence to the view that where discriminatory conduct is concerned, the only crime is to get caught. By this logic, racial redlining by bankers isn't racist unless people find out about it. And the crusading district attorney who uncovers previously hidden evidence of such discrimination isn't to be hailed as a friend of justice, after all: by bringing it to light, he was only activating the racist potential of those misdeeds. Lawrence's analysis of segregation reaches the same surprising conclusion: "The nonspeech elements are by-products of the main message rather than the message being simply a by-product of unlawful conduct."[61] By this logic, poverty is really about the *message* of class inequality rather than material deprivation. We might conclude, then, that the problem of economic inequality would most naturally be redressed by promulgating a self-affirmative lower-class identity along the lines of Poverty Is Beautiful. Words may not be cheap, but they must be less costly than AFDC and job training programs.

Something, let us agree, has gone very wrong here. In arguments of this sort, the pendulum has swung from the absurd position that words don't matter to the equally absurd position that *only* words matter. Critical race theory, it appears, has fallen under the sway of a species of academic nominalism. Yes, speech is a species of action. Yes, there are some acts that only speech can perform. But there are some acts that speech alone cannot accomplish. You cannot heal the sick by pronouncing them well. You cannot uplift the poor by declaring them to be rich.

In their joint manifesto, the authors of *Words That Wound* identify theirs as "a fight for a constitutional community where 'freedom' does not implicate a right to degrade and humiliate another human being."[62] These are heady words, but like much sweepingly utopian rhetoric, they also suggest a regime so heavily policed as to be incompatible with democracy. Once we are forbidden to degrade and humiliate, will we retain the moral autonomy to elevate and affirm?

In the end, the preference for the substantive liberties supposedly vouchsafed by the Fourteenth Amendment to the exclusion of the formal ones enshrined in the First Amendment rehearses without learning from the classic disjunction that Isaiah Berlin analyzed in his "Two Concepts of Liberty." His words have aged little since 1958. "Negative" liberty, the simple freedom from external coercion, seemed to him

> a truer and more humane ideal than the goals of those who seek in the great, disciplined, authoritarian structures the ideal of "positive" self-mastery by classes, or peoples, or the whole of mankind. It is truer, because it does, at least, recognize the fact that human goals are many, not all of them commensurable, and in perpetual rivalry with one another.[63]

More to the point, to suggest, as Lawrence and his fellow critical race theorists do, that equality must precede liberty is simply to jettison the latter without securing the former. The First Amendment will not, true enough, secure us substantive liberties, but neither will its abrogation. No one has come close to showing that First Amendment liberties are so costly that they significantly impede our chance of securing the equal protection guarantees of the Fourteenth Amendment. You cannot get the Fourteenth Amendment through the First, to be sure; but no one has persuaded me yet that you cannot have both.

Still, it isn't hard to explain the disenchantment among minority critics with such liberal mainstays as the "marketplace of ideas" and the ideal of public discourse. In the end, I take it to be an extension of a larger crisis of faith. The civil rights era witnessed the development of a national consensus—something hammered out noisily, and against significant resistance, to be sure—that racism, at least overt racism, was wrong. Amazingly enough, things like reason, argumentation, and moral suasion *did* play a significant role in changing attitudes toward "race relations." But what have they done for us lately?

For all his robust good sense, Harry Kalven Jr. was spectacularly wrong when he wrote: "One is tempted to say that it will be a sign that the Negro problem has basically been solved when the Negro begins to worry about group-libel protection."[64] On the contrary, the disillusionment with liberal ideology rampant among many minority scholars and activists stems from the lack of progress in the struggle for racial equality over the past fifteen years. Liberalism's core principle of formal equity seems to have led us so far, but no farther. It "put the vampire back in its coffin, but it was no silver stake," as Patricia J. Williams notes.[65] The problem may be that the continuing economic and material inequality between black and white America— and, more pointedly, the continuing immiseration of large segments of black America—cannot be erased simply through better racial attitudes. The problem, further, may be that in some ways we intellectuals have not yet caught up to this changing reality. It isn't only generals who are prone to fight the last war.

As analysts on the Left and Right alike have shown, poverty, white and black, can take on a life of its own, to the point that removing the conditions that caused it can do little to alleviate it. The eighties may have been the "Cosby Decade," as some declared, but you wouldn't know it from the South Bronx. What's become clear is that the political economy of race and poverty can no longer be reduced to a mirror of what whites think of blacks. But rather than responding by forging new and subtler modes of socioeconomic analysis, we have finessed the gap between rhetoric and reality by coming up with new and subtler definitions of the word "racism." Hence the new model of institutional racism—often just called racism—is one that can operate in the absence of actual racists. By progressively redefining our terms, we could always say of the economic gap between black and white America: the problem is still racism—and, by stipulation, it would be true.

But the grip of this vocabulary has tended to foreclose the more sophisticated and multivariate models of political economy we so desperately need. I cannot otherwise explain why some of our brightest legal minds believe that substantive liberties can be vouchsafed and substantive inequities redressed by punishing rude remarks. Or why their analysis of racism owes more to the totalizing theory of Catharine MacKinnon than to the work of scholar-investigators like Douglas Massey or William Julius Wilson or Gary Orfield—people who, whatever their disagreements, at least attempt to find out how things work in the real world, never confusing the empirical with the merely anecdotal.

Instead, critical theory is often allowed to serve as a labor-saving device.

For if racism can be fully textualized, if its real existence is in its articulation, then racial inequity can be prized free from the moss and soil of political economy. "Gender is sexual," MacKinnon told us in *Toward a Feminist Theory of the State*. "Pornography constitutes the meaning of that sexuality."[66] By extension, racist speech must prove to be the real content of racial subordination: banish it, and you banish subordination. The perverse result is a see-no-evil, hear-no-evil approach toward racial inequality. Alas, even if hate did disappear, aggregative patterns of segregation and segmentation in housing and employment would not. Conversely, in the absence of this material and economic gap, no one would much care about racist speech.

Beliefs cannot prosper that go untested and unchallenged. The critical race theorists must be credited with helping to reinvigorate the debate about freedom of expression; even if not ultimately persuaded to join them, the civil libertarian will be much further along for having listened to their arguments and examples. The intelligence, innovation, and thoughtfulness of their best work ask for and deserve a reasoned response, not, as so often happens, demonization and dismissal. And yet for all the passion and scholarship the critical race theorists have expended upon the hate speech movement, I cannot believe it will capture their attention for very much longer.

"It is strange how rapidly things change," Kalven wrote in 1965. "Just a little more than a decade ago we were all concerned with devising legal controls for the libeling of groups. . . . Ironically, once the victory was won, the momentum for such legal measures seemed to dissipate, and the problem has all but disappeared from view."[67] It *is* strange how rapidly things change—and change back. Still, I suspect the results will be similar this time around: advocates of speech restrictions will grow disenchanted not with their failures, but their victories, and the movement will come to seem just another curious byway in the long history of our racial desperation.

And yet it will not have been without its political costs. I cannot put it better than Lawrence himself, who writes: "I fear that by framing the debate as we have—as one in which the liberty of free speech is in conflict with the elimination of racism—we have advanced the cause of racial oppression and placed the bigot on the moral high ground, fanning the rising flames of racism."[68] Though he does not intend it as such, I can only read this as a harsh rebuke to the hate speech movement itself. As the critical race theory manifesto acknowledges, "this debate has deeply divided the liberal civil rights/civil liberties community"; and so it has. It has created hostility between old and fast allies and fissured longtime coalitions.

Somewhere along the way, I fear, we have lost touch with the Pragmatists' sturdily earthbound question: Was it worth it? For while the temporal benefits of its victories are at best conjectural, the political damage to the already fragile liberal alliance is apparent in the here-and-now. Meanwhile, Justice Hugo Black's sardonic words of dissent return to us like a tocsin: "Another such victory and I am undone."

NOTES

1. Catharine A. MacKinnon, *Only Words* (Cambridge, Mass.: Harvard University Press, 1993), pp. 76–77.

2. Mari J. Matsuda et al., *Words That Wound: Critical Race Theory, Assaultive Speech, and the First Amendment* (Boulder, Colo.: Westview Press, 1993), p. 4. The collection also reprints a provocative essay by UCLA's Kimberlè Williams Crenshaw, though one whose principal concerns—the conflicting allegiances posed by race and gender—place it beyond the ambit of this discussion.

3. See John Hart Ely, *Democracy and Distrust: A Theory of Judicial Review* (Cambridge, Mass.: Harvard University Press, 1980), p. 113 n.

4. Frederick Schauer, "Categories and the First Amendment: A Play in Three Acts," *Vanderbilt Law Review* 34 (1981): 270.

5. *Gitlow v. New York,* 268 US 652, 673 (1925).

6. *Chaplinsky v. New Hampshire,* 315 US 568, 572 (1942).

7. Matsuda et al., *Words That Wound,* p. 74.

8. Ibid., pp. 24, 92.

9. Ibid., pp. 68, 66.

10. "The Demise of the *Chaplinsky* Fighting Words Doctrine: An Argument for Its Interment," *Harvard Law Review* 106 (March 1993): 1129–46.

11. See *Lewis v. City of New Orleans* 408 US 913 (1972) and 415 US 130, 131 n. 1 (1974).

12. Kenneth Karst, "Equality As a Central Principle in the First Amendment," *University of Chicago Law Review* 43 (1975): 38.

13. Matsuda et al., *Words That Wound,* pp. 68, 9.

14. Ibid., p. 8.

15. See Patricia J. Williams, *The Alchemy of Race and Rights* (Cambridge, Mass.: Harvard University Press, 1991), pp. 98–130.

16. Matsuda et al., *Words That Wound,* pp. 107, 75.

17. *Beauharnais v. Illinois,* 434 US 250, 258 (1952).

18. Ibid., p. 275.

19. MacKinnon, *Only Words,* pp. 82, 51–52.

20. Respondent's Brief, *Beauharnais v. Illinois,* quoted in ibid., p. 131 n. 29.

21. See David Riesman, "Democracy and Defamation: Control of Group Libel," *Columbia University Law Review* 42 (1942): 727–80.

22. Matsuda et al., *Words That Wound,* p. 47.

23. Ibid., pp. 75, 65; emphasis added.

24. Ibid., p. 75.

25. Ibid., p. 100.

26. Ibid., p. 46.

27. Ibid., p. 36.

28. Ibid.

29. Stanley Fish, *There's No Such Thing as Free Speech and It's a Good Thing, Too* (New York: Oxford University Press, 1994), p. 130.

30. See Nadine Strossen, "Regulating Racist Speech on Campus: A Modest Proposal?" *Duke University Law Journal* (1990): 484–573.

31. Robert C. Post, *Constitutional Domains: Democracy, Community, Management* (Cambridge, Mass.: Harvard University Press, 1995), p. 322.

32. Anthony D'Amato, "Harmful Speech and the Culture of Indeterminacy," *William and Mary Law Review* 32 (1991): 331.

33. Matsuda et al., *Words That Wound*, pp. 18, 49, 95; emphasis added.

34. Thomas C. Grey, "Civil Rights vs. Civil Liberties: The Case of Discriminatory Verbal Harassment," *Social Philosophy and Policy* 8 (Spring 1991): 105.

35. Alexander Bickel, *The Morality of Consent* (New Haven, Conn.: Yale University Press, 1975), p. 75.

36. Matsuda et al., *Words That Wound*, pp. 49, 86.

37. Patrick Devlin, *The Enforcement of Morals* (London: Oxford University Press, 1965), p. 11.

38. Matsuda et al., *Words That Wound*, pp. 92–93.

39. Ibid., p. 74.

40. Ibid., p. 37.

41. David Cole, "Neutral Standards and Racist Speech," *Reconstruction* 2 (1992): 68.

42. Matsuda et al., *Words That Wound*, p. 7.

43. Ibid., p. 6.

44. Strossen, "Regulating Racist Speech," p. 557.

45. Matsuda et al., *Words That Wound*, p. 40.

46. Ibid., p. 86.

47. Ibid., pp. 50, 87.

48. David A. J. Richards, *Toleration and the Constitution* (New York: Oxford University Press, 1986), p. 192.

49. Grey, "Civil Rights vs. Civil Liberties," p. 105.

50. Matsuda et al., *Words That Wound*, p. 15.

51. Ibid., p. 13.

52. Ibid.

53. Ibid., p. 79.

54. Ibid., p. 95.

55. Ibid., p. 49.

56. Ibid., p. 62.

57. MacKinnon, *Only Words*, p. 82.

58. Post, *Constitutional Domains*, p. 177.

59. Ibid., pp. 317–18.

60. Matsuda et al., *Words That Wound*, p. 62.

61. Ibid., p. 60.

62. Ibid., p. 15.

63. Isaiah Berlin, *Four Essays on Liberty* (New York: Oxford University Press, 1969), p. 171.

64. Harry Kalven Jr., *The Negro and the First Amendment* (Chicago: University of Chicago Press, 1966), p. 11.

65. Williams, *The Alchemy of Race and Rights,* p. 120.

66. Catharine A. MacKinnon, *Toward a Feminist Theory of the State* (Cambridge, Mass.: Harvard University Press, 1989), p. 197.

67. Kalven, *The Negro and the First Amendment,* p. 7.

68. Matsuda et al., *Words That Wound,* p. 57.

SIX

Academic Freedom as an
Ethical Practice

Joan W. Scott

Fairly early in my life I began to learn about academic freedom. It was a complicated lesson. In my family, academic freedom was an unquestioned ideal, a matter of principle invoked repeatedly throughout the difficult years of the 1950s and early 1960s. At the same time, I had good reason to be skeptical of the power of the ideal, for I knew that it could be violated in practice. My father was a New York City high school teacher, suspended in 1951 (when I was 10) and fired in 1953 for refusing to cooperate first with a congressional committee, and then with the superintendent of schools, on their investigations into communist activity among teachers. Although formally tenured according to the rules of the board of education, my father lost his job because, in that moment of the early Cold War, his refusal to discuss his political beliefs and affiliations was taken as evidence that he was a communist and therefore unfit to teach. This despite the fact that he was a devoted fan of Thomas Jefferson, the Bill of Rights, and the Constitution, and that his students and their parents testified to the ways in which his history classes deepened their appreciation of American democracy.

In the tallying of losses he experienced in that period—his job, his pension, his financial security, many colleagues he had once considered friends—none was so painful as the loss of his academic freedom. At the same time, the existence of the principle was something he could hold on to, a right that was still his and to which he could appeal. I remember wondering why he cared so much about a principle that had failed to protect him from an arbitrary exercise of political power, but I also understood that the principle had some tangible existence for him independent of its ability to bring about the effects it was designed to secure.

Writing in 1955, Fritz Machlup, then of Johns Hopkins University, argued that academic freedom became a reality only when some scholars, having been accused of "abusing" their academic freedom, were nonetheless protected from those seeking to punish them for their presumed offenses. "When these pressures and temptations to interfere are resisted and the offenders are assured of their immunity, then, and only then, is academic freedom shown to be a reality. Thus, the occurrences of so-called abuses of academic freedom, far from being incompatible with the existence of academic freedom, are the only proofs of its existence."[1] In my father's case, the situation was the reverse: having failed to protect him from "these pressures and temptations to interfere," academic freedom existed nonetheless. Indeed, it was precisely in its loss that the abstract principle acquired concrete reality. And it was in the name of the defense of and subsequent pursuit of this lost object that my father justified his "insubordinate" behavior at the board of education, and sustained his moral outrage and his sense of righteous indignation at the betrayal represented by his treatment (and that of the some 350 other New York City schoolteachers who were forced out in those years). I can now say that academic freedom functioned as an "ethics" for my father, in the way Michel de Certeau has defined it. "Ethics," he writes, "is articulated through effective operations, and it defines a distance between what is and what ought to be. The distance designates a space where we have something to do."[2]

One of the confusing things about "academic freedom" for me in that period was that there was more than one meaning, indeed there were contradictory meanings, to be found for the term. My father understood academic freedom as an individual teacher's or scholar's right not to be judged by any criteria but the quality of his teaching or scholarship. Others thought that academic freedom pertained only to the actual pursuit of scholarly inquiry, protecting from outside interference only those who actually espoused unpopular or unorthodox views in writing or in the classroom. The board of education had yet another definition. It sometimes argued that in order to protect the autonomy of the teaching establishment from "outside" interference, it had to clean its own house by purging politically suspect teachers. In this definition, the greater good of the profession required the sacrifice of its most unconventional or troublesome members. All sides in this confrontation insisted that academic freedom had only one meaning and that that meaning was absolute.

In fact, I think that the concept of academic freedom carries many meanings (the defense of individual rights of inquiry, of unpopular ideas, and corporate autonomy), and that these meanings are (and have been) developed differently in different relationships of power and in different historical circumstances. Although in 1951 my vocabulary didn't include the notion either of paradox or ambiguity, I think they are what I was observing. Academic freedom, like any notion of freedom or rights, is (in the words of political theorist Wendy Brown) "neither a philosophical absolute nor a tangible entity, but a relational and contextual practice that takes shape in opposition to whatever is locally and ideologically conceived as unfreedom."[3] At the same time, its idiom is necessarily ahistorical and acontextual; indeed it is precisely because "academic freedom" is thought to stand outside specific political contexts, as a universal principle, that it can be invoked as a check on specific abuses of power. This tension between academic freedom as a historically circumscribed relationship and an enduring universal ideal cannot be resolved; it is what gives the concept its ethical and practical force. The effort to resolve the tension by insisting on only one true definition is to engage in an exercise of dogmatism that can only disarm the concept it purports to defend. By dogmatism I mean the claim to be authorized by some immutable truth or reality which can entertain no legitimate objection to itself, and to then impose laws—to determine inclusions and exclusions—in the name of that truth or reality.[4]

To acknowledge the inherent internal contradiction and the historical variability of a principle is not to give up on the possibility of making judgments. I have no difficulty condemning the board of education's actions, and not only because my father's dismissal profoundly affected my life. My condemnation is an interpretation of a set of circumstances in which, it seems to me, political hysteria substituted for reasoned action, no evidence of subversive activity—in or outside the classroom—was ever produced, and those most in need of protection (the political dissenters) were systematically denied it. When weighed against the harm done to an individual in this instance, arguments for the protection of corporate autonomy seem weak, if not beside the point (though I concede that, in other instances, different conclusions might be drawn). The point is that, although academic freedom is a principle, its content is never clear-cut. Specific cases are always complex and, as those of us who sit through the long meetings of Committee A (the AAUP committee charged with investigating violations of academic freedom) learn firsthand, they always involve contestation: differences of interpretation and therefore debate about what has happened and why. It is the debate about cases (and provisional agreement that allows for adjudication) that articulates historical meanings for academic freedom. This debate is the "effective operation" that takes place in the space "between what is and what ought to be" and so constitutes another example of what de Certeau means by "ethics."

If, as I have argued, the power of academic freedom lies precisely in the ambiguity of its existence as a universal principle and as a historically circumscribed relationship—in the distance between what ought to be and what is—and if dogmatism is the great threat to academic freedom because it seeks to banish ambiguity by appealing to absolute truth, we are not rid of the threat for having pointed it out. For the problem of dogmatism is not external to academic freedom but is another of those ambiguities at the very heart of the concept. Academic freedom protects those whose thinking challenges orthodoxy; at the same time the legitimacy of the challenge— the proof that the critic is not a madman or a crank—is secured by membership in a disciplinary community based upon shared commitment to certain methods, standards, and beliefs. While that commitment doesn't force agreement at every level of practice, it does resist assaults on its fundamental premises (in my field a reflective acceptance of a certain notion of "history" as the empirical object of study) and in this way functions as orthodoxy. The critic of orthodoxy thus, ironically, must find legitimation in the very discipline whose orthodoxy he or she challenges.

Let me illustrate this point a bit more. Academic freedom has meant (at least in this century and in this country) protection for the critical function of scholars and teachers who believed they were attempting to advance knowledge by calling into question widely held or accepted beliefs. This questioning, moreover, is not trivial or superficial, it is fundamental. It introduces ideas which are "unassimilable," which cannot be integrated into a prevailing corpus.[5] While Galileo was the archetypical example of this kind of unassimilable idea in the narrative of scientific progress, twentieth-century commentators worried more about protecting the expression of scholars in fields which could not make a full claim to scientific standing. Thus John Dewey, in his (from our end-of-the-century perspective) remarkably prescient 1902 essay "Academic Freedom," pointed to the lower scientific status of "the social and psychological disciplines and to some phases of linguistic and historical study—those most intimately associated with religious history and literature."[6] Scholars in these fields needed "the utmost freedom of investigation," he suggested, because they dealt more closely than technical scientists with "the problems of life," and were thus more likely to come up against "deep-rooted prejudice and intense emotional reaction": "These exist because of the habits and modes of life to which the people have accustomed themselves. To attack them is to appear to be hostile to institutions in which the worth of life is bound up."[7]

Dewey asserted, on the one hand, that academic freedom would result in the "advance" of these fields, but he also recognized, on the other, that they might remain "partial sciences," lacking the detachment and technical mastery that at once guaranteed popular acceptance of the authority of physics and chemistry and confined those fields to "problems of technical theory." (Because of debates about evolution, biology was still in a "transitional" state.) The urgency of social needs could not be met by technicians; Dewey thought that specialization, however scientific its allure, meant withdrawal from "the larger issues of life." It was a kind of privatization, the opposite of public action. To the mastery of science, Dewey counterposed the "virility" of social engagement. (Here masculinity marked public as opposed to private action.) Specialization, he insisted, posed an "immediate danger to courage, and the freedom that can only come from courage."

> Teaching, in any case, is something of a protected industry; it is sheltered. The teacher is set somewhat one side [*sic*] from the incidence of the most violent stresses and strains of life. His problems are largely intellectual, not moral; his associates are largely immature. There is always the danger of a teacher's losing something of the virility that comes from having to face and wrestle with economic and political problems on equal terms with competitors. Specialization unfortunately increases these dangers. It leads the individual, if he follows it unreservedly, into bypaths still further off from the highway where men, struggling together, develop strength. The insidious conviction that certain matters of fundamental import to humanity are none of my concern because outside of my *Fach,* is likely to work more harm to genuine freedom of academic work than any fancied dread of interference from a moneyed benefactor.[8]

The ideas that underlay men's virile struggles with economic and political problems could not claim the same kind of objectivity that technical science did. For this reason Dewey suggested that "the problem of academic freedom becomes to a very large extent a personal matter," involving the "style" and "manner" of an individual's presentation—things which could not easily be regulated and which were, moreover, not necessarily an indicator of the seriousness of a scholar's teaching.

Whenever scientific method is only partially attained the danger of undue dogmatism and of partisanship is very great. It is possible to consecrate ideas born of sheer partisanship with the halo of scientifically established belief. It is possible to state what is currently recognized to be scientific truth in such a way as to violate the most sacred beliefs of a large number of our fellow-men. The manner of conveying the truth may cause an irritation quite foreign to its own substance. This is quite likely to be the case whenever the negative rather than the positive aspect is dwelt upon; wherever the discrepancy between the new truth and established institutions is emphasized, rather than the intrinsic significance of the new conception. The outcome is disintegrating instead of constructive; and the methods inevitably breed distrust and antagonism.[9]

If polemic could be disguised as science, and science mistaken for partisanship, on what basis could the reliability of a professor's pronouncements be ascertained? Dewey cited University of Chicago president William Rainey Harper's 1900 convocation address as an answer. In addition to refraining from sensationalism and political partisanship in the classroom, Harper insisted that scholars restrict their expressions to their areas of competence, and refrain from promulgating as truth "ideas or opinions which have not been tested scientifically by . . . colleagues in the same department of research or investigation."[10] This notion of a disciplinary community of researchers held great promise for Dewey and he came back to it at the end of his essay. Such a community, he thought, would "solidify and reinforce otherwise scattered and casual efforts" of individual scholars and give them the courage to resist pressures, internal to the university, that dampened the autonomy needed for the pursuit of truth. Disciplinary communities (Dewey called them "scientific associations") were the guarantee both of the independence of the individual scholar in an increasingly centralized and oligarchic university, and of the integrity of his work. They were "an immediate resource counteracting the dangers threatening academic freedom."[11]

For Dewey, as for later commentators, the disciplinary community provided support for the individual, verifying his or her technical expertise and qualifications. Indeed, it was that communal self-regulation based in a certain expertise that made academic freedom different from other notions of individual rights. But there was little acknowledgment that there was also a tension between the regulatory authority of a disciplinary community and the autonomy of its individual members, that discipline was necessarily exclusionary and that that might mean that scholarly critique could be threatened from within. "Corporate scientific consciousness" Dewey defined glowingly as "the sense of the solidarity of truth. Whatever wounds the body of truth in one of its members attacks the whole organism."[12] Defining "academic freedom" in the 1937 edition of the *Encyclopedia of the Social Sciences,* Arthur Lovejoy also stressed the advantages for an individual scholar of subsumption in a disciplinary community. The individual scholar, he pointed out, checked by "qualified bodies of his own profession," was enabled to stand up against outside interference from "political or ecclesiastical authority, or from the administrative officials of the institution in which he is employed."[13] In the 1968 edition of the *International Encyclopedia of the Social Sciences,* Glenn Morrow developed the idea even further. The condition for the advance of knowledge, he wrote, rested on the impossibility of ever finally establishing the truth of a truth claim.

> Even after prolonged examination and testing, the claim can be accorded only a high degree of probability; and its status is never immune to later criticism. These conditions imply a community of scholars and scientists cooperating with one another through mutual criticism and selecting and recruiting new members through disciplined and systematic training. These very requirements tended to produce such a community, animated by a professional spirit and resentful of any attempts by incompetent outside authorities to control its activities or judge its results.[14]

Here academic freedom rests on the protection afforded individuals by their disciplines against "incompetent outside authorities." What is ignored is the possible conflict between "mutual criticism" and the selection of new members "through disciplined and systematic training." Morrow, like Dewey, makes the correction of error, argument about interpretation, and the "approval and disapproval" of peers an entirely positive dimension of scholarly activity. But the inseparable other side of that regulatory and enabling authority is that it secures consensus by exclusion. And the grounds for exclusion can be, historically have been, *difference*—difference from some representative type (John Dewey's "virile"—and I would add white—male, for example, as the prototypical social scientist or humanist) or difference from the reigning philosophical and methodological assumptions (about causality, say, or intentionality, or the transparency of fact in the writing of history).

The ambiguity of discipline is unavoidable: the institution of the discipline, which protects the academic freedom of individuals, also operates to deny some of them that freedom. Put in other terms, discipline is at once productive—it permits the organization of knowledge and it authorizes knowledge producers—and confining—it installs explicit and tacit normative standards which, when they are understood to be provisional, can serve important mediating functions, but which, when they are taken as dogmatic precepts, become instruments of punishment. The two aspects cannot be disentangled; discipline functions in a necessarily paradoxical way.

That freedom and subjection are two sides of the same coin is not a new insight, but it bears repeating at a time when the whole issue of disciplinarity has been thrown open to question by epistemological challenges to disciplinary foundations, and by debates about the politics of knowledge and the relationship between the pursuit of knowledge and contemporary political concerns. These debates date at least to the 1960s, a time of enormous expansion of universities and the beginnings of the diversification of their faculties and student bodies, and of the politicization of university life by the Vietnam War. In that context, the question of the "relevance" of disciplinary authority was repeatedly posed. I remember long arguments with fellow graduate students at the University of Wisconsin about whether "history from the bottom up" was the only socially responsible history to write and about whether, indeed, one could justify one's desire for graduate training at all.[15] In the end, most of us got degrees and became university teachers, accepting the need for discipline even as we hoped to make our history more relevant by overturning canonical teachings and exposing their (conservative) foundational premises. Without discipline, there was no way to articulate the problematics that concerned us, no historical frame within which to pose our questions and search for answers, no structure in terms of which (and against which) fundamental critical challenges could be posed. Disciplines carried with them a whole intellectual history of contest about the legitimacy of questions and the frameworks for answering them and so provided the conditions of possibility for their own critical transformation. They also provided the conditions of possibility for interdisciplinarity—at its best the use of articulated structures of inquiry to address problems in new or different domains.

If there is a more intense "crisis" today than when I was a graduate student, it has to do with the suppression of the intellectual history of disciplines (and their portrayal as increasingly refined techniques or methodologies) and the attempt to resolve the necessary tension between discipline and critical challenge by forcing a choice between them. The extreme polarization of opinion about the role disciplines ought to play in the organization of academic knowledge is everywhere apparent: in the debates about the status of canonical and noncanonical texts, about the truth of competing historical narratives, about the relevance of the standpoint or identity or personal experience of the speaker to the authority of his or her knowledge, about the relationship between freedom of expression and the exercise of power, about the place of interdisciplinary programs in the curriculum, and about the uses and abuses of scholarly authority (including its erotic aspects) for classroom pedagogy.[16] Discipline usually figures in these debates either as that which must be restored in its most dogmatic form—foundational assumptions are taken to have fixed, enduring, and inherent value—or as that which must be exposed as the mask of oppressive power and replaced by a more emancipatory politics whose authority is based in personal experience. Discipline is either fetishized as immutable or rejected as an instrument of repression.

In this polarized atmosphere there is no middle ground; that is the reason the "culture wars" metaphor is so apt. The positions are not only entrenched and mutually exclusive, making reconciliation or persuasion impossible, they are also characterized by intense moralism. Moralism is an expression of resentment and anger; it is hope gone sour and analysis that has lost its bearings. It individualizes social problems, blaming those who would point them out for having caused them in the first place. And moralism, as Wendy Brown has so skillfully described it, "tends to be intensely antagonistic toward . . . a richly agonistic political or intellectual life. . . . The identity of the moralist is . . . staked against intellectual inquiry which might tear up the foundations of its own premises; its survival is imperilled by the very practice of open-ended intellectual inquiry."[17] As moralism gains the day, so does dogmatism, and the basis for academic freedom is seriously undermined. This is because dogmatism insists that its truths are immune to criticism or change. Dogmatism denies the need that scholars have to pursue a logic of inquiry wherever it might lead.

As examples, there is, on the one hand, the furious assault on, indeed the demonization of, those challenging disciplinary premises as "postmodernists."[18] As if postmodernists were the cause of all the problems of disciplinary uncertainty scholars are now facing; as if their banishment would end the questions about difference posed by demographic changes in university populations, by the emergence of postcolonial critiques of colonial assumptions, by developments in the history of philosophy that reach back to at least the nineteenth century, by the more recent end of the Cold War, and by the extraordinary economic constraints of the last years. The attack on so-called postmodernists as Nazi sympathizers, communists, nihilists, and moral relativists is revealing for the way in which it politicizes contests about knowledge. It makes the presumed political implications of one's scholarly ideas, not the ideas themselves, the ultimate ground for exclusion. The deflection of the issue not only offers a political test for what is being defended as objective knowledge, it also precludes serious discussion of the more difficult philosophical matters that are at stake. This refusal to engage serious philosophical critique, moreover, plays into anti-intellectual currents in the society at large and thus into the hands of those attacking the university from outside (whether the attacks come in the form of congressional scrutiny or massive defunding).

The virulent attack being waged on postmodernists is only one example of the way upholders of orthodoxy seek to bar from the field critics of foundational disciplinary premises. By denying these critics the legitimacy that disciplinary membership confers, such attacks preclude claims by them that their academic freedom has been violated. Ironically, the tables are sometimes turned as the defenders of orthodoxy invoke the protection of academic freedom against internal critics as if the critics were outsiders, effectively banishing them. (In a recent instance, a conservative author who received a negative book review claimed that her academic freedom had been violated by the reviewer, depicted as an outsider, who was in fact a scholar with expertise on the subject matter of the book but who held a different political position from her own.)[19] The point is that boundaries of inclusion and exclusion are being rigidly drawn, not only to deal with current critics but to warn future generations of the high price of apostasy. It is dogmatism in action.

On the other hand, there are the critics of orthodoxy who blame the mistreatment of minorities both in the curriculum and in the society at large on the oppressive influence of disciplinary authority. Thus, in a recent article in the *Chronicle of Higher Education,* a white literary critic, replying to charges by African-American women that her color disqualified her from writing about novels like Toni Morrison's *Beloved,* argued that it was not color that was the problem but the disciplinary training that had supplied her with "the tricks of textual mastery." By attempting to "master" texts with rigorous theoretical analyses "constructed by white male critics," she thought women such as herself were unthinkingly reenacting the subjugation and the oppressive domination of blacks by whites. As an alternative, she urged white women to disavow "mastery" and write about their emotional responses to the text. The goal ought to be to "focus more on pondering the way our historical, cultural, and personal identities connect" with stories such as *Beloved*. This "pondering" happens best without external direction; in this way personal emotional experience substitutes for disciplinary authority.[20] The practice as well as the purpose of reading texts is reduced to a process of self-discovery that seems to me not only to contradict the author's stated political aim of understanding and respecting difference but also to end the need for education, conceived as the training of minds and the imparting of new knowledge to them. In place of her disciplinary expertise, the teacher has the certainty of her political beliefs. What authority she has in her classroom rests on her dogmatic assertion of those beliefs and her expectation that they ought to be shared by her students. When that is not the case, there is no protection from the charge that she is "silencing" the opinions of some of her dissenting students, no way to prove that her criticisms of their work have not denied them freedom of speech. The invocation of "academic freedom" in what may be speech cases, but certainly are not academic freedom cases (as when students claim violation of *their* academic freedom because the teacher disagreed with their opinions), testifies to the weakening, if not the disappearance, of the idea of disciplinary legitimation for classroom pedagogy.

Despite their opposition to one another, these two examples (the attack on postmodernism and the attack on disciplinarity) both represent attempts to build community—in one case a disciplinary community, in the other a political community—on a foundation of immutable truth.[21] The proponents of disciplinary orthodoxy take for granted the enduring value—the fixed truth—of their discipline's current epistemological foundations. For historians now this is the idea that history is an empirical object that can be studied more or less objectively. Interpretation of specific events such as the French Revolution may vary as may attributions of causality, but consensus about the existence of "history" as a discoverable sequence of events with a correct interpretation is taken to be the ground of membership in the community of historians. Some historians, otherwise students of ineluctable change, have inconsistently resisted the idea that this concept of history could change (although, as the intellectual history of the field shows, it has in the past). They prophesy anarchy as the very least of the consequences that will follow from even engaging with philosophical critiques of "history." Israel, to paraphrase Peter Novick's anguished cry, will lose its king.[22]

An important strain of opposition to disciplinarity bases its community on the shared belief that knowledge is instrumental politics.[23] This is a very different position from the one that says that there is a politics that is a set of historically specific institutional, ideological, and personal contests, necessarily associated with the production of knowledge. The instrumentalist view is far more reductive, conflating the politics of knowledge with politics in general, so that, for example, an expansion of the literary canon is seen as a direct political empowerment of previously excluded persons, or the overthrow of the idea of objectivity is seen as crucial to the advancement of women. Although literary canons and strong claims to objectivity may indeed be related to the entrenchment of white male privilege, it is not at all clear that there is a direct relationship between them. At the very least, the histories of canons and of objectivity are also disciplinary histories that cannot be reduced to simple morality tales about power and politics. When they are, when there is assumed to be a one-to-one correspondence between thought and its political impact, scholarly differences are inevitably taken to be political differences; those who think this is not the case are considered naive or complicit, enemies because they stand outside the consensus on which the community of righteousness must be based.[24]

In the standoff between these two communities, the functions of discipline and criticism are separated from one another; the one is reduced to dogmatic policing of standards and norms, the other limited to political advocacy. Their interaction is precluded, even as the existence of each is predicated on the exclusion of the other. And yet it is precisely the interaction of discipline and criticism—the necessary contests between them—that, ideally, academic freedom mediates. This is the reason, I would submit, for the current sense of crisis felt by those committed to the ethical practice that is academic freedom.

Since disciplines are often referred to as "communities of the competent," it is worthwhile trying to think about the two terms—discipline and community—together, specifically about whether the dogmatic form I have been describing is the only one available. I don't think it is, but I also think that elaborating an alternative requires something more than pious nods to pluralism and tolerance.

Communities assume some kind of consensus and thus are necessarily exclusionary; discipline separates the trained from the untrained. Disciplinary communities consist of people who agree to follow a certain set of rules in order to be trained. The key to thinking about nonorthodox disciplinary communities may lie not in the abandonment of these rules but in the clarification of how the rules are conceived: whether they are considered immutable, whether they are thought to implement a set of fixed beliefs, whether they countenance the kinds of contests that would lead to their own transformation.

If we think of communities and disciplines not as common essences, not as bodies of people who are the same (whether that sameness comes from shared identity or from shared belief in metaphysical truth), but as provisional entities called into being to organize relations of difference, then standards and rules become heuristic practices around which argument is expected and change anticipated.[25] What disciplinary communities share, in this view of them, is a common commitment to the autonomous pursuit of knowledge and a common agreement that such pursuit requires regulation. It might be better to say here that what is pursued is not truth or even knowledge (both of which imply some settled package of uncontestable information), but understanding (which retains the notion that there is something to be known that is apart from the scholar, and at the same time conveys the idea that interpretation always structures what is known).[26]

Disciplinary communities, then, share a common commitment to the autonomous pursuit of understanding, which they both limit and make possible by articulating, contesting, and revising the rules of such pursuits and the standards by which outcomes will be judged. (Understanding, after all, requires the same rigor and must be subjected to the same evaluation as knowledge; it is not based entirely on empathy or experience.) The problem of exclusion doesn't disappear from this more provisional notion of a disciplinary community, but its functional and arbitrary nature are clearly recognized. This recognition insists on a place for criticism and critical transformation at the very heart of the conception of a discipline and so guarantees the existence of that scholarly critical function that discipline is meant to legitimate and that academic freedom is designed to protect.

But what is the practical relationship of academic freedom to this conception of a discipline? Can academic freedom protect from the tendency to orthodoxy within a discipline the critical function on which it most depends? What role does a claim of academic freedom have in mediating relations between defenders and critics of orthodoxy on matters of the quality of work or the granting of tenure? Is academic freedom useful only as a protection against interference from outside the discipline, from government agencies, trustees, administrators, affirmative action officers, and sexual harassment counselors? Or can it be deployed to settle intradisciplinary conflicts? The answers are difficult and not clear-cut, intensifying the sense of crisis occasioned by the current tendency to equate discipline with orthodoxy and criticism with politics.

On the one hand, Committee A is on record as having rejected the idea that belief in the governing principles of a profession or discipline ought to be a condition of employment. In 1985 it stated clearly that academic freedom must protect even those deemed "nihilists" by their colleagues for their skepticism about the very foundations of the discipline.

> In many instances a show of disrespect for a discipline is, at the very same time, an expression of dissent from the prevailing doctrines of that discipline. There is more than a sonant connection between respectfulness and respectability; there is no wide gap between respectability and ideological conventionalism. Thus, while a litmus test of belief in the worth of a subject as a minimum qualification for appointment to a position where one is expected to teach it or teach about it may seem modest in the abstract, on reflection it may prove to be very mistaken; it may end by barring those most likely to have remade the field.

The report concluded this way:

> It is not merely that the long history of academic freedom teaches that charges of irreverence can readily serve as covers to objections to unorthodoxy; rather, it is that it is all but impossible to extenuate the one without abetting the other.[27]

As a statement of principle, this 1985 document suggests broad scope for academic freedom in mediating disciplinary disputes. But, in practice, Committee A has not treated all exercises, or even abuses, of disciplinary power (the granting of tenure, for example, or the decision to substitute one methodological or interpretive approach for another, or the phasing in or out of whole areas of study) as violations of academic freedom. This is because such intervention would bring questions of individual scholarly rights into arenas where they do not belong, arenas where the collective political battles that implement and challenge hierarchy, and so effect disciplinary change, must be waged. Even though these are exactly the battles which may constitute (racial, gender, ethnic, religious, epistemological) difference as an implicit ground for hierarchy, and in that way limit a scholar's freedom, they cannot be said to violate academic freedom. For to analyze disciplinary power only in terms of academic freedom is to reduce complex structural and intellectual processes (that must be analyzed and engaged with as such) to questions of individual rights. One may impinge on the other, but they cannot be addressed or remedied in the same way. So, paradoxically, if academic freedom is to remain an effective protection for individual critical scholarly inquiry, it cannot be invoked in most of the battles about the rules and standards that underwrite the individual scholar's open-ended pursuit of understanding. In the collective process that articulates disciplinary power, academic freedom is not usually the most appropriate intervention.

And yet, of course, there are always the gray areas that must be interpreted, that cannot be decided in advance (the negative tenure case that does violate academic freedom, for example). For that reason, it seems to me, academic freedom must include substantive, not just procedural judgments. Academic freedom is committed to an ideal of the unfettered pursuit of understanding that exists beyond structures of inequality or domination, yet it always addresses concrete situations (within disciplines and between scholars and "outsiders") that involve difference and power. At its best, academic freedom doesn't simply monitor such situations for the exercise of due process (although due process is a necessary condition for the unfettered pursuit of understanding), but intervenes to point out the ways in which certain (but not all) of the practices that enforce exclusions interfere with an individual's ability to pursue his or her inquiry wherever it leads. The adjudicatory function of academic freedom is to decide, in the context of specific cases, which are and which aren't violations. By imagining autonomy to be an individual right, academic freedom attempts to negotiate the necessarily relational and conflictual nature of the actual pursuit of understanding. Strategically, academic freedom endorses an ideal of scholarly activity that is blind to power in order to be able to see how power is abused in particular cases and whether those abuses constitute violations of academic freedom. Blindness and insight are thus crucially interdependent, enabling the kind of critical specificity that separates ethics from dogma.

Academic freedom lives in the ethical space between an ideal of the autonomous pursuit of understanding and the specific historical, institutional, and political realities that limit such pursuits. Its existence recognizes the complexity and necessary conflict that inhere in the activities of so-called truth seekers, and the dangers that follow from consolidation around any particular truth (including an idea of truth itself). Academic freedom can never be boiled down to an essence; it is instead an ethical practice aimed not only at the protection of individuals, but at (what Dewey and his associates thought of as) the advancement of our collective well-being.

At this moment in our history cynicism seems to have become the national ethos, a result at least in part of the loss of belief in the master narrative of progress that once sustained my father in his principled refusal to compromise his rights.[28] One symptom of this loss is, I would suggest, an enormous outpouring of nostalgia for the substantive values of family, decency, "standards of excellence," morality, commonality, and truth. The cure for the seemingly insoluble problems of the present is thought to be a return to a past in which meanings were self-evident and universally shared, a past, in other words, that is dogmatically conceived.

The problems we confront *are* tremendously difficult: an increasing imbalance in the distribution of economic resources nationally and globally, an increasing impotency of citizens in the political sphere, an inability to negotiate the seemingly irreducible differences among contending groups in the society. But the answer does not consist in the infusion of "values" into the national psyche. Along that path lies the elimination of enemies and the enforcement of orthodoxy, the end of history and the final solution. The insistence on a return to "values" precludes precisely what is probably the only answer we have: a notion of ethical practice. While "values" represent closed meanings, "ethical practice" is an operation open to change. In de Certeau's definition with which I began this essay, the effective operation of ethics "defines a distance between what is and what ought to be. This distance designates a space where we have something to do." That distance is the open space of history. Not the history of grand teleological promises, but the history that inscribes time as the embodiment of changing human relationships, changing in relation to a changing set of ideals that are as elusive in practice as they are practical in their effects.

It may be self-serving, or at least entirely predictable, for a historian to offer history as the best way to think about academic freedom. But that is what I want to do. I will be forgiven, perhaps, if I say that I am not offering prevailing professional sentiment, but that I speak as a critic embattled within her own field.

Academic freedom is a tense mediation of relationships, an imperfect contest about issues that can never be totally resolved. As such, it is a commitment to time and to history. With it, we are not always spared the punishment that orthodoxy metes out to its critics; without it, the critical function of scholarship and the possibility it represents for change would be lost. Academic freedom, then, is both a guarantor and an exemplification of the ethical practice that constitutes history, the relentless striving to close the distance between what is and what ought to be.

NOTES

I wish to thank Wendy Brown, Judith Butler, Stefan Collini, Christopher Fynsk, Peter Galison, Tony Scott, and the members of the Twentieth Century Seminar at the CUNY Graduate Center for their critical suggestions.

1. Fritz Machlup, "On Some Misconceptions Concerning Academic Freedom" (1955), in Louis Joughin, ed., *Academic Freedom and Tenure: A Handbook of the American Association of University Professors* (Madison: University of Wisconsin Press, 1969), p. 192.

2. Michel de Certeau, "History: Science and Fiction," in *Heterologies: Discourse on the Other,* trans. Brian Massumi (Minneapolis: University of Minnesota Press, 1986), p. 199.

3. Wendy Brown, "Introduction," *States of Injury: Studies in Power and Freedom in Late Modernity* (Princeton, N.J.: Princeton University Press, 1995), p. 6.

4. See de Certeau, "History: Science and Fiction," p. 199.

5. William Haver, "Après moi le Deleuze: The Question of Practice" (n.p., 1992), p. 29.

6. John Dewey, "Academic Freedom," in *John Dewey: The Middle Works, 1899–1924* (Carbondale: Southern Illinois University Press, 1976), 2:56.

7. Ibid., 2:58.

8. Ibid., 2:64.

9. Ibid., 2:59.

10. Ibid., 2:60.

11. Ibid., 2:65–66.

12. Ibid., 2:66.

13. Arthur O. Lovejoy, "Academic Freedom," *Encyclopedia of the Social Sciences,* ed. E. R. A. Seligman (New York: Macmillan, 1937), 1:384–87, quote from p. 384.

14. Glenn Morrow, "Academic Freedom," *International Encyclopedia of the Social Sciences,* ed. David L. Sills (New York: Macmillan and The Free Press, 1968), 1:4–9, quote from pp. 5–6.

15. On the question of "relevance," see Jesse Lemisch, "Radical Scholarship as Scientific Method and Anti-Authoritarianism, Not 'Relevance,'" *New University Conference Papers* 2 (1970). See also the discussion of the debates in this period in Peter Novick, *That Noble Dream: The "Objectivity Question" and the American Historical Profession* (New York: Cambridge University Press, 1988), pp. 415–68. See also Bruce Robbins, *Secular Vocations: Intellectuals, Professionalism, Culture* (London: Verso, 1993), esp. pp. 80–83.

16. On the erotic component of pedagogy, see Jane Gallop, "Sex and Sexism: Feminism and Harassment Policy," *Academe* 80 (September/October 1994): 16–23.

17. Wendy Brown, "Toward a Genealogy of Contemporary Political Moralism," in *Democracy, Community, Citizenship,* ed. Tom Keenan and Kendall Thomas (London: Verso, 1995).

18. For examples of this kind of "postmodernist" bashing, see Joyce Appleby, Lynn Hunt, and Margaret Jacob, *Telling the Truth about History* (New York: Norton, 1994), and Paul R. Gross and Norman Levitt, *Higher Superstition: The Academic Left and Its Quarrels with Science* (Baltimore: Johns Hopkins University Press, 1994).

19. On this, see the symposium on "Who Stole Feminism?" by Christina Hoff Sommers, a special issue of *Democratic Culture* (the newsletter of Teachers for a Democratic Culture), vol. 3 (Fall 1994). The articles by Nina Auerbach, "Christina's World," and Rebecca Sinkler, "The Choice of Nina Auerbach," detail the episode about the book review.

20. Katherine J. Mayberry, "White Feminists Who Study Black Writers," *The Chronicle of Higher Education,* October 12, 1994, p. A48.

21. See Haver, "Après moi le Deleuze," p. 2.

22. See Novick, *That Noble Dream,* chap. 16.

23. I want to point out here that not all critics of disciplinarity are political instrumentalists or fundamentalists.

24. For a compelling analysis of this issue, see John Guillory, *Cultural Capital: The Problem of Literary Canon Formation* (Chicago: University of Chicago Press, 1993).

25. I wish to thank Tony Scott for his help with these formulations. On the question of community, see Jean-Luc Nancy, *The Inoperative Community* (Minneapolis: University of Minnesota Press, 1991); and *Community at Loose Ends,* ed. Miami Theory Collective (Minneapolis: University of Minnesota Press, 1991), esp. the article by Christopher Fynsk, "Community and the Limits of Theory," pp. 19–29.

26. On understanding as the goal of humanistic scholarship, see Stefan Collini, "Research in the Humanities," *TLS,* April 3, 1987, pp. 349–50.

27. "Response to an Inquiry by Professor Paul Brest," in "Report of Committee A for 1985–86," *Academe* 72 (September 1986): 13a, 19a; cited in *Academe* 74 (September/October 1988): 55.

28. On the loss of the teleological historical narrative, see Brown, "Toward a Genealogy of Contemporary Political Moralism."

SEVEN

We Need a New Interpretation of Academic Freedom

Ronald Dworkin

I. INTRODUCTION

The phrase "academic freedom" collects different images and associations now than it did thirty, or maybe even ten, years ago. We thought, then, about leftist teachers and McCarthyite legislators and loyalty oaths and courageous and cowardly university presidents. Liberals and radicals were all for academic freedom. Many conservatives thought it overrated or even part of the conspiracy to paint America red. Now it is the party of reform that talks down academic freedom and conservatives who call it a bulwark of Western civilization. Now the phrase makes us think of insensitive professors and of speech codes that might protect students from their insensitivity. We wonder whether academic freedom forbids such protection and, if so, whether academic freedom is as important as liberals once thought.

Some examples will be useful to bear in mind. I do not mean that incidents like these are everyday occurrences on American campuses, as some right-wing critics of universities suggest, or even that they have actually occurred as I describe them; I cite them because they are the kinds of events, real or exaggerated, that have generated new suspicion about and new enthusiasm for academic freedom. A professor is disciplined because he teaches that blacks are inferior to whites. Another is punished because he teaches that Jews are the enemy of blacks. A professor is severely criticized because he assigns the journals of slave-owning plantation managers as reading in a course on American history, and he does not receive what many of his colleagues consider appropriate support from university officials when students complain. Another professor is disciplined because, to illustrate a complex point in contract law, he quotes Byron's line in *Don Juan* about the woman who, whispering "I shall ne'er consent," consented, and another because he describes belly dancing as like holding a vibrator under a plate of Jell-O. The University of Michigan adopts a speech code which prohibits "Any behavior, verbal or physical, that stigmatizes or victimizes an individual on the basis of race, ethnicity, religion, sex, sexual orientation, creed, national origin, ancestry, age, marital status, handicap, or Vietnam-era veteran status, and that . . . creates an intimidating, hostile or demeaning environment for educational purposes." Stanford University adopts a different speech code, which forbids speech if it "(1) is intended to insult or stigmatize an individual or a small number of individuals on the basis of their sex, race, color, handicap, religion, sexual orientation, or national and ethnic origin, (2) is addressed directly to the individual or individuals whom it insults or stigmatizes, and (3) makes use of insulting or 'fighting' words or nonverbal symbols." Each of these various events is widely deplored and is said to constitute a violation of academic freedom.

This shift in causes célèbres has produced a new uncertainty about what academic freedom actually is. This is not surprising. Political values take their meaning from paradigms of their application, and when these shift, values that seemed obvious suddenly resist clear statement. But if the dimensions and goals of academic freedom are now uncertain, it is important that we attempt to redefine them. We must construct a fresh account of academic freedom that meets two tests. First, it must fit well enough with general understandings of what academic freedom does and does not require so that it can provide a new interpretation of an established value, not a new value altogether. Second, it must justify those general understandings as well as they can be justified; it must show why academic freedom *is* a value, so that we can judge how important it is, and whether and when it should yield to other, competing values.[1]

This interpretive project seems particularly timely when we consider the emotional dimension of the contemporary controversies. According to the most popular view of the matter, these disputes force us to choose between two values: equality—in particular, racial and gender equality—on the one hand and academic freedom on the other. This seems an emotional mismatch. Racial injustice and gender stereotyping have done terrible harm, and many American institutions rightly think it imperative to try to eradicate at least their worst consequences. These efforts, particularly in universities, make great demands on many students. Blacks, for example, are expected to compete in universities from which members of their race were largely excluded, and to pursue studies centered on cultures that they had long been taught owed nothing to and offered nothing for them. We know how raw the sensibilities of some such students must be, and we think it only right to do whatever we can to make their situation less difficult. Academic freedom, in contrast, seems an abstract and bloodless value, something to worry about, if at all, only in the long term, after these more urgent problems have been resolved.

Academic freedom has another, different, disadvantage in this supposed encounter. It is often defended on the ground that scholars must be free if they are to discover objective truth. But the very possibility of objective truth is now itself under challenge from an anti-truth-squad of relativists, subjectivists, neo-Pragmatists, postmodernists, and similar critics now powerful in the unconfident departments of American universities. According to these critics academic freedom is not just bloodless but fraudulent. This relativist challenge is deeply confused. But its popularity contributes to—and is yet more evidence of—the weakness of the grip that academic freedom now has on the sentiments even of many academics.

II. CONTOURS

Two Levels of Insulation
We begin reinterpreting academic freedom by reminding ourselves of what, historically, it has been understood to require and not to require. It imposes two levels of insulation. First, it insulates universities, colleges, and other institutions of higher education from political institutions like legislatures and courts and from economic powers like large corporations. A state legislature has, of course, the right to decide which state universities to establish—whether, for example, to add an agricultural or a liberal arts college to the existing university structure. But once political officials have established such an institution, fixed its academic character and its budget, and appointed its officials, they may not dictate how those they have appointed should interpret that character or who should teach what is to be taught, or how. Second, academic freedom insulates scholars from the administrators of their universities: university officials can appoint faculty, allocate budgets to departments, and in that way decide, within limits, what curriculum will be offered. But they cannot dictate how those who have been appointed will teach what has been decided will be taught.

These might seem odd lines to draw. If a legislature may decide that a liberal arts college is what the community needs, and what budget it should have, why should it not also decide what, in detail, should be taught there, and how? Why is the latter decision not simply a continuation and elaboration of the former ones? But academic freedom makes distinctions like these—distinctions between what academic posts should be created and who should fill them, on the one hand, and how those appointed to those posts should acquit their responsibilities, on the other—critically important. Any competent interpretation must explain and justify those distinctions.

Academic Freedom and Free Speech

Academic freedom is plainly related to a more general and better known political value, which is freedom of speech, and various American courts have held that central forms of academic freedom are protected by the Constitution's First Amendment. It might therefore seem natural to treat academic freedom as just the application of that more general right to the special case of academic institutions. But that would obscure much that is special about academic freedom. Free speech is a moral right—and in America a legal right, as well—for everyone. But it doesn't provide for everyone what academic freedom provides for scholars. Free speech is not, except in very special circumstances, a right to speak one's mind in a position maintained and supported by others. Legally, of course, the First Amendment applies only against government: it is not violated when private institutions impose speech restrictions as a condition of employment. Even the moral right of free speech is not normally violated by such conditions—it is not violated, for example, when a department store fires someone for denigrating its products, or when a church does not allow one of its priests to preach a rival faith from its pulpit. Free speech, at its core, is the right not to be altogether prevented from saying something, not the right to continue to be supported and aided while saying it by those who think it false or undesirable.

In that respect, academic freedom, which does require certain institutions to support and help people no matter what they write or say or teach, is stronger than the more general right of free speech. In other respects, however, it is less clearly a right, because no one is morally entitled to the status which brings that extra protection. No one is entitled to demand that a particular form of college or university be founded or remain in business. Nor is anyone entitled to an academic or administrative office within those that do exist. Indeed, apart from tenure, which is held only by some, no one is entitled to remain in such an office, even once appointed, beyond the length of a stipulated term. It seems better, therefore, not to count academic freedom as derivative from a more general right to free speech, or, indeed, to count it as involving a right at all. I shall try to show, however, that the two institutions—academic freedom and a right to free speech—are closely connected in a different way: they form important parts of a system of ideas and institutions that creates a culture of individual intellectual responsibility and that protects it from disintegrating into a culture of intellectual conformity.

III. THE INSTRUMENTAL GROUND

We must construct an interpretation of academic freedom that fits these general contours and justifies the ideal they presuppose. The conventional justification of academic freedom treats it as instrumental in the discovery of truth. According to this view, a system of independent academic institutions and scholars who are independent within them provides the best chance of collectively reaching the truth about a wide range of matters, from science to art to politics. We have a better chance of discovering what is true, it declares, if we leave our academics and their institutions free from external control to the greatest degree possible.

This conventional defense of academic freedom echoes John Stuart Mill's famous defense of freedom of speech. Mill argued that truth emerges best from a marketplace of ideas from which no opinion is excluded. Though most American lawyers accept Mill's argument as the best justification for the First Amendment, that argument does not provide a convincing defense of much of the protection that the First Amendment in fact offers and that partisans of freedom of speech think right.[2] It does not adequately explain why we permit pornography, or even why we tolerate Nazis or certain fundamentalists who, if they did persuade a sufficient number of people to join their terrorism, would destroy liberty thereafter. Mill's kind of defense does seem stronger when it is applied to academic freedom than to free speech generally, however, because those whom academic freedom insulates are less likely to act from nakedly political or ideological motives than are those whose power it insulates them from. Certainly science and probably every other study in the university is more successful, judged in purely academic terms, when it is free from either political control or the dominion of commerce.

But we must nevertheless concede that on many occasions certain compromises of academic freedom might well provide even more efficient truth-seeking strategies, particularly if we want to discover not just what is true but also what is useful or important. Universities do well not to hire scholars, no matter how clever or persuasive, who are committed to ideas their colleagues think patently wrong, or trivial, or of no intellectual importance. It is unobjectionable for a biology department not to hire a creationist, or a history department someone who denies the Holocaust, or an economics department someone who will devote his career only to the special economics of the baseball card market. University resources are limited and should not be spent on those who will occupy their time developing arguments for what is plainly false or researching what is obviously of no serious interest. Of course we know that sometimes a theory or program now dismissed as wrong or trivial will turn out to be true or crucial. But, overall, given that academic resources are limited, it is better that they be allocated to scholars whose work strikes other academics as promising, rather than only on the basis of, say, the raw intelligence of researchers. This argument would not justify forbidding creationists or negationists or baseball card economists to publish their views or to roar them out at Hyde Park Corner. But it does justify university officials deciding to hire other scholars in their place. If that is so, however—if we advance truth and useful discussion by not wasting scarce academic resources on plainly false opinions or trivial projects—then why would we not advance truth even more securely by preventing scholars already in place from teaching those opinions or pursuing those projects if they were converted to them after their appointment? Academic freedom forbids this, but the Millian explanation does not seem to show why.

There is a standard reply to these worries. It is said that even if on some occasions protecting academic freedom does inhibit the search for truth, it would be worse for truth in the long run to allow any exceptions, because we could not be sure that these would be made wisely or that their effects would be limited. The only safe conditions for academic research, according to this view, are those in which academic freedom is protected without exception and with passionate commitment. That might be right, but it does involve a leap of faith. Of course some useful research would be lost if university officials had more power to direct the work of academic faculty, but some useful research would also be gained, and we cannot have any great confidence that the balance would be negative. We think the balance positive when hiring or promotion decisions must be made against scarce resources, even though we know, as I said, that officials will sometimes make mistakes. Dictating to those already on staff is different in various ways, but not so different as to make the opposite judgment compelling.

Even if we were to accept this familiar argument and suppose that complete academic freedom will advance truth in the long run if the run is long enough, that instrumental assumption does not seem strong enough, on its own, to justify the emotional power that many of us feel academic freedom has, and that it must have if it is to hold its own now, against the moral urgency of the competing goals and ideals I mentioned. Why is it not worth some speculative loss of knowledge, at the margin of research, in order to protect people who have been victims of great social injustice from further insult, or to make their opportunity to help themselves and other members of their race or gender more genuine and effective? In a cosmic instant or two our sun will explode and all our libraries, museums, and palaces will be intergalactic ash. By then human beings and any other intelligent species that have joined us will have come to know only a tiny fraction of what might be known. How can it matter so much if we allow that fraction to be just a little tinier in order to protect some people from injury? If we want to defend academic freedom, we need a ground that better matches its emotional importance for us, and the outrage we feel when it is violated, even in the name of causes we share.

IV. THE ETHICAL GROUND

So though the conventional, instrumental defense of academic freedom is important, and at least in general valid, it is not enough. We must connect that defense to something deeper, less contingent and speculative, and more personal. I shall now argue that academic freedom plays an important ethical role not just in the lives of the few people it protects, but in the life of the community more generally. It is an important, structural part of the culture of independence that we need in order to lead the kind of lives that we should. An invasion of academic freedom is insulting and harmful for some because it frustrates satisfying important responsibilities, and it is dangerous for everyone because it weakens the culture of independence and cheapens the ideal that culture protects.

I mean the ideal of ethical individualism.[3] This insists, among its other components, that we each have responsibility for making as much of a success of our lives as we can, and that this responsibility is personal, in the sense that we must each make up our own mind, as a matter of felt personal conviction, about what a successful life for us would be. Ethical individualism is the inspiration behind the institutions and attitudes of political liberalism. It supports the central core of liberal ideas that includes both freedom of speech and academic freedom, not just as a wise environment for academic discovery, but as encouragement of and protection for the primacy of individual conviction.

People who accept ethical individualism accept consequent responsibilities. The first is the responsibility not to profess what one believes to be false. This duty is protected, in liberal societies, by a right of conscience that forbids forcing people to religious or moral or political declaration against their will. The second is a more positive responsibility of affirmation: it is a duty to speak out for what one believes to be true. According to ethical individualism, we all have that duty as citizens: it is wrong to remain silent when our society must make a collective decision and we believe we have information or opinion it should take into account. We have that responsibility even when we know that our opinion will not be heeded—when the state acts unjustly, for example, and we know we can only bear witness to our anger at what it does in our name. That sense of responsibility, and of the moral damage done when we are prevented from exercising it, is part of the medley of reasons that together make it so important to us, as individuals, that we have a general right of free speech on political matters.

Some social roles and professions incorporate heightened versions of this personal responsibility. The character of that special responsibility varies. Salesmen should not lie, but need not give their customers commercially neutral advice. Priests are responsible for the whole truth, but need not remain in the pulpit, after they have lost their faith, to explain why their parishioners should abandon that faith as well. Doctors' duties are more inalienable: they must tell their patients what they believe it is in the patient's best interests to hear, and must not accept any external limit on that responsibility. That is one reason why the Reagan administration's order forbidding federally financed doctors from even discussing abortion with their patients was so outrageous. The Supreme Court, in a widely criticized decision, upheld that regulation, on the ground that it is no invasion of the First Amendment to condition the receipt of federal funds on not speaking in defined ways.[4] That was a mistake in law, I believe, but the administration's order was a disgrace in any case, because it ignored the deep responsibility of the moral role of a physician, and the moral harm that follows from frustrating it.[5] The regulation forced doctors to choose between ignoring one of two responsibilities, each cardinal to their professional ethics: not to abandon patients, and to care for them in the way that they, the doctors, think best. So the administrative order, which was withdrawn as one of the first acts of the Clinton administration, violated the principle we might call medical freedom.

Professors and others who teach and study in universities have an even more general and uncompromising responsibility. They have a paradigmatic duty to discover and teach what they find important and true, and this duty is not, even to the degree that medical responsibility may be, subject to any qualification about the best interests of those to whom they speak. It is an undiluted responsibility to the truth, and it is, in that way, the closest a professional responsibility can come to the fundamental ethical responsibility each of us has, according to the ideals of ethical individualism, to live our lives in accordance with our own felt convictions.

V. THE CULTURE OF INDEPENDENCE

We have just noticed part of the ethical justification for academic freedom: the institution protects people in a particular role—students and scholars—from the moral damage of frustration in their special responsibilities. But those responsibilities are imposed by conventional understandings—by institutional assignments that might have been different—so we must now consider whether they serve an important purpose and so should be maintained and protected. Why should we have academic institutions whose professors and students and officials are dedicated to discovering and transmitting truth as they individually, one by one, see it?

Ethical individualism needs a particular kind of culture—a culture of independence—in which to flourish. Its enemy is the opposite culture—the culture of conformity, of Khomeini's Iran, Torquemada's Spain, and Joe McCarthy's America—in which truth is collected not person by person, in acts of independent conviction, but is embedded in monolithic traditions or the fiats of priesthood or junta or majority vote, and dissent from that truth is treason. That totalitarian epistemology—searingly identified in the finally successful campaign of Orwell's dictator to make his victim believe, through torture, that $2 + 2 = 5$—is tyranny's most frightening feature.

Liberal public education, freedom of speech, conscience, and religion, and academic freedom are all parts of our society's support for a culture of independence and of its defense against a culture of conformity. Academic freedom plays a special role because educational institutions are pivotal to those efforts. They are pivotal, first, because they can so easily become engines of conformity, as every totalitarian regime has realized, and, second, because they can provide important encouragement and skills for a life of personal conviction. Part of the point of education, in a liberal society, is learning the importance and depth of an allegiance to personal rather than collective truth. Academic freedom is also important symbolically, because in a free academy the example and virtues of ethical individualism are so patently on display. In no other occupation is it so plainly and evidently the responsibility of professionals to find and tell and teach the truth as they see it. Scholars exist for that, and only for that. A culture of independence values learning "for its own sake" because such learning is also, in that way, for that culture's sake as well.

I should summarize this part of the argument. Academic freedom represents and reinforces the ideals of ethical individualism. It exhibits those ideals in the most appropriate context by creating a theater in which personal conviction about truth and value is all that matters, and it trains scholars and students alike in the skills and attitudes essential to a culture of independence. So any violation of academic freedom is damaging in manifold ways. It is morally harmful to those whose freedom to speak or write or teach is restricted, because a deep responsibility is thereby thwarted. It is morally harmful to those whose learning is corrupted by the same restriction. It damages the general culture of independence that academic freedom nourishes, because any invasion of academic freedom is not only harmful in itself but makes future invasions more likely. And it insults, for everyone, the ideals of ethical individualism, because the scholar serving only his own vision of the truth is a crucial symbol as well as an important progenitor of that ethical ideal. All this is at stake and put in jeopardy every time a teacher is told what or what not to teach or how to teach it.

That is the ethical justification of academic freedom, and it provides a complementary and more comprehensive justification than the conventional, explicitly instrumental, Millian justification. The ethical justification supplies the emotional weight that the instrumental argument cannot. It may now be said that the symbolic and other roles I just claimed for academic freedom are real for only a small fraction of the population—only, perhaps, for a minority even of those who have been university students. I suspect, to the contrary, that the pride that people with no higher education take in local and national universities indicates that a much wider community shares the values I am trying to describe. But if I am wrong, and only a minority now believes that academic freedom has ethical importance, that argues for more rather than less attention to the ethical argument. We hope, after all, that the best forms of education will be available to an ever growing share of the community, and the ideals of personal conviction, intellectual integrity, and ethical independence are essential to that goal.

We may now return to the crucial test that I said any competent interpretation of academic freedom must meet. That ideal insists on distinctions that, as I said, might seem bizarre at first sight. The key distinction, as I stated it, is between the power of politicians and university officials and colleagues to design institutions and appoint scholars, which academic freedom allows, and their power to control what those scholars do once appointed, which academic freedom prohibits. That distinction might indeed seem odd if we thought that academic freedom served only the instrumental goal of encouraging discovery. Then we might have to concede, as I said, that if it is wise to let officials appoint on the basis of their own judgment about the importance of what a scholar is likely to do, it must also be wise to allow them to correct for mistakes, so far as possible, by disciplining someone already appointed. But from the different ethical perspective we have now developed, the distinction is not only sensible but central. The principle of individual responsibility is not violated when politicians choose university presidents or presidents choose professors on the basis of some collective or institutional opinion about where truth lies. But it is violated when they dictate to faculty after appointment, because then people whose responsibility is to speak and write and teach truth as they see it are prevented from doing so. It is the frustration of responsibility in place that seems so outrageous and so offensive to the ethical ideals we ought to cherish.

VI. SHOULD ACADEMIC FREEDOM BE COMPROMISED?

Limits of Academic Freedom

Though academic freedom is a profound value, for all the reasons we have now noticed, it is nevertheless only one value among many. We wanted a new interpretation of academic freedom in order to respond to new challenges to that old ideal. How do we choose when academic freedom conflicts with something else that is also important, like equality or decency? We should notice, first, an important distinction between two different kinds of argument for resisting the claim of a conceded value. The first argues for a limit to that value: it suggests that on the best interpretation its point or underlying justification has no application in the case at hand. That is the claim someone makes, for example, when he insists that the sanctity of human life, which is normally outraged by any deliberate killing, is not outraged when a doctor administers a lethal injection to a terminally ill patient who genuinely wants to die. On this view, the conflict is illusory, because the sanctity of life, properly understood, is not violated by such a killing.[6] The second is an argument not for recognizing the limits of a value but for accepting a compromise of it because, though the point of the value does extend to the case in question, its force is nevertheless overridden by a competing value. That is the claim of those who accept free speech as an important value but nevertheless endorse censorship when it is necessary to protect national security. The distinction is important in our present context, because many of the cases in which people feel strongly that academic freedom must yield to a competing value are actually cases in which the rationale for academic freedom does not apply: they are cases defining the limits of that rationale, not cases suggesting any degraded importance when it really is at stake.

Deliberate insults—by which I mean statements or displays whose principal motive is to cause injury or distress or some other kind of harm— are not even in principle covered by the idea of academic freedom, on either the instrumental or ethical understandings of that value. So when a university prohibits or discourages such insult, it is recognizing the limits of the doctrine, not compromising it. But we must take very great care to distinguish such cases, when the insult is intentional, from cases in which it is not, though the wound may be as great. Intentional harm is generally graver than nonintentional harm; as Oliver Wendell Holmes once said, even a dog knows the difference between being kicked and stumbled over. But the distinction is important now not for that reason but because though intentional insult is not covered by academic freedom, negligent insult must be.

The distinction between the two is often hard to draw in practice, not only because motives are often obscure and hidden even from the agent whose motives they are, but because people often act with mixed motives: someone who declares that women are weak in abstract reasoning may at once express a biological opinion he sincerely believes and at the same time hope to outrage and insult part of his audience. But since we are describing a limit to an important protection, we should define intentional insult narrowly. We should use the counterfactual test: Would the speaker have said what he did if he did not believe it would cause distress? It is easy to answer the question in some contexts. Few people would bother to burn crosses if they believed that blacks would simply be amused at the sight; few people would shout "nigger" or "kike" at someone they thought would be charmed by the sound of the word. The person, whoever it was, who nailed a laundry list to the door of a Chinese-American student at Stanford was not indifferent to whether seeing it there it would cause her pain. I am not of course urging this test as a limit to the general right of free speech, or to the legal protection of the First Amendment. It would be a clear violation of that right for the legislature to outlaw all speech designed to wound. But the distinct point and virtues of academic freedom would not then be in play. A university may properly demand an atmosphere of decency in which neither faculty nor groups of students act with the intention of intimidating or embarrassing or hurting anyone in the community, and insofar as speech codes banned only such behavior they would be consistent with academic freedom even when (because the university in question was a public institution) they violated the First Amendment. We can safely extend this limit to academic freedom to include language or display that might be called insulting per se, because its meaning in contemporary diction includes insult. Addressing a black student as "boy" or "girl," or wearing a white hood to class, or blazoning a swastika or a *Playboy* centerfold on the wall of an office which students are invited or expected to visit is in itself an insult, and a university can reasonably demand, consistently with academic freedom, that its students and faculty express their opinions in other ways.

Most of the cases that have attracted recent attention, however, are cases in which a student or professor is accused not of wounding some student or group of students intentionally, in the strong sense that the counterfactual test picks out, or of using language that is insulting per se, but of acting with what has come to be called, in a new runic phrase, "insensitivity"— acting, that is, without due consideration of the injury his remarks are likely to cause. The examples of allegedly offensive remarks I cited earlier all fall into that category. The professors who assigned slave owners' journals or quoted Byron or talked about vibrators were accused of insensitivity, and it is extremely implausible that any of them even expected let alone intended to injure. In other cases, though a teacher with any sense would indeed expect to injure or offend by defending some thesis—that women are not as good at abstract reasoning as men, for example—he would probably not intend that harm either. He would prefer, however unreasonable or silly or unlikely this might be, that women not be offended by his remarks, but take them in a constructive spirit. So the exception for remarks intended to wound, while important, does not reach the cases that have provoked the greatest controversy and pose the most important threats to academic freedom.

What Should Override Free Speech?
So we come, finally, to what is undoubtedly the crucial question. What should academic officials do about culpable insensitivity? Compare the hate

speech code that Stanford University adopted with that of the University of Michigan, which was held unconstitutional. The former forbids speech if it "(1) is intended to insult or stigmatize an individual or a small number of individuals on the basis of their sex, race, color, handicap, religion, sexual orientation, or national and ethnic origin, (2) is addressed directly to the individual or individuals whom it insults or stigmatizes, and (3) makes use of insulting or 'fighting' words or nonverbal symbols." If "intended to insult or stigmatize" is given the strong sense I described—if no one intends to insult or stigmatize unless he would not have spoken as he did if he did not think the target of his remarks would feel insulted or stigmatized—then the Stanford code does not offend against academic freedom, though, as I said, it is a different question whether it violates the broader and more general moral right of free speech.[7] Michigan, on the other hand, forbade "any behavior, verbal or physical, that stigmatizes or victimizes an individual on the basis of race, ethnicity, religion, sex, sexual orientation, creed, national origin, ancestry, age, marital status, handicap, or Vietnam-era veteran status, and that . . . creates an intimidating, hostile or demeaning environment for educational purposes." There is no requirement of intention in the strict sense I described, so Michigan's code would presumably have allowed the university to punish a lecturer on colonial history who defended the motives of plantation owners or a student's honest statement that he could not help but think that homosexuals defy nature's laws. The unvarnished expression of either of these opinions in a classroom might well be felt as insulting and stigmatizing and might well create a hostile and demeaning environment for some and perhaps many students. Nevertheless their expression falls within academic freedom. Prohibiting or punishing such opinions would violate the principle that people must be free to state what they believe to be important and true, in language they believe most precise and apt.

But that is not the end of the story. For academic freedom is, as I said, only one value among many, and we can recognize and honor it while nevertheless insisting that it must sometimes be compromised to protect what is, in context, a more important or urgent one. The argument that it should be compromised now, to protect students from racial or gender insensitivity, can take two very different forms. The first is an argument of policy. Our political, civil, and commercial societies still suffer from the effects of racism and sexism. In some ways the situation is worse than ever: the gap between white and black income and share of wealth continues to increase, for example. Universities have a critical role in helping to reduce the injustice: many of them have changed their admissions policies and their curricula to admit and welcome students who would formerly have been excluded and to increase the awareness in all students of problems, contributions, and cultures that were formerly virtually ignored. But the insensitivity of some professors and fellow-students undermines these important goals. It makes students who should be welcomed feel unwelcome, and it reinforces racist and sexist attitudes that universities aim to marginalize. So, according to this argument of policy, it is irrational to tolerate academic insensitivity, because that is arming the enemy we mean to fight.

Ethical values like academic freedom should yield to public policy only when the need for them to yield is both great and evident, and we do not have clear enough ground for thinking that speech codes or other weapons of censorship would do much to help reduce prejudice. There is no real evidence either way, but it seems equally likely that such measures exacerbate prejudice by allowing its more subtle forms to mask as outrage against censorship. In any case, censorship plainly is the enemy not the friend of equality in the long run. For as long back as we care to inspect, intellectuals and academics have crowded the bow of the egalitarian movement, and those who hate equality have made it a priority to try to silence them. Times change, of course, but not in that respect. If critics of academic freedom succeed in teaching the public at large that that ideal is overrated, and may be set aside in the interests of attractive social goals, the lesson will be studied in other than egalitarian constituencies. If some people think racial and gender equality are urgent goals, others—and there are more of them— think it more urgent that the decline in family values and traditional virtues be halted, and they will be glad of a chance to dictate that university curricula emphasize those virtues and avoid texts that ridicule them, particularly those in which homosexuality and other "different" styles of life are celebrated. I am, I agree, only repeating an old liberal warning. But it is a warning that cannot be repeated often enough. Censorship will always prove a traitor to justice.

The second version of the argument for compromising academic freedom is very different. It is not an argument of policy, which can only trump an important value if the beneficial results are crucial and evident, but an argument of principle which, if it is sound, has much more imperative force. People in a pluralistic society have a right, this argument of principle insists, to work and study and live in an environment that is free from statements or displays they reasonably take to be denigrating or humiliating. On this view, whatever compromises in academic freedom are required to prevent insensitive insults are not limited and temporary adjustments to a special and urgent need, as they are according to the argument of policy. They are rather permanent, structural features of any just community.

This argument of principle has an impressive shape, because it appeals to a competing right rather than an overriding policy, and we know that the closely related value of free speech is sometimes properly compromised out of concern for competing rights. A great literature, it is true, attempts to treat cases in which freedom of speech is set aside as cases of limit rather than compromise. It attempts, for example, to define "speech" so that occasions when censorship is permissible can be treated as cases in which free speech has not been denied. Someone who uses "fighting words" that are very likely to produce immediate violence, for example, is not protected by the First Amendment, and it is often said, by way of justifying that exemption, that he has crossed the line that separates "speech" from "action." But the most energetic constitutional scholarship has not been able to clarify this distinction; in fact these and similar examples are better understood as cases of compromise of the right of free speech in deference to other rights that are, in context, more urgently or centrally at stake. We have a right to physical security, for example, and it is that right, rather than any mysterious infusion of "action" into "speech," that best explains why shouting "Lynch him!" to a mob with a rope, or putting out a Mafia contract, or falsely shouting "Fire!" in a crowded theater cannot be protected.

The argument of principle I just described, however, goes far beyond justifying limited constraints on speech like these. It demands prohibiting any expression or display that might reasonably be thought to embarrass anyone or lower others' esteem for them or their own self-respect. The idea that people have *that* right is absurd. Of course it would be good if everyone liked and respected everyone else who merited that response. But we cannot recognize a right to respect, or a right to be free from the effects of speech that makes respect less likely, without wholly subverting the central ideals of the culture of independence and denying the ethical individualism that that culture protects. The dominant opinions and prejudices of any society will always be hurtful to some of its members. Terrible insults are offered everyday, in some American community or other, to creationists and religious fundamentalists, to people who believe that homosexuality is deeply sinful or that sex is proper only within marriage, to those who think that God forbids surgery or penicillin or demands holy wars, to people who think that Norman Rockwell was the only great artist of the century, or that Hallmark cards are moving or that Sousa marches are great music, to people who are short or fat or just plain slow. Think of the writers who would have to be censored if there really were a right not to be insulted by other people's opinions: they include Rabelais, Voltaire, Rushdie, Galileo, Darwin, Wilde, and Mencken. People of a thousand different convictions or shapes or tastes are ridiculed or insulted by every level of speech and publication in every decent democracy in the world.

A culture of independence almost guarantees that this will be so. Certainly ridicule is often unjust: people should be ridiculed and despised for some things, but not for others. But we cannot accept a right that would entitle some people to demand that others systematically stifle their opinions about anything. We should be decent to one another, and bigotry is despicable. But if we really came to think that we violated other people's rights whenever we reported sincere views that denigrated them in their own or others' eyes, we would have shattered our own sense of what it is to live honestly. We must find other, less suicidal, weapons against racism and sexism. We must, as always, put our faith in freedom not repression.[8]

I will attempt no new summary of my argument but offer a short exhortation instead. I have been guilty of what must seem an absurd degree of professional hubris and cheerleading. I claim that my own profession—the weak battalions of university teachers—carries much of the responsibility for maintaining a magnificent ethical tradition, and that we must defend our freedom, with passion and whatever strength we all together have, on that ground. We have lately become less confident of our importance and less ready to insist on our independence. We have allowed academic freedom to seem pale and abstract and even fraudulent. But we must now remember how easy it has proved, elsewhere, for that freedom to be lost, and how hard it is to regain once lost. We do carry a great responsibility, and it is time we carried it once again with pride.

NOTES

1. I mean interpreting the social institution of academic freedom, not just identifying how far the law (including, in America, the Constitution) defines and protects that social institution, though the former is pertinent to the latter. There is, so far as I know, no law against the donor of an academic chair reserving the right to name its holders; but that would violate academic freedom. Nor is academic freedom the same as wise academic policy. It might be silly for a university English department to turn itself entirely over to a trendy new form of criticism. But it would be a violation of academic freedom for the legislature to forbid this.

2. See the chapters about freedom of speech in my book *Freedom's Law* (Cambridge, Mass.: Harvard University Press, 1966).

3. For a description of ethical individualism (though not under that name), see my *Foundations of Liberal Equality,* Tanner Foundation Lecture Series, vol. 11 (Salt Lake City: University of Utah Press, 1990).

4. *Rust v. Sullivan,* 111 U.S. 1759 (1991).

5. For an explanation of the idea of "moral harm," see my essay "Principle, Policy, Procedure," *A Matter of Principle* (Cambridge, Mass.: Harvard University Press, 1985).

6. See my *Life's Dominion: An Argument about Abortion, Euthanasia, and Individual Freedom* (New York: Knopf, 1993).

7. A lower court in California recently invalidated the Stanford code as violating a state statute forbidding universities to impose stricter speech regulations than governments could impose. See "Court Overturns Stanford University Code Barring Bigoted Speech," *New York Times,* March 1, 1995, p. B8.

8. People do have special rights not to suffer from discrimination, which is different from ridicule or offense. They have a right not to be denied employment because they are blacks or women or creationists or people of no imagination or very bad taste, for example, except when these properties would interfere with their work.

EIGHT

Science and Its Critics

Evelyn Fox Keller

Many of the authors in this volume focus on the implications of postmodernist critiques of Enlightenment values, particularly as these have gained ascendancy in the humanities, for the ideal of academic freedom. My focus is somewhat different. By training I am a scientist (a physicist, in fact) and even though I no longer work as a scientist—neither in a lab, nor in the production of scientific theory—science retains the place in my intellectual life of a first love, and it remains the central focus of my scholarship. I have become, in a word, part of that enterprise—an even more recent arrival than academic freedom—that takes the study of science rather than the study of nature as its central mission. Accordingly, my focus in this paper is the recent tensions that have been evoked by the arrival of this new venture, loosely called "science studies."

Like the very term "science," "science studies" is a broad and imprecise term. It covers many disciplinary approaches (philosophical, historical, sociological, even literary) and proceeds from an equally broad spectrum of philosophical positions. And the label "postmodern," so frequently invoked in relation to science studies, is even broader and more difficult to define. With these caveats, I conservatively suggest that science studies may be said to be postmodern in a historical sense—that is, in the sense that it is new, that it has arisen on the heels of all of the eras that have variously been called modern. More specifically, science studies is a product only of the last three decades.

There is of course also another sense in which the term "postmodern" is sometimes invoked in this context, and that has to do with the authority claimed by students of science studies outside, and often independent, of the sciences. What invites some authors to use the label here is the particular claim that science studies makes to independent authority to analyze, to criticize, to speak about the natural sciences, and the conflation of this claim with the repudiation of Enlightenment values for which postmodernism is famous. Even ignoring its other problems,[1] I would suggest that this usage of the label rests on an unacceptably myopic view of history: While scientists have sought for their ventures autonomy and immunity from external criticism since the seventeenth century, I would argue that it is only in the twentieth century, and especially in the years immediately following World War II, that full autonomy and immunity have come to be taken for granted by working scientists, have come to be assumed as natural and inalienable rights.

No discussion of the current state of the sciences in relation to their critics can reasonably begin without first taking due note of the phenomenal political and institutional growth experienced by the natural sciences in the aftermath of World War II and the consequent redistribution of power in the university. We might note, for example, that the arts and the humanities accounted for almost 20 percent of all doctoral degrees awarded in the decades immediately prior to World War II. In the subsequent decades, however, as the total number of doctorates sharply increased (elevenfold between 1940 and 1973), the proportion of degrees in arts and the humanities experienced a steady decline (accounting for only 11 percent of all degrees in the 1950s). Comparing degrees in letters with those in natural science and engineering, we see letters accounting for 5.7 percent of 1970 degrees, 4.1 percent for 1980, and 3.3 percent for 1989, while natural science and engineering account for approximately one-third of all degrees in the same years. The distribution of resources would, of course, tell an even more dramatic story. (E.g., measured in real dollars, the budget of the National Endowment for the Humanities declined by about 20 percent between 1979 and 1991, while that of the National Science Foundation doubled.)[2] In other words, what I have been calling the new enterprise of science studies arose out of a context that must itself be recognized as new, that is, in response to the conspicuous growth in the status and power of the scientific disciplines, both in the academy and in the world at large, that has taken place since 1940.

Thomas Kuhn's *Structure of Scientific Revolutions,* published in 1962, is often credited with providing the opening wedge; the work of the Edinburgh school (SSK, as it has come to be known)—especially that of David Bloor, Barry Barnes, David Edge, Donald MacKenzie, Andy Pickering, and

Steven Shapin—began to appear in the seventies; Bruno Latour and Steve Woolgar published their *Social Construction of a Scientific Fact* in 1979; and the first feminist critiques of science emerged in the late seventies. It is worth noting, at least parenthetically, that most of the authors of these efforts had themselves come out of the sciences. The often very heated debates these works generated among their various authors attest to their serious philosophical (as well as political) differences, and my grouping of them together under a single banner is certainly not intended to obscure such differences. It is simply to note that, collectively, this work had an enormous impact on the ways in which intellectuals of all sorts—including historians, philosophers, sociologists, and even literary theorists—think about science.

Largely as a result of their more careful historical and sociological studies of what scientists actually do, these works led to a major upset in the received wisdom (roughly consonant with scientists' own understanding of their endeavor) that had prevailed among historians, philosophers, and sociologists of science prior to the 1960s. Time-honored concepts of rationality, of objectivity, of evidence and proof, even of truth and reality were revealed to be considerably more problematic than they had earlier seemed to be: they were shown to be subject to historical and social contingency and, accordingly, as irremediably resistant to clear and stable definition. With the advent of such studies, therefore, what had once looked like a clear boundary between internal (i.e., scientific) and external (i.e., social or extrascientific) factors in the development of scientific knowledge has given way to the growing conviction that scientific knowledge is infiltrated by social and historical factors on every level. Close analysis of how questions are posed, of how research programs come to be legitimated, of how theoretical disputes are resolved, of "how experiments end"[3] has revealed the untenability of any clear and stable demarcation between scientific and social, between fact and value, knowledge and ideology, even between right and might. What makes a particular question "the right question to ask," or one explanation more persuasive and satisfying than another, may—indeed, generally does—seem conspicuously obvious for working scientists, but, from the vantage point of even a slight distance, it becomes even more obvious that consensus about these issues is created not merely by compelling evidence or logic, but by all sorts of social (economic, political) pressures as well. The principal point that emerges from three decades of careful historical and sociological analysis is that, on every level, choices are made—of what it is that we want to know, of how we proceed, of what counts as knowledge— and that these choices are social even as they are cognitive and experimental.

As Steven Shapin provocatively puts it, "there is as much society inside science as outside."[4]

Of course, just how to reconcile these insights with the conspicuous and manifest successes of science, with the fact, as they say, that "science works," is a serious and difficult problem, and it remains an ongoing challenge for science studies as well as a focus of active, sometimes intense, debate. Nonetheless, there is one point on which this broad field of inquiry is unified, and it is a crucial one: Virtually all scholars in science studies take as their starting point the need to attend to the historical and social contingency of the particular kinds of human practices that, at any given time or place, are said to constitute "doing science."

For the most part, however, working scientists—those whose business it is to "do" science, to construct theories about nature rather than about science—have not read this work. My own work might be taken as a case in point. While many biologists read my biography of Barbara McClintock when it appeared in 1983, they tended to read it as a straight scientific biography, wisely refraining from reading into that work any simplistic message about a "feminist science" that some nonscientists sought in the book. By contrast, very few scientists read my much more theoretical work *Reflections on Gender and Science,* appearing only two years later, just as most had earlier taken little note of Latour and Woolgar, of the work of the Edinburgh school, or even of Kuhn. True to the demands of their professions, they kept their eyes on the business at hand and refused to be distracted. I should emphasize that this is not intended as a criticism but merely as an observation about the nature of scientific work.

In other words, up until the last few years, relations between scientists and their critics proceeded in the established fashion of academic scholarship, with claims of independent authority, even about science, treated with that mix of laissez-faire and disinterest we sometimes think of as indicative of academic freedom. Certainly there was concern in the scientific community with "scientific illiteracy" in the public at large, especially with the rise of religious fundamentalism, creationism, and New Age philosophy, all of which were seen as antithetical, if not actually hostile, to the ethos of science. But inside the academy, tolerance of the new scholarship, even if not respect, tended to prevail. After all, nothing anyone in science studies was writing—none of these theoretical inquiries into the historical and social contingency of scientific values—had much effect on the progress of their enterprise.

In these last few years, however, this tradition of passive tolerance has begun to unravel. In the minds of at least some scientists, the activities of scholars writing about science from the other side of the two-culture divide has suddenly come to seem dangerously potent, sufficiently threatening to their own endeavor to warrant their being drawn into an unfamiliar fray. As a result, the "academic wars" of recent years can now count on some very ardent new recruits, self-designated defenders of science and the Enlightenment taking arms in what they regard as the war being waged against science by their colleagues in the humanities and social sciences. Explicitly linking their caricature of science studies with postmodernism, "PC" (read feminism and multiculturalism), and the generic threat to the integrity of the academy with which recent trends in the humanities had earlier been charged, these new skirmishes raise sharply the question of whether anyone, apart from working scientists, can claim intellectual license to read, analyze, and perhaps even judge the texts and practices of science. By way of illustration, I might cite physicist Steven Weinberg's recent attacks on social constructionism and postmodernism (in his *Dreams of a Final Theory* [1994] and in a recent conference at Boston University); or the effort undertaken by physicists and mathematicians at the Institute for Advanced Studies at Princeton to successfully block the appointment of Bruno Latour in the School of Social Sciences, where he had been unanimously endorsed; or even my own stunningly unsuccessful attempt at initiating a public dialogue on these matters at MIT (of which more later).

Yet more recent was the publication of a book-length tirade, a self-described "crusade," against what the authors Paul Gross and Norman Levitt (a biologist and a mathematician) call the "muddle-headedness of the Academic Left" in its "quarrels with science." Although the authors of *Higher Superstition* never quite define what they mean by "Academic Left," and they acknowledge the internal diversity of this "large and influential community," of one thing they are certain: "To put it bluntly, the academic left [which, for them, includes virtually all critics of scientific realism, though with a special animus reserved for feminists] dislikes science." Gross and Levitt are outraged and have responded, as they themselves write, by "accusing a powerful faction in modern academic life of intellectual dereliction."[5] Not surprisingly, many readers are delighted. Jonathan Rauch, for example, in his review of *Higher Superstition* for the *Wall Street Journal,* writes:

> As far as I know, this book is the first by working scientists to pull up the PC attack on science by its roots and shake it hard. The results are refreshing. Most of what has been written about PC and its offshoots focuses on the

movement's left-wing politics and authoritarian style. Messrs. Gross and Levitt level a different charge: That, at least where science is concerned, the radicals don't have any idea what they're talking about.[6]

How comforting!

This is not the place to undertake a careful examination of the charges made by Messrs. Gross and Levitt, or of Mr. Rauch for that matter (perhaps, especially, of his easy invocation of PC as shorthand for postmodernism, social constructionism, feminism, and multiculturalism), but it may be the place to register some general observations about what seems to be going on.

First, it will surely come as a surprise to many of the particular authors Gross and Levitt take on, as it does to me, to find themselves/ourselves in one and the same political bed, especially grouped under the common denominator of our "dislike" of science. But I suppose it is in the nature of war to insist on camps, to reduce a complex terrain to two sides, in which one must be in one camp or the other. This, it seems to me, is the real tragedy of the academic wars, and if I must take a side, that side would have to be against the war itself. I want here to take the opportunity of insisting on the freedom to inhabit other spaces. For my particular concerns, these are the spaces in which one can be, on the one hand, both "for" science and "for" the need to engage in the study of science at some remove from the daily work of scientists, and, on the other hand, "against" doctrinaire claims issuing from any particular camp or school. Call it academic freedom, if you will.

The problem is straightforward enough, raising issues of both competence and respect, the two structural preconditions for any ideal of academic freedom. The question of competence arises first, especially since it has already been so forcefully raised by the critics of science studies, but it is not quite as simple a matter as these critics would have. Certainly, any claim to authority in the study of science (at least if it is to be credible) must rest on some measure of competence to read the texts of science with comprehension and discernment. But, like any other interdisciplinary venture, it also requires other kinds of competence. In particular, it requires some measure of competence in historical, philosophical, and sociological analysis, enough, say, to read that literature with comprehension. But even with my waffle, "some measure of competence," this is a tall order. Inevitably, the question arises, How much competence? What does it even mean to have "expertise" in so many different areas? And by what (or by whose) standards are these multiple competencies to be judged?

These are, of course, familiar problems, inherent to any interdisciplinary effort, and they are the principal reason why interdisciplinarity has been such a thorn in the side of the modern university throughout its history. But, with whatever discomfort, universities have coped, largely because of the necessity of interdisciplinary challenges to maintaining the vitality of disciplines. Today, however, new challenges have arisen for measures of competence and notions of "standards." Some would even say that these challenges are tantamount to abandoning the idea of Truth, and if we can't talk about Truth, how can we talk about standards?

There has been a great deal of discussion about the erosion of the philosophical foundations on which the ideal of academic freedom rests, resulting particularly from the critical theories of knowledge and interpretation usually associated with postmodernism. As Louis Menand puts it (see chap. 1),

> It is this state of intellectual affairs that has made it seem so difficult to argue that professors need the protections associated with the concept of academic freedom, since so many professors . . . now . . . assert that their work is not about reaching the truth about a field, but about intervening politically in a conversation—a "discourse"—that is already partial and political.

Furthermore, some would add, if our work is not about "reaching the truth," in what terms are we even to talk about measures of competence or standards?

I suggest that we may have something of a red herring here. While it is undoubtedly the case that past justifications for academic freedom, as well as past talk about competence and standards, have leaned heavily on notions both of intellectual inquiry as a "neutral and disinterested activity," of Truth as a certain and unambiguous goal, and of Reason as a disembodied, transcendent, and exceedingly privileged attribute, and it is equally true that confidence in these Enlightenment ideals has taken a severe beating in recent years, I would argue that the relevance of such observations to the current crisis in the academy has been severely overrated. Indeed, I would suggest that our measures of scholarly competence have never depended on Truth as an ontological category but rather on something I might call social truth.[7]

Shared measures of competence, some degree of consensus about standards, and some notion of academic freedom are certainly necessary to the viability of intellectual inquiry. But, as others before me have observed, these need not depend on the survival of Truth and Reason (capital T and R). Respect for truth (small t) and reason (small r)—and especially, as Rorty puts it earlier in this volume, confidence in truth-telling—will suffice. Indeed, without such respect and confidence, we could hardly proceed. These may not be popular words in the current intellectual climate of the humanities or of much of the social sciences, yet they nonetheless provide a kind of ground upon which even the most ardent poststructuralists continue to rely, a baseline demonstrably sufficient for at least locally agreed upon measures of competence and standards. Only the most casual (might one say, incompetent?) reading of, say, Foucault and Derrida (the culprits most often cited) will miss the density of philosophical reasoning and historical facticity on which their arguments are based (or on which their arguments can be criticized) and fail to see that it is the *abuse* of absolute notions of Truth and Reason with which these authors take issue. But my concern here is, finally, not with the merits or difficulties in the writings of either Foucault or Derrida. The simple fact is (as a merely cursory look at the historical record will remind us) that, interestingly enough, the claims of science studies to independent authority were (especially in its first two decades) almost entirely uninformed by developments in French poststructuralist thought. The crucial feature of these claims was not in fact any grand repudiation of Enlightenment ideals, and certainly not any disregard for truth or reason, but precisely their independence of received wisdom within the natural sciences, that is, the essentially inter- (or extra-) disciplinary nature of their claim to authority. The critiques that emerged from these efforts—of proof, of truth and rationality, even of objectivity—rested critically not on the abandonment of these values but rather on their deployment in forms of analysis in which scientists themselves were neither expert, nor to which, for the most part, they were even privy.

For many (beginning with Kuhn), it was careful historical analysis that provided enlightenment; for others, it was the empirical evidence provided by sociological and ethnographic studies; to feminists, it was reasoning informed not so much by the methods of established disciplines in other parts of the academy as it was by a close attention to marks of gender that had gone unnoticed by virtually all intellectual historians. The crucial point is that these other vantage points—and other kinds of evidence (or data) they elicited—provided access to an understanding of the workings of science not readily available to working scientists precisely because of their investment, generally obligatory, in the daily demands of their own technical agendas.

I have already remarked on the fact that very few scientists read this work. In fact, this work was not for the most part even intended for a scientific audience. It was aimed at the ways in which science is understood (by nonscientists and by scientists) rather than at its internal workings. Almost no one in science studies argued with the efficacy of science, though many took issue with conventional modes of accounting for that efficacy. Similarly, I do not know of anyone who has sought to obstruct or otherwise interfere with the actual practices of scientists (though a very few—myself for one—have explicitly sought to enlarge their agendas). In other words, despite our rejection of the view of science as "outside society," for all practical purposes the operative boundary between that particular social activity we call science and other activities more traditionally recognized as social remained surprisingly intact. Small wonder, then, that scientists saw little reason to read this work or to feel threatened by its presence in the academy: As they quite rightly perceived, their own enterprise—how they ran their labs, their seminars, or their classes—was scarcely touched by it. Why then bother with what their less enlightened brothers (or sisters) in the academy might be up to?

Given the particular character of the recent outbursts of some scientists, one might think that the tacit contract that had previously been in place should have been very welcome to practitioners of science studies, and undoubtedly to many it was. But not to me. Not only did such a state of passive tolerance, or, more accurately, of inattention, preclude the possibility of any constructive impact from this work on the actual conduct of science, but, in my view, that inattention must also take at least partial blame for the more irresponsible excesses that can in fact be found in some of the writings of science studies. If scientists were insulated from the analyses of their critics, now it must be said that those who had taken the understanding of science as their mission have, especially in recent years, become increasingly insulated from the concerns of their subjects. This inattention on both sides of the divide—each to the activities of the other—has been as damaging as it has been complicitous. It has made it virtually impossible to find the kind of dialogue that is so vital to the health of any interdisciplinary venture. Indeed, it might be said that none of the conditions of exchange required to secure the integrity of interdisciplinary scholarship are in place.

The deepest failure is, of course, the absence of respect. In its absence we can begin to see—again, on both sides of the divide—the cultivation of active disrespect, a disdain that is increasingly coming to serve as substitute, and even as justification, for the failure to acquire those extradisciplinary competencies required for constructive dialogue. Where is the animus coming from? And how novel is it? Is it in fact so different from academic contests of the past? As we well know, the academy has always been a contentious place, but still I think an important dimension of the current state of affairs is new. However imperfectly, universities have a long history of coping, more or less well, with the problems raised by interdisciplinary challenges. And to the extent that they were able to do so, it was because representatives of the various disciplines involved could count on at least a minimum level of mutual respect simply by virtue of their simultaneous membership in that larger protected and privileged community we call the academy. I suggest that part of the problem we encounter today is that the academy is no longer either quite so protected or so privileged as it used to be.

I am reminded of an incident which can perhaps serve as a useful allegory: Some years ago, having just moved from New York City to Cambridge, Massachusetts, I enrolled my daughter in a wonderful, quintessentially Cantabrigian private school called Shady Hill. We were utterly charmed by the niceties of life around us, but nothing impressed us quite so much as the novel solution Shady Hill had developed for dealing with the painful problem of inclusion/exclusion almost inevitably raised by private, at-home, birthday parties: Invitations were simply posted on the bulletin board! It was only over time that I came to understand how deeply this ostensibly inclusive and democratic solution depended on the underlying and taken-for-granted exclusivity of the school.

In one sense at least, the walls of academe are conspicuously like those of Shady Hill: their efficacy in securing internal confidence and respect is in direct proportion to their height. And in the turbulent, and yes, multicultural, world of the 1990s, the academy is manifestly no longer the gentleman's club it once was. The influx of new constituencies, particularly as these find expression in feminism and multiculturalism, looms large in today's academic wars, and one must at least ask: How much of the evident animus of these wars reflects that most primitive fear of outsiders in the realm? Or, to paraphrase David Hollinger, how wide can we draw the academic circle of "we"? Can these new members of the community be relied on to conform, to adhere to and uphold the established codes? And when they don't, when disagreements inevitably do arise, can these disagreements—especially with those who don't even look like gentlemen—possibly be expected to remain gentlemanly?

Evidently not. Indeed, it is the nastiness, the pervasive mistrust, and the absence of even reasonable efforts at mutual understanding that most conspicuously characterize these recent exchanges, as much so between science and science studies as in the academic wars in the humanities. In my own field, what has all along been most troubling is the absence of sufficient respect to even bother trying to understand the intellectual issues at stake in debates internal to disciplines, or schools, beyond one's own. Now that some scientists have begun to attend to the work of science studies, they express outrage at the failures of technical comprehension in the writings of some of its authors, and I sympathize. But the notion that these works might themselves depend on distinctions which scientists on their own part are rarely equipped to make—or that a response to science studies requires intellectual effort of any kind—rarely registers.

Again, an incident from my own experience may be useful. Earlier I alluded to a panel discussion I organized, two years ago, at MIT in an effort to explore issues of mutual misunderstanding between scientists and their critics, volunteering my own services as mediator or, rather, as translator. What happened, however, in lieu of the discussion I had hoped would take place, was that I myself became the object of an unbridled attack from the scientists on the panel—as it happens, for claims I have not only never made but had frequently (even on that very occasion) explicitly disputed. Later, in an offstage conversation with a colleague of mine in the history of science, the leader of the charge remarked that he had never found enlightenment from any work in science studies. My colleague asked the obvious question, "What have you read?" And sure enough, after pressing the point some, she managed to elicit the confession that he had read none of the books standard in a science studies curriculum, not even my own works that he had just attacked. As a number of authors have noted, knowledge is not the only available coinage of power; ignorance can serve quite as well.

By contrast, it must be granted that Gross and Levitt, the authors of *Higher Superstition,* have done a great deal of reading, going beyond the media accounts to the texts themselves. Their comprehension may be less than could be hoped for, but in at least some cases they are able to make criticisms that could, and indeed should, be addressed. And for this they surely deserve credit. But unfortunately Gross and Levitt are not interested in initiating a dialogue. The notion of dialogue implies the symmetry of exchange—interlocutors talking to each other. And there is neither symmetry here nor any expectation of a two-way exchange. Gross and Levitt are not suggesting that their understanding of the history or philosophy of science might be up for either evaluation or discussion, only that of those— anyone?—not actually working as scientists. They are not interested in hearing back from the authors they critique; in fact, they are not even talking to them. Their audience, and their concerns, lie elsewhere. As they themselves explain:

> The academic left's rebellion against science is unlikely to affect scientific practice and content. . . . The danger, for the moment at least, is not to science itself. What is threatened is the capability of the larger culture, which embraces the mass media as well as the more serious processes of education, to interact fruitfully with the sciences.[8]

Their audience, in other words, is, finally, not the "academic left," as they call it, but the nonscientific culture at large. Nor is their concern with the practice or content of science, or even, for that matter, with the integrity of the academy. It is with the public perception of science—especially with how the "larger culture" might "interact with the sciences." And here, perhaps, we begin to see what most crucially distinguishes the debates between scientists and their critics from the academic wars more generally, that is, what gives these debates their particular edge.

I noted earlier that it is only in the last few years that work in science studies has come to be perceived (at least by some scientists) as actually threatening, enough so to warrant their active attention. The obvious question is, Why now? The answer, I fear, may be equally obvious and perhaps even banal. For all the talk about the autonomy of science, the basic fact is that science, especially big science, is in a position of utter and absolute dependency. Without the continuing support of the nonscientific public, the institution of science as we have come to know it, and as working scientists have come to take for granted, would end. It is thus hardly surprising that scientists would want the public to perceive their ventures in the best possible light, even wish to dictate that perception. But as their current budgets so palpably indicate, their ability to do so has weakened considerably in the past few years. After decades of growth, the funding of basic research has leveled off, and in some areas (e.g., particle physics), it has even declined. The cancellation of the Superconducting Super Collider came as a particularly visceral shock to the scientific community, and many are now alarmed.

Does this have anything to do with the writings of science studies? Clearly, their critics think that it does. But what exactly is the connection? Perhaps an argument for some such connection can be based on the one concern that those in science studies do in fact share with their colleagues in the natural sciences. Despite their failure to talk to each other and the frequency with which they talk past each other, both groups are concerned with what used to be called "the contract between science and society."

Where they differ is in their assumptions about the nature of this contract. Few if any scholars in science studies believe that social support for science should be unconditional. Rather, they take the contingency of the social approval on which scientific research so manifestly depends as both necessary and appropriate.

Even so, however, we are still a long way from a direct link between the work of science studies and the current funding crisis. This work may well have had a major influence on the ways in which many scholars in the humanities and social sciences think about the natural sciences, but I don't think anyone believes that its often quite abstruse arguments have had anywhere near the breadth or degree of influence it would take to cause this particular crisis. Nonetheless, it makes for an easy and obvious target: First, it is close by. Even if it poses no threat to the practice of science "in the short run" (as Gross and Levitt themselves admit), the obvious fear is that, over the long run, it might. Furthermore, this threat, unlike many others, is housed within the academy, thus putting it in the domain in which scientists have accumulated palpable power over the last few decades. From the anxious perspective of scientists alarmed by recent trends in funding, science studies comes to look like the "enemy within." And fortuitously enough, especially when this endeavor is linked with feminism, multiculturalism, and poststructuralism, there is the invaluable resource of ready allies from the academic wars already raging, and a large and avid constituency waiting eagerly to see all these new developments, along with their proponents, discredited, or better yet, banished.

This may make good political logic, but it is in the name of scientific logic and objectivity that these arguments are usually made. I suggest that if the work of science studies has any merit, it is precisely here, in its effort to distinguish between the two kinds of logic, where that merit is to be found. One might even say that the arguments deployed by Gross and Levitt, or by others with similar concerns, provide an ideal case for analysis of the political and ideological uses to which the rhetoric of objectivity so easily lends itself.

Rorty is right: invocations of epistemology are beside the point; indeed, they are simultaneously misleading and counterproductive. The crisis we face today is real enough, but it has far less to do with arguments about the locus or status of ontological Truth than it has to do with current social, political, and economic realities. Terms like "objectivity" and "PC" have become weapons in the social, political, and economic struggles in which we are all embedded.

In closing, it might be useful to recall that the term "PC" actually originated on the Left, as an expression inviting a certain self-mockery and at least implicit self-criticism. Employed as originally intended—self-reflexively—it is in fact a useful term, one that we might all invoke to protect ourselves from the dangers of complacency and orthodoxy to which we are, merely by virtue of our disciplinary identifications, inevitably subject. But when invoked as a slur or attack on the discipline and disciplines of others, it has the opposite effect of polarizing debate, foreclosing dialogue, and blinding us to ideological abuses of reason on our own part, in our own domains.

The tension between scientists and their critics in science studies is real enough, and it will not go away. But it has little if anything to do with political correctness. What it is primarily about is the disparity between the blank check that working scientists want (some would say, need) for the conduct of their enterprise, and what the rest of us need in order to evaluate and respond appropriately to both their claims and their demands. The work of science studies makes abundantly clear the need to reexamine the social contract on which science depends, and this is not welcome news to working scientists. All too understandably, they would prefer their demands for complete autonomy to go unchallenged. But if this is not possible, as I think it clearly is not, how are we, as members of a responsible academy, to deal with the conflicts that inevitably ensue? Is it too naive to believe that traditional ideals of analysis, dialogue, and respectful criticism can suffice? If the raison d'être of the university rests on its unwillingness to sanction ignorance, then the most serious threat to its future is to be found in our willingness to tolerate the substitution of diatribe for criticism and our failure to censure any abrogation of conventional intellectual standards—even by those who may, in other contexts, have earned our respect.

NOTES

1. E.g., the very problem of "authority" that has been raised by postmodernist critiques.

2. These data have been taken from the *Digest of Educational Statistics,* 1992, U.S. Department of Education, Office of Educational Research and Improvement, NCES 02-097, and Seymour E. Harris, *A Statistical Portrait of Higher Education,* Report for the Carnegie Commission on Higher Education (New York: McGraw-Hill, 1972).

3. To borrow the title of Peter Galison, *How Experiments End* (Chicago: University of Chicago Press, 1987).

4. See Steven Shapin, *A Social History of Truth: Gentility, Credibility, and Scientific Knowledge in Seventeenth-Century England* (Chicago: University of Chicago Press, 1994).

5. See Paul Gross and Norman Levitt, *Higher Superstition: The Academic Left and Its Quarrels with Science* (Baltimore: Johns Hopkins University Press, 1994).

6. Jonathan Rauch, "Academic Left vs. Science," *Wall Street Journal,* April 19, 1994, p. A18.

7. See, e.g., Shapin, *A Social History of Truth.*

8. See Gross and Levitt, *Higher Superstition.*

NINE

Identity, Authority, and Freedom:
The Potentate and the Traveler

Edward W. Said

Discussion concerning academic freedom is not only different in each society but also takes very different forms, one version of which in American universities today concerns the nature of the curriculum. For at least the past decade, a debate has been going on between those, on the one hand, who feel that the traditional curriculum of the liberal arts—in particular the core of Western humanities courses—has been under severe attack, and those on the other side, who believe that the curriculum in the humanities and the social sciences should more directly reflect the interests of groups in society who have been suppressed, ignored, or papered over with high-sounding formulas. For it is a fact that everywhere in the United States, which is after all an immigrant society made up of many Africans and Asians as well as Europeans, universities have finally had to deal with non-Western societies, with the literature, history, and particular concerns of women, various nationalities, and minorities; and with unconventional, hitherto untaught subjects such as popular culture, mass communications and film, and oral history. In addition, a whole slew of controversial political issues like race, gender, imperialism, war, and slavery have found their way into lectures and seminars. To this extraordinary, almost Copernican change in the general intellectual consciousness, responses have often been very hostile. Some critics have reacted as if the very nature of the university and academic freedom has been threatened because unduly politicized. Others have gone further: for them the critique of the Western canon, with its panoply of
214 what its opponents have called Dead White European Males (for example,

Aristotle, Shakespeare, and Wordsworth), has rather improbably signaled the onset of a new fascism, the demise of Western civilization itself, and the return of slavery, child marriage, bigamy, and the harem.

In most cases, however, the actual changes in the canon that reflect the interests of women or African or Native Americans have been pretty mild: Western humanities courses now often include Jane Austen or Toni Morrison, and they might also have added novels by Chinua Achebe, García Márquez, and Salman Rushdie. There have been a few extreme cases of silliness: younger teachers and scholars publicly attacking more senior scholars as racists, or pillorying their peers for not being "politically correct." Yet all of this discussion and controversy underlines the general fact that what goes on in school or university is somehow privileged, whether on the one hand it is supposed to appear "above" parochial interests, changes in fashion or style, and political pressure, or on the other hand, whether the university is meant to be engaged intellectually and politically with significant political and social change, with improvements in the status of subaltern or minority populations, and with abuses of power and lapses in morality, which the university must remedy, criticize, and align itself in opposition to.

Although a thousand qualifications and conditions can enter into a discussion of either or both sides, one assumption is common to both: the idea that the status of university or school as well as what goes along with them intellectually and socially is special, is different from other sites in society like the government bureaucracy, the workplace, or the home. I believe that all societies today assign a special privilege to the academy that, whether the privilege exempts it from intercourse with the everyday world or involves it directly in that world, says that unique conditions do, indeed ought to, prevail in it. To say that someone is educated or an educator is to say something having to do with the mind, with intellectual and moral values, with a particular process of inquiry, discussion, and exchange, none of which is encountered as regularly outside as inside the academy. The idea is that academies form the minds of the young, prepare them for life, just as—to look at things from the point of view of the teacher—to teach is to be engaged in a vocation or calling having principally to do not with financial gain but with the unending search for truth.

These are very high and important matters, and for those of us who have made education our life, they testify to the genuine aura surrounding the academic and intellectual enterprise. There *is* something hallowed and consecrated about the academy; there *is* a sense of violated sanctity experienced by us when the university or school is subjected to crude political pressures. Yet, I believe, to be convinced of these genuinely powerful truths is not entirely to be freed of the circumstances—some would call them encumbrances—that impinge on education today, influence our thinking about it, and shape our efforts in the academy. The point I want to make is that as we consider these situational or contextual matters, the search for academic freedom, to which this occasion is so manifestly dedicated, becomes more important, more urgent, more requiring of careful and reflective analysis. So whereas it is universally true that contemporary societies treat the academy with seriousness and respect, each community of academics, intellectuals, and students must wrestle with the problem of what academic freedom in that society at that time actually is and should be.

In the United States, where I live and work, there has been a distinct change in the academic climate since I was a student a generation ago. Until the late 1960s, it was assumed by most people that what took place within university precincts was removed from any steady, or collaborative, or—in the worst case—collusive association with the world outside. Yet because the experience of the war in Vietnam was so powerful, and because there was so much traffic between the academy and the institutions of government and power, the veil was rent, so to speak. No longer was it taken for granted that political scientists or sociologists were sage-like theoreticians or impartial researchers; many of them were discovered to be working, sometimes secretly and sometimes openly, on such topics as counterinsurgency and "lethal research" for the State Department, the CIA, or the Pentagon.

Yet after the university's apartness was seen as an idea to have been abandoned, an equal and opposite set of reactions set in. It became almost a cliché that the university was to be regarded only as an arm of the government, that it reflected only the interests of corporations and establishment power and should therefore be wholly transformed into a place where students would be educated as reformers or revolutionaries. Relevance was the new watchword. And while a new set of materials was introduced into the academy for the first time—I refer once again to women's studies, minority studies, studies that deal with the effects of war, racism, and class and gender oppression—there did in fact seem to be a new worldliness in the university that denied it the relative aloofness it once seemed entitled to.

As a reaction to all this, academic freedom was the phrase given to the movement that claimed to want to return the university to a now very much regretted sort of impartiality to, and distance from, the everyday world. But here all sorts of exaggerations and polemical distortions were introduced. During the 1980s, the American university was portrayed as being in the possession of a Marxist revolutionary conspiracy. This of course was a ludicrously false notion. Also, the argument put forward in the name of academic freedom claimed that because so many new courses and ideas had been introduced into the traditional curriculum, the university's age-old standards had diminished, had fallen prey to outside political pressures. To restore the university's true freedom from everyday life meant returning to courses, ideas, and values that derived exclusively from the mainstream European thinkers—Plato, Aristotle, Sophocles, Descartes, Montaigne, Shakespeare, Bacon, Locke, and so on. One of the most famous and commercially successful books of the past decade was *The Closing of the American Mind,* a long diatribe against an assorted set of villains, including Nietzsche, feminism, Marxism, and Black Studies; the author of this work, who had been a professor at Cornell University when for a short time the university had been shut down by a group of armed African-American students, was so embittered by his experience that his book argued quite frankly for the university's freedom to educate not large numbers of the deprived and disadvantaged but a small, carefully prepared and instructed elite. The result would be, as the book was quite explicit in explaining, that only a handful of works by the Greeks and some French Enlightenment philosophers would survive the rigorous tests for inclusion in the newly "liberated" curriculum.

But the prescription for curing the university of its woes, for liberating it from political pressures is in a sense worse than the malady. Surely one would have thought that to use the concept of freedom about the academy is not on the face of it to talk mainly about exclusion but about inclusion, and surely it would seem to be true that the university ought to be the place not where many vigorous and exciting intellectual pursuits should be forbidden but where they ought to be encouraged on as wide a front as possible. I will grant, as everyone must, that the concept of freedom cannot be a license for, as Matthew Arnold put it in another context, entirely doing as one likes. But it must be the case, I think, that advocates of freedom for university communities to undertake intellectual pursuits cannot spend most of their time arguing that only a handful of approved books, ideas, disciplines, and methods are worthy of serious intellectual attention. The realities of social life are viewed in this perspective as sordid and demeaning, although it needs to be noted that professors such as the author of *The Closing of the American Mind* have no difficulty accepting money from corporations and foundations outside the university who happen to espouse their own deeply conservative views. To say of such practices that they represent a double standard is no exaggeration. For you cannot honestly impugn people as enemies of academic freedom just because they welcome worldly concerns into the academy while, when you do more or less the same thing, you consider yourself to be "upholding standards."

An altogether different challenge to the concept of academic freedom is found in national universities in the Arab world, which is where I originally come from. I speak here of most of the large public universities in countries like Jordan, Syria, Iraq, Egypt, Morocco, Saudi Arabia, and other Gulf states. Most of these countries are in fact run by secular governments, although some—like Saudi Arabia—have secular governments with a religious mandate. What is important to understand, however, is that with few exceptions Arab universities are not only nationalist universities but are also political institutions, for perfectly understandable reasons. For several centuries, the Arab world has been dominated by Ottoman or European colonialism. National independence for countries like Egypt and Syria, say, meant that young people at last could be educated fully in the traditions, histories, languages, and cultures of their own particular Arab countries. In my own case, for instance, I was educated entirely in British colonial schools in Palestine and Egypt, where all study focused on the history of British society, literature, and values. Much the same was true in the main British and French colonies, such as India and Algeria, where it was assumed that native elites would be taught the rudiments of intellectual culture in idioms and methods designed in effect to keep those native elites subservient to colonial rule, the superiority of European learning, and so forth. Until I was about sixteen I knew a great deal more about the eighteenth-century enclosure system in England than I did about how the Islamic *waqfs* operated in my own part of the world, and—irony of ironies—colonial preconsuls like Cromer and Kitchener were more familiar to me than Haroun al-Rashid or Khalid ibn al-Walid.

When independence was achieved as a result of anticolonial struggles, one of the first areas to be changed was education. I recall, for instance, that after the Revolution of 1952 in Egypt a great deal of emphasis was placed on the Arabization of the curriculum, the Arabization of intellectual norms, the Arabization of values to be inculcated in schools and universities. The same was true in Algeria after 1962, where an entire generation of Muslims were for the first time entitled and enjoined to study Arabic, which had been forbidden except as a language in mosques while Algeria was considered and ruled as a department of France. It is important to understand, therefore, the passion that went into reclaiming educational territory that for so long had been dominated by foreign rulers in the Arab world, and it is equally important to understand the tremendous spiritual wound felt by many of us because of the sustained presence in our midst of domineering foreigners who taught us to respect distant norms and values more than our own. Our culture was felt to be of a lower grade, perhaps even congenitally inferior and something of which to be ashamed.

Now it would be wrong and even absurd to suggest that a national education based on Arabic norms is in and of itself either trivial or impoverished. The Arab-Islamic tradition is one of the great cultural contributions to humanity, and in the old universities of Fez and al-Azhar as well as the various *madrasas* throughout the Arab world, a rich educational experience has been provided to uncounted generations of students. Yet it is also true to say that in the newly independent countries of the Arab world, the national universities were reconceived, I believe, as (rightly or wrongly) extensions of the newly established national security state. Once again it is clear that all societies accord a remarkable privilege to the university and school as crucibles for shaping national identity.

Yet all too often in the Arab world, true education was short-circuited, so to speak. Whereas in the past young Arabs fell prey to the intervention of foreign ideas and norms, now they were to be remade in the image of the ruling party, which, given the Cold War and the Arab-Israeli struggle, became also the party of national security—and in some countries, the only party. Thus adding to the vastly increased pressure on universities to open their doors to everyone in the new society—an extremely admirable policy—universities also became the proving ground for earnest patriots. Professorial appointments were, as they are in many places in the world today, civil service appointments. Alas, political conformity rather than intellectual excellence was often made to serve as a criterion for promotion and appointment, with the general result that timidity, a studious lack of imagination, and careful conservatism came to rule intellectual practice. Moreover, because the general atmosphere in the Arab world of the past three decades has become both conspiratorial and, I am sorry to say, repressive—all in the name of national security—nationalism in the university has come to represent not freedom but accommodation, not brilliance and daring but caution and fear, not the advancement of knowledge but self-preservation.

Not only did many brilliant and gifted people leave the Arab world in a massive brain-drain, but I would say that the whole notion of academic freedom underwent a significant downgrading during the past three decades. It became possible for one to be free in the university only if one

completely avoided anything that might attract unwelcome attention or suspicion. I do not want to make a long, anguished recital of how badly demor-
alized and discouraged a place the Arab university, in most of its contemporary aspects, has become, but I do think it is important to link its depressed
situation with the lack of democratic rights, the absence of a free press, and
an atmosphere bereft of well-being and confidence elsewhere in the society.
No one can say that these things are not connected to each other, because
they so obviously are. Political repression has never been good for academic
freedom, and, perhaps more importantly, it has been disastrous for academic
and intellectual excellence. My assessment of Arab academic life is that too
high a price has been paid in sustaining nationalist regimes that have allowed
political passions and an ideology of conformity to dominate—perhaps even
to swallow up—civil institutions such as the university. To make the practice
of intellectual discourse dependent on conformity to a predetermined political ideology is to nullify intellect altogether.

For all its problems, however, the American academy is a very different
place from its counterpart in the Arab world. To suggest that there are any
obvious similarities at all would be to misrepresent each seriously. Yet I do
not want to celebrate the greater manifest freedom of inquiry, the generally
higher level of intellectual attainment, the quite extraordinary range of interests demonstrated in the American academy at the expense of the much
more obvious constraints and difficulties in Arab universities, which after
everything is said share the fate of many other universities in the Third
World. That sort of almost bullying praise of the virtues of Western education today would be too easy and far too simple.

Nevertheless it is important to show the connection between such
different circumstances as those that obtain in the Middle East and in the
United States by remarking how it is that in both a very great premium is
placed upon the cultural and national *identity* of the education being offered.
I spoke earlier about the debate between upholders and opponents of the
Western canon in the American university; I also spoke of how in the post-
independence, postcolonial Arab universities a great degree of emphasis was
placed on the *Arabness* of what was being offered. In both cases therefore,
ordinarily so different and so far removed from each other, one idea—that
of national identity—shines through. It is precisely this idea, American
and Western in one case, Arab and Islamic in the other, that plays an aston-
ishingly important role as authority and as point of reference in the whole
educational process. I want to raise the question of how the central
importance and authority given the national identity impinges on and

greatly influences, surreptitiously and often unquestioningly, academic freedom—that is, what transpires in the name of academic freedom.

When I discussed earlier how the specific social and cultural circumstances of the academic situation in each society define the problem of academic freedom, national identity was very much what I had in mind. Certainly this is true of a society like that of South Africa, now undergoing particularly difficult and stressful transformation. But as one looks elsewhere in the world, one finds that many places are experiencing much the same contest over what the national identity is or ought to be. This contest, almost more than anything else, defines the political and cultural situation of the late twentieth century: that as the world grows smaller and more interdependent economically, environmentally, and through the revolution in communications, there is a greater sense that societies interact, often abrasively, in terms of who or what their national identities are. Consider on a global level the importance today of the Western European community as one large cultural block interacting with the Eastern European community and the former Soviet Union, with Japan and the United States, and with many parts of the Third World. Similarly, look at the contest between the Islamic world and the West, in which national, cultural, and religious self-images and self-definitions play so powerful a role. To speak of hegemony, attempts at domination, and the control of resources in this global struggle is, I strongly believe, to speak in very accurate (if also melodramatic) terms.

But that is not all. Within societies such as this one and those in the Western, African, Asian, and Islamic worlds, there is also a contest as to which concept of national identity ought to prevail. Although this question is principally of philosophical and historical derivation, inevitably it leads one to the urgent political issue of how, given the definition of identity, the society is to be governed. To look closely at the recent history of imperialism and decolonization is to grasp the centrality of the debate. In Algeria, as the works of Frantz Fanon eloquently testify, Algerians were viewed by the French as a subordinate race, fit only for colonial and subaltern status. Even the distinguished humanistic writer Albert Camus, who was a native-born member of the French settler population, embodied the Algerian in his fiction as an essentially nameless, threatening creature; during the late fifties Camus explicitly said in his *Algerian Chronicles* that there was no Algerian Muslim nation. Of course there was. After the liberation in 1962 one of the principal tasks of the FLN was to reestablish the integrity, the centrality, the paramountcy and sovereignty of the Muslim Algerian identity.

With the creation of a new governmental structure in Algeria came an educational program focused first on the teaching of Arabic and on Algerian history, formerly either banned or subordinated to programs stressing the superiority of French civilization. The subsequent disastrous course of events in Algeria, the rise of Islamists and military groups, is too well known for me to do more than allude to it.

Surely in South Africa much the same dynamic will be and doubtless already is embodied in the nature of the educational program, as the country moves out of apartheid into a new system of democratic, racially unbiased government. However, there are some further points I wish to make about all this, as it has a bearing on the question of academic freedom.

The first is that in a condition in which cultural conflict is, to all intents and purposes, universal, the relationship between the national identity and other national identities is going to be reflected in the academy. The question is how. All cultures teach about themselves, and all cultures naturally assert their supremacy over others. To study the tradition, the masterpieces, the great interpretive methods of a culture inclines members of that culture to reverence, respect, loyalty, and even patriotism. This of course is understandable. But my point is that no culture exists in isolation, and since it is a matter of course that the study of one's own tradition in school and university is taken for granted, we must look at what of *other* cultures, *other* traditions, *other* national communities also is communicated as one's own culture is studied. I should like to argue that if the authority granted our own culture carries with it the authority to perpetuate cultural hostility, then a true academic freedom is very much at risk, having as it were conceded that intellectual discourse must worship at the altar of national identity and thereby denigrate or diminish others.

Let me explain. Historically, every society has its Other: The Greeks had the barbarians, the Arabs the Persians, the Hindus the Muslims, and on and on. But since the nineteenth century consolidated the world system, all cultures and societies today are intermixed. No country on earth is made up of homogeneous natives; each has its immigrants, its internal "Others," and each society, very much like the world we live in, is a hybrid. Yet a discrepancy exists at the very heart of this vital, complex, and intermingled world. I have in mind the discrepancy between the heterogeneous reality and the concept of national identity, to which so much of education is in fact dedicated. If we recall once again the two examples I gave earlier of debate about what is Western in the American university and of politicization of the Arabness of the Arab university, we will note that in both instances a faltering and outdated concept of a single national identity more or less lords it over the true variety and manifold diversity of human life. In both cases a kind of supernational concept—that of the West in the United States, and that of the Arabs or Islam in countries like Algeria, Syria, and Iraq (each of which has large minority populations)—is pressed into service. This scarcely improves things, since in both a combination of authority and defensiveness inhibits, disables, and ultimately falsifies thought. What finally matters about the West or the Arabs, in my opinion, is not what these notions exclude but to what they are connected, how much they include, and how interesting are the interactions between them and other cultures.

I do not have an easy way of resolving this very serious discrepancy. I do know, nevertheless, that the meaning of academic freedom cannot simply be reduced to venerating the unexamined authority of a national identity and its culture. For in its essence the intellectual life—and I speak here mainly of what I know about the social sciences and the humanities—is about the freedom to be critical: criticism *is* intellectual life and, while the academic precinct contains a great deal in it, its spirit is intellectual and critical, and neither reverential nor patriotic. One of the great lessons of the critical spirit is that human life and history are secular—that is, actually constructed and reproduced by men and women. The problem with the inculcation of cultural, national, or ethnic identity is that it takes insufficient note of how these identities are constructions, not god-given or natural artifacts. If the academy is to be a place for the realization not of the nation but of the intellect—and that, I think is the academy's reason for being—then the intellect must not be coercively held in thrall to the authority of the national identity. Otherwise, I fear, the old inequities, cruelties, and unthinking attachments that have so disfigured human history will be recycled by the academy, which then loses much of its real intellectual freedom as a result.

I would put the crucial question this way: what kind of authority, what sort of human norms, what kind of identity do we allow to lead us, to guide our study, to dictate our educational processes? The question is especially relevant in cases where after years of repression—South Africa and Palestine are excellent cases in point—the prospects of liberation and independence entitle us to ask the question for the first time. Do we say: now that we have won, that we have achieved equality and independence, let us elevate ourselves, our history, our cultural or ethnic identity above that of others, uncritically giving this identity of ours centrality and coercive dominance? Do we substitute for a Eurocentric norm an Afrocentric or Islamo- or Arabocentric one? Or, as happened so many times in the postcolonial world, do we get our independence and then return to models for education derived lazily, adopted imitatively and uncritically, from elsewhere? In short, do we use the freedom we have fought for merely to replicate the mind-forged manacles that once enslaved us, and having put them on do we proceed to apply them to others less fortunate than ourselves?

Raising these questions means that the university—more generally speaking the academy, but especially, I think, the university—has a privileged role to play in dealing with these matters. Universities exist in the world, although each university, as I have suggested, exists in its own particular world, with a history and social circumstances all of its own. I cannot bring myself to believe that, even though it cannot be an immediately political arena, the university is free of the encumbrances, the problems, the social dynamics of its surrounding environment. How much better to take note of these realities than blithely to talk about academic freedom in an airy and insouciant way, as if real freedom happens, and having once happened goes on happening undeterred and unconcerned. When I first began teaching about thirty years ago, an older colleague took me aside and informed me that the academic life was odd indeed; it was sometimes deathly boring, it was generally polite and in its own way quite impotently genteel, but whatever the case, he added, it was certainly better than working! None of us can deny the sense of luxury carried inside the academic sanctum, as it were, the real sense that as most people go to their jobs and suffer their daily anxiety, we read books and talk and write of great ideas, experiences, epochs. In my opinion, there is no higher privilege. But in actuality no university or school can really be a shelter from the difficulties of human life and more specifically from the political intercourse of a given society and culture.

This is by no means to deny that, as Newman said so beautifully and so memorably,

> [A university] has this object and this mission; it contemplates neither moral impression nor mechanical production; it professes to exercise the mind neither in art nor in duty; its function is intellectual culture; here it may leave its scholars, and it has done its work when it has done as much as this. It educates the intellect to reason well in all matters, to reach out towards truth, and to grasp it.[1]

Note the care with which Newman, perhaps with Swift the greatest of English prose stylists, selects his words for what actions take place in the pursuit of knowledge: words like *exercise, educates, reach out,* and *grasp.* In none of these words is there anything to suggest coercion, or direct utility, or immediate advantage or dominance. Newman says in another place,

> Knowledge . . . [is] something intellectual, something which grasps what it perceives through the senses; something which takes a view of things; which sees more than the senses convey; which reasons upon what it sees, and while it sees; which invests it with an idea.

Then he adds:

> Not to know the relative disposition of things is the state of slaves or children; to have mapped out the universe is the boast, or at least the ambition, of philosophy.[2]

Newman defines philosophy as the highest state of knowledge.

These are incomparably eloquent statements, and they can only be a little deflated when we remind ourselves that Newman was speaking about English men, not women, and then also about the education of young Catholics. Nonetheless the profound truth in what Newman says is, I believe, designed to undercut any partial or somehow narrow view of education whose aim might seem only to reaffirm one particularly attractive and dominant identity, that which is the resident power or authority of the moment. Perhaps like many of his Victorian contemporaries—Ruskin comes quickly to mind—Newman was arguing earnestly for a type of education that placed the highest premium on English, European, or Christian values in knowledge. But sometimes, even though we may mean to say something, another thought at odds with what we say insinuates itself into our rhetoric and in effect criticizes it, delivers a different and less assertive idea than on the surface we might have intended. This happens when we read Newman. Suddenly we realize that although he is obviously extolling what is an overridingly Western conception of the world, with little allowance made for what was African or Latin American or Indian (or even Irish, since he was speaking in Dublin) his words let slip the notion that even an English or Western identity wasn't enough, wasn't at bottom or at best what education and freedom were all about.

Certainly it is difficult to find in Newman anything like a license either for blinkered specialization or for gentlemanly aestheticism. What he expects of the academy is, he says,

> the power of viewing many things at once as one whole, of referring them severally to their true place in the universal system, of understanding their respective values, and determining their mutual dependence.[3]

This synthetic wholeness has a special relevance to the fraught political situations of conflict, the unresolved tension, and the social as well as moral disparities that are constitutive to the world of today's academy. He proposes a large and generous view of human diversity. To link the practice of education—and by extension, of freedom—in the academy directly to the settling of political scores, or to an equally unmodulated reflection of real national conflict is neither to pursue knowledge nor in the end to educate ourselves and our students, which is an everlasting effort at understanding. But what happens when we take Newman's prescriptions about viewing many things as one whole or, referring them severally to their true place in the universal system, we transpose these notions to today's world of embattled national identities, cultural conflicts, and power relations? Is there any possibility for bridging the gap between the ivory tower of contemplative rationality ostensibly advocated by Newman and our own urgent need for self-realization and self-assertion with its background in a history of repression and denial?

I think there is. I will go further and say that it is precisely the role of the contemporary academy to bridge this gap, since society itself is too directly inflected by politics to serve so general and so finally intellectual and moral a role. We must first, I think, accept that nationalism resurgent, or even nationalism militant, whether it is the nationalism of the victim or of the victor, has its limits. Nationalism is the philosophy of identity made into a collectively organized passion. For those of us just emerging from marginality and persecution, nationalism is a necessary thing: a long-deferred and long-denied identity needs to come out into the open and take its place among other human identities. But that is only the first step. To make all or even most of education subservient to this goal is to limit human horizons without either intellectual or, I would argue, political warrant. To assume that the ends of education are best advanced by focusing principally on *our own* separateness, our own ethnic identity, culture, and traditions, ironically places us where as subaltern, inferior, or lesser races we had been placed by nineteenth-century racial theory, unable to share in the general riches of human culture. To say that women should read mainly women's literature, that blacks should study and perfect only black techniques of understanding and interpretation, that Arabs and Muslims should return to the Holy Book for all knowledge and wisdom is the inverse of saying, along with Carlyle and Gobineau, that all the lesser races must retain their inferior status in the world. There is room for all at the rendezvous of victory, said Aimé Césaire; no race has a monopoly on beauty or intelligence.

A single overmastering identity at the core of the academic enterprise, whether that identity be Western, African, or Asian, is a confinement, a deprivation. The world we live in is made up of numerous identities interacting, sometimes harmoniously, sometimes antithetically. Not to deal with that whole—which is in fact a contemporary version of the whole referred to by Newman as a true enlargement of mind—is not to have academic freedom. We cannot make our claim as seekers after justice that we advocate knowledge only of and about ourselves. Our model for academic freedom should therefore be the migrant or traveler: for if, in the real world outside the academy, we must needs be ourselves and only ourselves, inside the academy we should be able to discover and travel among other selves, other identities, other varieties of the human adventure. But, most essentially, in this joint discovery of self and Other, it is the role of the academy to transform what might be conflict, or contest, or assertion into reconciliation, mutuality, recognition, and creative interaction. So much of the knowledge produced by Europe about Africa, or about India and the Middle East, originally derived from the need for imperial control; indeed, as a recent study of Roderick Murchison by Robert Stafford convincingly shows, even geology and biology were implicated, along with geography and ethnography, in the imperial scramble for Africa.[4] But rather than viewing the search for knowledge in the academy as the search for coercion and control over others, we should regard knowledge as something for which to *risk* identity, and we should think of academic freedom as an invitation to give up on identity in the hope of understanding and perhaps even assuming more than one. We must always view the academy as a place to voyage in, owning none of it but at home everywhere in it.

It comes, finally, to two images for inhabiting the academic and cultural space provided by school and university. On the one hand, we can be there in order to reign and hold sway. Here, in such a conception of academic space, the academic professional is king and potentate. In that form you sit surveying all before you with detachment and mastery. Your legitimacy is that this is your domain, which you can describe with *authority* as principally Western, or African, or Islamic, or American, or on and on. The other model is considerably more mobile, more playful, although no less serious. The image of traveler depends not on power, but on motion, on a willingness to go into different worlds, use different idioms, and understand a variety of disguises, masks, and rhetorics. Travelers must suspend the claim of customary routine in order to live in new rhythms and rituals. Most of all, and most unlike the potentate who must guard only one place and defend its frontiers, the traveler *crosses over,* traverses territory, and abandons fixed positions, all the time. To do this with dedication and love as well as a realistic sense of the terrain is, I believe, a kind of academic freedom at its highest, since one of its main features is that you can leave authority and dogma to the potentate. You will have other things to think about and enjoy than merely yourself and your domain, and those other things are far more impressive, far more worthy of study and respect than self-adulation and uncritical self-appreciation. To join the academic world is therefore to enter a ceaseless quest for knowledge and freedom.

NOTES

1. John Cardinal Newman, *The Idea of a University* (1853, 1858; New York: Double-day and Co., 1962), p. 149.
2. Ibid., p. 138.
3. Ibid., p. 158.
4. Robert A. Stafford, *Scientist of Empire: Sir Roderick Murchison, Scientific Exploration, and Victorian Imperialism* (Cambridge: Cambridge University Press, 1989).

RONALD DWORKIN is Professor of Law at New York University and University Professor of Jurisprudence at Oxford University. His books include *Taking Rights Seriously* (1979), *A Matter of Principle* (1985), *Law's Empire* (1986), *Life's Dominion* (1993), and *Freedom's Law* (1996). He is a member of the British Academy and the American Academy of Arts and Sciences.

HENRY LOUIS GATES JR is W. E. B. Du Bois Professor of the Humanities and Chair of the Department of Afro-American Studies at Harvard University. He is the coeditor, with K. Anthony Appiah, of *Transition: An International Review*. His books include *Figures in Black* (1987), *The Signifying Monkey* (1988), *Loose Canons: Notes on the Culture Wars* (1992), *Colored People* (1994), and, with Cornel West, *The Future of the Race* (1996).

THOMAS L. HASKELL is Samuel G. McCann Professor of History at Rice University. He is the winner of five G. R. Brown Awards for Superior Teaching. He is the author of *The Emergence of Professional Social Science* (1977) and *Explanatory Schemes* (forthcoming, in 1997), and the editor of *The Authority of Experts* (1984) and, with Richard Teichgraeber, *The Culture of the Market* (1993).

EVELYN FOX KELLER is Professor of the History and Philosophy of Science at the Program of Science, Technology, and Society at the Massachusetts Institute of Technology. She is a MacArthur Fellow. Her books include *A Feeling for the Organism: The Life and Work of Barbara McClintock* (1983), *Reflections on Gender and Science* (1985), *Secrets of Life, Secrets of Death* (1992), and *Refiguring Life: Metaphors of Twentieth-Century Biology* (1995); and she is the editor, with Helen Longino, of *Feminism and Science* (1996).

LOUIS MENAND is Professor of English at the Graduate Center of the City University of New York. He is Contributing Editor of *The New York Review of Books* and a vice-president of PEN-American Center. He is the author of *Discovering Modernism: T. S. Eliot and His Context* (1987) and the editor, with A. Walton Litz and Lawrence Rainey, of volume 7 of *The Cambridge History of Literary Criticism* (forthcoming).

LINDA RAY PRATT is Professor of English and Chair of the Department of English at the University of Nebraska at Lincoln. She was President of the American Association of University Professors from 1992 to 1994.

RICHARD RORTY is University Professor of Humanities at the University of Virginia. He has been a MacArthur Fellow and a president of the Eastern Division of the American Philosophical Association, and he is a member of the American Academy of Arts and Sciences. His books include *Philosophy and the Mirror of Nature* (1979), *Consequences of Pragmatism* (1982), *Contingency, Irony, and Solidarity* (1988), and two volumes of *Philosophical Papers* (1991).

EDWARD W. SAID is University Professor at Columbia University. He is a fellow of the American Academy of Arts and Sciences and a member of the Council on Foreign Relations. He was a member of the Palestine National Council from 1977 to 1991. His books include *Beginnings: Intention and Method* (1975), *Orientalism* (1978), *The Question of Palestine* (1979), *The World, the Text, and the Critic* (1983), *Musical Elaborations* (1991), *Culture and Imperialism* (1993), and *Representations of the Intellectual* (1994).

JOAN W. SCOTT is Professor of Social Science at the Institute for Advanced Study. Her books include *The Glassworkers of Carmaux: French Craftsmen and Political Action in a Nineteenth-Century City* (1974), *Gender and the Politics of History* (1988), and *Only Paradoxes to Offer: French Feminists and the Rights of Man* (1996). She is also the author, with Louise A. Tilly, of *Women, Work, and Family* (1978), and the editor, with Judith Butler, of *Feminists Theorize the Political* (1992).

CASS R. SUNSTEIN is Karl N. Llewellyn Distinguished Service Professor of Jurisprudence and Co-Director of the Center on Constitutionalism in Eastern Europe at the University of Chicago. He is a member of the American Academy of Arts and Sciences. His books include *The Partial Constitution* (1993), *Democracy and the Problem of Free Speech* (1993), and *Legal Reasoning and Political Conflict* (1996).

power (*continued*)
knowledge and, 48, 57, 85nn.9, 10.
See also politics
Powers, H. H., 49
Pragmatism: in AAUP's founding documents, viii, ix; Chesterton's criticism
of, 33, 34, 40n.14; on conditions
of intelligibility, 42n.18; on intrinsic
versus observer-relative properties,
39n.9; James, 65, 69; Lovejoy on, 65;
on objectivity as intersubjectivity, 38;
Rorty's revival of, 68; on rules and
principles, 134, 135; on significance
of philosophical controversies, 32–33.
See also Dewey, John; Peirce, Charles
Sanders; Rorty, Richard
professions: academic faculty as professionals, 7, 8, 46–47, 53–54, 86n.22;
academic freedom and professionalization, 53–54; Fish's defense of professionalism, 74–76; research university as paradigm of professionalism, 8;
as self-regulating, 7, 8, 46
professors. *See* faculty
Putnam, Hilary, 25, 26, 39n.5, 68

race. *See* critical race theory
racist speech. *See* hate speech codes
Rauch, Jonathan, 203–4
R.A.V. v. St. Paul, 103, 104, 105, 109,
132
realism: antirealism, 64, 70, 72–74; deconstruction contrasted with, 36–37;
Hesse's moderate version of, 89n.64;
of Peirce, 62, 70; in Western Rationalistic Tradition, 25
recovery movement, 148–49
relativism, epistemological: academic
freedom and, viii, 12–13, 21–22, 183;
in attacks on the university, 4; in
Dewey, 13; in Fish, 77; historicism,
57, 72; and poststructuralism, 11;
Silber on, 41n.16
relevance, 170, 216
representationalism: ambiguity in,

30–32; antirepresentationalism, 31,
35, 71–72
Richards, David A. J., 146
Rieff, Philip, 81
Riesman, David, 130
Rorty, Richard: antiprofessionalism of,
74, 76; antirealism of, 64, 70; antirepresentationalism of, 31, 35, 71–72; on
communities of inquiry, 69, 89n.60;
on edification versus confrontation,
66–68; on invocations of epistemology, 211; Kuhn's criticism of, 88n.45;
Lovejoy criticized by, 64–66; Peirce
compared with, 61, 62, 69; Peirce
criticized by, 68–70; practice versus
rhetorical posture of, 73–74; Pragmatism of, 68; on truth in liberal society, 69
Ross, Edward A., 44, 48–53, 80
Roth v. United States, 125
Russell, Bertrand, 40n.14

Scalia, Antonin, 132
Schauer, Frederick, 124, 136
science, 199–213; contract with society,
210–11; dependency of, 210; efficacy
of, 207; evolution, 55–56, 167; political and institutional growth of, 200;
science studies' responsibility for
funding crisis in, 210–11; scientific
conception of knowledge, 11–12,
41n.17; social and historical factors
in, 201–2; social sciences, 18, 86n.22,
166–67, 214, 223; working scientists
and science studies, 202–4, 206–7.
See also science studies
science studies, 199–213; competence
in, 204–5; defined, 199; Edinburgh
school, 200–201; on efficacy of science, 207; feminism and multiculturalism associated with, 203, 211;
Kuhn, 200; origins of, 200–201; political correctness in, 203–4; as postmodern, 199–200, 203; and poststructuralism, 206, 211; responsibility for

funding crisis in science, 210–11;
working scientists and, 202–4, 206–7
Searle, John, 25, 26, 29–32, 36–37,
39n.9, 41nn. 17, 18
Seligman, Edward R. A., 51, 53, 56, 57,
58, 59–60
Shapin, Steven, 201, 202
Silber, John, 40n.16
Skokie march, 97, 136
Small, Albion, 52
Smith, John E., 63
Snow, C. P., 41n.17
social sciences, 18, 86n.22, 166–67, 214,
223
specialization, 167
speech: commercial speech, 97, 98, 123;
formative power of language, 153;
low value and high value speech,
96–99; speech-conduct distinction,
97–98, 153, 196; struggle with racism
waged through language, 152. *See
also* freedom of expression; political
speech
speech acts, 153
speech codes. *See* hate speech codes
Stafford, Robert, 227
Stanford, Mrs. Jane Lothrop, 49, 50,
51, 80
Stanford University: hate speech code,
109, 126, 146–47, 182, 194, 198n.7;
Ross case, 48–53, 80
Stevens, John Paul, 104
Strossen, Nadine, 137, 144, 145
students: academic freedom for, 14–17,
173; and professor's authority, 55

Taussig, Frank, 49
Taylor, Charles, 90n.81, 151
tenure: AAUP support for, 87n.31; aca-
demic freedom and, 175; as element
of academic life, 8; and intellectual
freedom, 9
Terminiello decision, 137
Thomas, Laurence, 134
Toulmin, Stephen, 87n.38, 89n.64
Trilling, Lionel, 15

trustees, 58, 60, 73
truth: academic freedom and relativity
of, viii, 12–13, 21–22, 183; academic
freedom as instrumental in discovery
of, 185–87; as communal, 57, 60–64;
Dewey on absolute, 33–36; Dewey
on function of the university as the
truth function, 35, 68, 89n.57; emerging from marketplace of ideas, 52,
185; fallibilism, 68, 70–72; philosophical debates about as irrelevant for
practice, 24; poststructuralist skepticism about, 13; and relativism, 4,
183; Rorty on truth in liberal society,
69; science studies' critique of, 201;
social truth, 205. *See also* correspondence theory of truth; knowledge;
objectivity

university, the. *See* academy, the
University of Connecticut, 149–50
University of Michigan, 101, 103, 139–
40, 145, 182, 194
University of Pennsylvania, 121

values, 177–78
Van Alstyne, William, 44
viewpoint and content neutrality, principle of, 103–5, 131–38, 142

Walzer, Michael, 6
Weinberg, Steven, 203
Westbrook, Robert, 40n.14
White, Andrew Dickson, 7, 43
Williams, Patricia J., 127, 155
Wilson, James Q., 138
Wilson, William Julius, 155
Wittgenstein, Ludwig, 36, 37
Wolf, Friedrich August, 84n.6
*Words That Wound: Critical Race Theory,
Assaultive Speech, and the First Amend-
ment* (Matsuda et al.), 121

Yeats, William Butler, 71

Zionism, 144–45